CULTURAL LITERACY

CULTURAL LITERACY

WHAT EVERY AMERICAN NEEDS TO KNOW

E. D. Hirsch, Jr.

With an Updated Appendix

WHAT LITERATE AMERICANS KNOW

E. D. Hirsch, Jr.
Joseph Kett
James Trefil

Vintage Books
A DIVISION OF RANDOM HOUSE
NEW YORK

To the memory of my father.

First Vintage Books Edition, May 1988

 Published in the United States by Random House, Inc., New York. Originally published, in hardcover, by Houghton Mifflin Company, in 1987.

Library of Congress Cataloging-in-Publication Data
Hirsch, E. D. (Eric Donald), 1928–
Cultural literacy.
Bibliography: p.
Includes index.
1. Educational anthropology — United States.
2. Culture. 3. Intercultural education — United States. 4. Literacy — United States.
I. Kett, Joseph F. II. Trefil, James S., 1938– . III. Title.
LB45.H57 1988 370.19 87-40478
ISBN 0-394-75843-9 (pbk.)

Manufactured in the United States of America
10 9 8 7

CONTENTS

ACKNOWLEDGMENTS

Many long-time friends and colleagues have encouraged and helped me in writing this book. The project has also been an occasion for forming new friends and new, deep obligations.

I have been pursuing the ideas set forth in these pages since the late 1970s and was first encouraged to publish them by Mina Shaughnessy as we talked for several hours shortly before her death in 1978. It therefore seemed appropriate to present those ideas at a 1980 conference dedicated to her memory. That talk, later published in the *Journal of Basic Writing* as "Culture and Literacy," contained the seeds of everything said in these pages. The seeds began to germinate during the academic year 1980–1981, while I was on a fellowship at the Center for Advanced Study in the Behavioral Sciences. I am grateful to the center and to the National Endowment for the Humanities for making that year possible.

In December 1981 I gave a brief sketch of my evolving ideas at a conference of the Modern Language Association, and Gerald Graff urged me to develop and publish the material. He sent the manuscript of my talk to Joseph Epstein, editor of *The American Scholar,* who was afterward relentless in his reminders that I owed him a full essay.

After "Cultural Literacy" appeared in *The American Scholar* in 1983, the tenor of my life began to change. I received a letter from Robert Payton, president of the Exxon Education Foundation, encouraging me to start acting on my perceptions rather than just writing them down. Payton's kindly and idealistic challenge pulled me away from my ordinary scholarly concerns and into educational activism.

Under his influence, and with the help of the funds his foundation provided, I joined forces with Joseph Kett and James Trefil to make a preliminary list of the items of cultural literacy. To these two friends I owe many hours of warm collegiality and intellectual stimulation. They join me in thanking the many reviewers of our list, including three who examined and commented on it in minute detail — John Casteen, then secretary of education of the Commonwealth of Virginia, Bernard Gifford, dean of the Graduate School of Education at Berkeley, and Diane Ravitch, educational historian and professor at Teachers College, Columbia University.

My two colleagues and I particularly wish to acknowledge the help, the labor, and the concrete suggestions of the team that has worked and is working with us to compile the larger dictionary of cultural literacy — Gardner Campbell, Tricia Emlet, Ruth Estep, Luis Gamez, Diana Smith, Michael Stanford, and Paul Vanderham. We are also grateful to Kieran Egan and Kate Kessler for their help.

The single greatest impetus to writing this book came from Diane Ravitch, who said simply that I ought to write a book, that I ought to call it *Cultural Literacy*, and that I ought to get it out as soon as possible. These suggestions, coming from someone whose work I deeply admire, proved irresistible. Without Professor Ravitch's original suggestions and continuing support, I might not have undertaken the book at all.

Encouragement came also from Professor Richard C. Anderson, director of the Center for the Study of Reading at the University of Illinois, and chairman of the Commission on Reading of the National Academy of Education. Because I admire his work, I sought his counsel whenever conferences brought us together. I am grateful for his advice on technical points. I am also grateful to another distinguished member of the Commission on Reading, Professor Jeanne Chall, director of the Reading Laboratory at the Harvard Graduate School of Education, who, in her generous comments on my ideas, as well as in her scholarly work, has been a source of energy and confidence.

I am grateful to Liz McPike, editor of *American Educator*, for astute advice about the first chapter; to Scott Miller of the Exxon Education Foundation for general comments and encouragement; and to Houghton Mifflin for its excellent and detailed annotations.

The book has benefited from the advice of three exceptional people who, because of their strong interest in educational reform, were willing to review the first draft in its entirety, despite their extremely demanding schedules — Joseph Epstein; Chester E. Finn, assistant secretary of education for educational research in the U.S. Department of Education; and Nathan Glazer, professor of education and sociology at Harvard. All three have made astute and useful suggestions. Of course, I alone take responsibility for what is said in this book.

To Polly Hirsch, who has read every word of the manuscript and, as always, has offered unfailingly sound advice and good sense, I am more grateful than she in her loving modesty is willing to believe.

Finally, I have dedicated this book to the memory of my father, because I learned from him the courage to follow ideas whither they lead.

E. D. HIRSCH, JR.
Charlottesville, Virginia

PREFACE TO THE VINTAGE EDITION

The only revisions in this edition (other than typographical corrections and improvements in the gloss on "Waltzing Matilda") are changes in the appendix, "What Literate Americans Know." We have studied about three thousand suggestions sent to us by more than two hundred readers. These have yielded a net increase of 343 items. The additions come from history, technology, literature, politics, science, and geography. The deletions are few, totaling only about twenty-five, e.g., "Edict of Nantes" and "Occam's razor," and other items that were questioned by several readers independently. Although exactitude is impossible in forming such a compilation, the many comments on the list have enabled us to make it a more reliable index to American literate culture than it was before. We wish to thank all those who have already responded to our request for suggestions, and we repeat the request to readers of this edition.

The idea of cultural literacy does not embrace the whole of education. This book focuses sharply on the background knowledge necessary for functional literacy and effective national communication. This limited educational goal, while not the whole story, is one that needs special emphasis today. American literacy has been declining at a time when our changed economy requires that our literacy should rise. American education can be credited with real achievements, but high national literacy has not been one of them.

The body of background knowledge that is taken for granted in literate national communication changes very slowly. This conservatism of literacy has no inherent connection with political conservatism. It reflects, rather, the universal reluctance of people to change their linguistic habits. Some elements of literate culture do not change at all. Spelling, for example, is extraordinarily conservative: no matter how energetically reformers like G. B. Shaw have tried to rationalize our spellings, and no matter how absurd they actually are, as in "enough" and "doubt," we are destined to keep those absurdities. Why? Because so many people have learned the traditional forms, and so many books have recorded them, that successful spelling reform would require orthographical thought-police. (Consider how hard it has been for us to convert to the metric system.) Other contents of literate culture exhibit a similar inertia for similar reasons.

This conservatism of literate culture is not, of course, total. New elements are constantly coming in, and old ones falling from use. Americans are right to press for reforms such as greater representation of women and minorities and of non-Western cultures, and to insist that literate culture keep up with historical and technical change. Indeed, such changes are generously reflected in our list. Yet the materials in the list that are of recent origin constitute less than 20 percent of the total. *Eighty percent of the listed items have been in use for more than a hundred years!*

Such cultural conservatism is useful for purposes of national communication. It enables grandparents to communicate with grandchildren, southerners with midwesterners, whites with blacks, Asians with Hispanics, and Republicans with Democrats — no matter where they were educated. If each local school system imparts the traditional reference points of literate culture, then everybody will be able to communicate with strangers. In the modern age, effective communication with strangers is altogether essential to promote the general welfare and to insure domestic tranquility. The inherent conservatism of literacy leads to a subtle but unavoidable paradox: the goals of political liberalism require educational conservatism. We make social and economic progress *only* by teaching myths and facts that are predominantly traditional.

E.D.H., JR.
November 1987
Charlottesville, Virginia

PREFACE

> Rousseau points out the facility with which children lend themselves to our false methods: . . . "The apparent ease with which children learn is their ruin."
>
> — JOHN DEWEY

> There is no matter what children should learn first, any more than what leg you should put into your breeches first. Sir, you may stand disputing which is best to put in first, but in the meantime your backside is bare. Sir, while you stand considering which of two things you should teach your child first, another boy has learn't 'em both.
>
> — SAMUEL JOHNSON

To be culturally literate is to possess the basic information needed to thrive in the modern world. The breadth of that information is great, extending over the major domains of human activity from sports to science. It is by no means confined to "culture" narrowly understood as an acquaintance with the arts. Nor is it confined to one social class. Quite the contrary. Cultural literacy constitutes the only sure avenue of opportunity for disadvantaged children, the only reliable way of combating the social determinism that now condemns them to remain in the same social and educational condition as their parents. That children from poor and illiterate homes tend to remain poor and illiterate is an unacceptable failure of our schools, one which has occurred not because our teachers are inept but chiefly because they are compelled to teach a fragmented curriculum based on faulty educational theories. Some say that our schools by themselves are powerless to change the cycle of poverty and illiteracy. I do not agree. They *can* break the cycle, but only if they themselves break fundamentally with some of the theories and practices that education professors and school administrators have followed over the past fifty years.

Although the chief beneficiaries of the educational reforms advocated in this book will be disadvantaged children, these same reforms will also enhance the literacy of children from middle-class homes. The educational goal advocated is that of mature literacy for *all* our citizens.

The connection between mature literacy and cultural literacy may already be familiar to those who have closely followed recent discussions of education. Shortly after the publication of my essay "Cultural Literacy," Dr. William Bennett, then chairman of the National Endowment for the Humanities and subsequently secretary of education in President Ronald Reagan's second administration, championed its ideas. This endorsement from an influential person of conservative views gave my ideas some currency, but such an endorsement was not likely to recommend the concept to liberal thinkers, and in fact the idea of cultural literacy has been attacked by some liberals on the assumption that I must be advocating a list of great books that every child in the land should be forced to read.

But those who examine the Appendix to this book will be able to judge for themselves how thoroughly mistaken such an assumption is. Very few specific titles appear on the list, and they usually appear as words, not works, because they represent writings that culturally literate people have read about but haven't read. *Das Kapital* is a good example. Cultural literacy is represented not by a *prescriptive* list of books but rather by a *descriptive* list of the information actually possessed by literate Americans. My aim in this book is to contribute to making that information the possession of all Americans.

The importance of such widely shared information can best be understood if I explain briefly how the idea of cultural literacy relates to currently prevailing theories of education. The theories that have dominated American education for the past fifty years stem ultimately from Jean Jacques Rousseau, who believed that we should encourage the natural development of young children and not impose adult ideas upon them before they can truly understand them. Rousseau's conception of education as a process of natural development was an abstract generalization meant to apply to all children in any time or place: to French children of the eighteenth century or to Japanese or American children of the twentieth century. He thought that a child's intellectual and social skills would develop naturally without regard to the specific content of education. His content-neutral conception of educational development has long been triumphant in American schools of education and has long dominated the "developmental," content-neutral curricula of our elementary schools.

In the first decades of this century, Rousseau's ideas powerfully influenced the educational conceptions of John Dewey, the writer who has most deeply affected modern American educational theory and practice. Dewey's clearest and, in his time, most widely read book on education, *Schools of To-morrow,* acknowledges Rousseau as the chief source of his educational principles. The first chapter of Dewey's book carries the telling title "Education as Natural Development" and is sprinkled with quotations from Rousseau. In it Dewey strongly seconds Rousseau's opposition to the mere accumulation of information.

> Development emphasizes the need of intimate and extensive personal acquaintance with a small number of typical situations with a view to mastering the way of dealing with the problems of experience, not the piling up of information.[1]

Believing that a few direct experiences would suffice to develop the skills that children require, Dewey assumed that early education need not be tied to specific content. He mistook a half-truth for the whole. He placed too much faith in children's ability to learn general skills from a few typical experiences and too hastily rejected "the piling up of information." Only by piling up specific, communally shared information can children learn to participate in complex cooperative activities with other members of their community.

This old truth, recently rediscovered, requires a countervailing theory of education that once again stresses the importance of specific information in early and late schooling. The corrective theory might be described as an anthropological theory of education, because it is based on the anthropological observation that all human communities are founded upon specific shared information. Americans are different from Germans, who in turn are different from

Japanese, because each group possesses specifically different cultural knowledge. In an anthropological perspective, the basic goal of education in a human community is acculturation, the transmission to children of the specific information shared by the adults of the group or polis.

Plato, that other great educational theorist, believed that the specific contents transmitted to children are by far the most important elements of education. In *The Republic* he makes Socrates ask rhetorically, "Shall we carelessly allow children to hear any casual tales which may be devised by casual persons, and to receive into their minds ideas for the most part the very opposite of those which we shall wish them to have when they are grown up?" Plato offered good reasons for being concerned with the specific contents of schooling, one of them ethical: "For great is the issue at stake, greater than appears — whether a person is to be good or bad."[2]

Time has shown that there is much truth in the durable educational theories of both Rousseau and Plato. But even the greatest thinkers, being human, see mainly in one direction at a time, and no thinkers, however profound, can foresee the future implications of their ideas when they are translated into social policy. The great test of social ideas is the crucible of history, which, after a time, usually discloses a one-sidedness in the best of human generalizations. History, not superior wisdom, shows us that neither the content-neutral curriculum of Rousseau and Dewey nor the narrowly specified curriculum of Plato is adequate to the needs of a modern nation.

Plato rightly believed that it is natural for children to learn an adult culture, but too confidently assumed that philosophy could devise the one best culture. (Nonetheless, we should concede to Plato that within our culture we have an obligation to choose and promote our best traditions.) On the other side, Rousseau and Dewey wrongly believed that adult culture is "unnatural" to young children. Rousseau, Dewey, and their present-day disciples have not shown an adequate appreciation of the need for transmission of specific cultural information.

In contrast to the theories of Plato and Rousseau, an anthropological theory of education accepts the naturalness as well as the relativity of human cultures. It deems it neither wrong nor unnatural to teach young children adult information before they fully understand it. The anthropological view stresses the universal fact that a human group must have effective communications to function effectively, that effective communications require shared culture, and that shared culture requires transmission of specific information to children. Literacy, an essential aim of education in the modern world, is no autonomous, empty skill but depends upon literate culture. Like any other aspect of acculturation, literacy requires the early and continued transmission of specific information. Dewey was deeply mistaken to disdain "accumulating information in the form of symbols."[3] Only by accumulating shared symbols, and the shared information that the symbols represent, can we learn to communicate effectively with one another in our national community.

CHAPTER I

Literacy and Cultural Literacy

THE DECLINE OF LITERATE KNOWLEDGE

This book explains why we need to make some very specific educational changes in order to achieve a higher level of national literacy. It does not anatomize the literacy crisis or devote many pages to Scholastic Aptitude Test scores. It does not document at length what has already been established, that Americans do not read as well as they should. It takes no position about methods of initial reading instruction beyond insisting that content must receive as much emphasis as "skill." It does not discuss teacher training or educational funding or school governance. In fact, one of its major purposes is to break away entirely from what Jeanne S. Chall has called "the great debate" about methods of reading instruction. It focuses on what I conceive to be the great hidden problem in American education, and I hope that it reveals this problem so compellingly that anyone who is concerned about American education will be persuaded by the book's argument and act upon it.

The standard of literacy required by modern society has been rising throughout the developed world, but American literacy rates have not risen to meet this standard. What seemed an acceptable level in the 1950s is no longer acceptable in the late 1980s, when only highly literate societies can prosper economically. Much of Japan's industrial efficiency has been credited to its almost universally high level of literacy. But in the United States, only two thirds of our citizens are literate, and even among those the average level is too low and should be raised. The remaining third of our citizens need to be brought as close to true literacy as possible. Ultimately our aim should be to attain universal literacy at a very high level, to achieve not only greater economic prosperity but also greater social justice and more effective democracy. We Americans have long accepted literacy as a paramount aim of schooling, but only recently have some of us who have done research in the field begun to realize that literacy is far more than a skill and that it requires large amounts of specific information. That new insight is central to this book.

Professor Chall is one of several reading specialists who have observed that "world knowledge" is essential to the development of reading and writing skills.[1] What she calls world knowledge I call cultural literacy, namely, the network of information that all competent readers possess. It is the background information, stored in their minds, that enables them to take up a newspaper and read it with an adequate level of comprehension, getting the point, grasping the implications, relating what they read to the unstated context which alone gives meaning to what they read. In describing the contents of this neglected domain of background information, I try to direct attention to a new opening that can help our schools make the significant improvement in education that has so far eluded us. The achievement of high universal literacy is the key to all other fundamental improvements in American education.

Why is literacy so important in the modern world? Some of the reasons, like the need to fill out forms or get a good job, are so obvious that they needn't be discussed. But the chief reason is broader. The complex undertakings of modern life depend on the cooperation of many people with different specialties in different places. Where communications fail, so do the undertakings. (That is the moral of the story of the Tower of Babel.) The function of national literacy is to foster effective nationwide communications. Our chief instrument of communication over time and space is the standard national language, which is sustained by national literacy. Mature literacy alone enables the tower to be built, the business to be well managed, and the airplane to fly without crashing. All nationwide communications, whether by telephone, radio, TV, or writing are fundamentally dependent upon literacy, for the essence of literacy is not simply reading and writing but also the effective use of the standard literate language. In Spain and most of Latin America the literate language is standard written Spanish. In Japan it is standard written Japanese. In our country it is standard written English.

Linguists have used the term "standard written English" to describe both our written and spoken language, because they want to remind us that standard spoken English is based upon forms that have been fixed in dictionaries and grammars and are adhered to in books, magazines, and newspapers. Although standard written English has no intrinsic superiority to other languages and dialects, its stable written forms have now standardized the oral forms of the language spoken by educated Americans.[2] The chief function of literacy is to make us masters of this standard instrument of knowledge and communication, thereby enabling us to give and receive complex information orally and in writing over time and space. Advancing technology, with its constant need for fast and complex communications, has made literacy ever more essential to commerce and domestic life. The literate language is more, not less, central in our society now than it was in the days before television and the silicon chip.

The recently rediscovered insight that literacy is more than a skill is based upon knowledge that all of us unconsciously have about language. We know instinctively that to understand what somebody is saying, we must understand more than the surface meanings of words; we have to understand the context as well. The need for background information applies all the more to reading and writing. To grasp the words on a page we have to know a lot of information that isn't set down on the page.

Consider the implications of the following experiment described in an article in *Scientific American*.[3] A researcher goes to Harvard Square in Cambridge, Massachusetts, with a tape recorder hidden in his coat pocket. Putting a copy of the *Boston Globe* under his arm, he pretends to be a native. He says to passers-by, "How do you get to Central Square?" The passers-by, thinking they are addressing a fellow Bostonian, don't even break their stride when they give their replies, which consist of a few words like "First stop on the subway."

The next day the researcher goes to the same spot, but this time he presents himself as a tourist, obviously unfamiliar with the city. "I'm from out of town," he says. "Can you tell me how to get to Central Square?" This time the tapes show that people's answers are much longer and more rudimentary. A typical one goes, "Yes, well you go down on the subway. You can see the entrance over there, and when you get downstairs you buy a token, put it in the slot, and you go over to the side that says Quincy. You take the train headed for Quincy, but you get off very soon, just the first stop is Central Square, and be sure you get off there. You'll know it because there's a big sign on the wall. It says Central Square." And so on.

Passers-by were intuitively aware that communication between strangers requires an estimate of how much relevant information can be taken for granted in the other person. If they can take a lot for granted, their communications can be short and efficient, subtle and complex. But if strangers share very little knowledge, their communications must be long and relatively rudimentary.

In order to put in perspective the importance of background knowledge in language, I want to connect the lack of it with our recent lack of success in teaching mature literacy to all students. The most broadly based evidence about our teaching of literacy comes from the National Assessment of Educational Progress (NAEP). This nationwide measurement, mandated by Congress, shows that between 1970 and 1980 seventeen-year-olds declined in their ability to understand written materials, and the decline was especially striking in the top group, those able to read at an "advanced" level.[4] Although these scores have now begun to rise, they remain alarmingly low. Still more precise quantitative data have come from the scores of the verbal Scholastic Aptitude Test (SAT). According to John B. Carroll, a distinguished psychometrician, the verbal SAT is essentially a test of "advanced vocabulary knowledge," which makes it a fairly sensitive instrument for measuring levels of literacy.[5] It is well known that verbal SAT scores have declined dramatically in the past fifteen years, and though recent reports have shown them rising again, it is from a very low base. Moreover, performance on the verbal SAT has been slipping steadily *at the top*. Ever fewer numbers of our best and brightest students are making high scores on the test.

Before the College Board disclosed the full statistics in 1984, antialarmists could argue that the fall in average verbal scores could be explained by the rise in the number of disadvantaged students taking the SATs. That argument can no longer be made. It's now clear that not only our disadvantaged but also our best educated and most talented young people are showing diminished verbal skills. To be precise, out of a constant pool of about a million test takers each year, 56 percent more students scored above 600 in 1972 than did so in 1984. More startling yet, the percentage drop was even greater for those scoring above 650 — 73 percent.[6]

In the mid 1980s American business leaders have become alarmed by the lack of communication skills in the young people they employ. Recently, top executives of some large U.S. companies, including CBS and Exxon, met to discuss the fact that their younger middle-level executives could no longer communicate their ideas effectively in speech or writing. This group of companies has made a grant to the American Academy of Arts and Sciences to analyze the causes of this growing problem. They want to know why, despite breathtaking advances in the technology of communication, the effectiveness of business communication has been slipping, to the detriment of our competitiveness in the world. The figures from NAEP surveys and the scores on the verbal SAT are solid evidence that literacy has been declining in this country just when our need for effective literacy has been sharply rising.

I now want to juxtapose some evidence for another kind of educational decline, one that is related to the drop in literacy. During the period 1970–1985, the amount of shared knowledge that we have been able to take for granted in communicating with our fellow citizens has also been declining. More and more of our young people don't know things we used to assume they knew.

A side effect of the diminution in shared information has been a noticeable increase in the number of articles in such publications as *Newsweek* and the *Wall Street Journal* about the surprising ignorance of the young. My son John, who recently taught Latin in high school and eighth grade, often told me of experiences which indicate that these articles are not exaggerated. In one of his classes he mentioned to his students that Latin, the language they were studying, is a dead language that is no longer spoken. After his pupils had struggled for several weeks with Latin grammar and vocabulary, this news was hard for some of them to accept. One girl raised her hand to challenge my son's claim. "What do they speak in Latin America?" she demanded.

At least she had heard of Latin America. Another day my son asked his Latin class if they knew the name of an epic poem by Homer. One pupil shot up his hand and eagerly said, "The Alamo!" Was it just a slip for *The Iliad*? No, he didn't know what the Alamo was, either. To judge from other stories about information gaps in the young, many American schoolchildren are less well informed than this pupil. The following, by Benjamin J. Stein, is an excerpt from one of the most evocative recent accounts of youthful ignorance.

> I spend a lot of time with teen agers. Besides employing three of them part-time, I frequently conduct focus groups at Los Angeles area high schools to learn about teen agers' attitudes towards movies or television shows or nuclear arms or politicians. . . .
>
> I have not yet found one single student in Los Angeles, in either college or high school, who could tell me the years when World War II was fought. Nor have I found one who could tell me the years when World War I was fought. Nor have I found one who knew when the American Civil War was fought. . . .
>
> A few have known how many U.S. senators California has, but none has known how many Nevada or Oregon has. ("Really? Even though they're so small?") . . . Only two could tell me where Chicago is, even in the vaguest terms. (My particular favorite geography lesson was the junior at the University of California at Los Angeles who thought that Toronto must be in Italy. My second-favorite geography lesson is the junior at USC, a pre-law student, who thought that Washington, D.C. was in Washington State.) . . .
>
> Only two could even approximately identify Thomas Jefferson. Only one could place the date of the Declaration of Independence. None could name even one of the first ten

amendments to the Constitution or connect them with the Bill of Rights. . . .

On and on it went. On and on it goes. I have mixed up episodes of ignorance of facts with ignorance of concepts because it seems to me that there is a connection. . . . The kids I saw (and there may be lots of others who are different) are not mentally prepared to continue the society because they basically do not understand the society well enough to value it.[7]

My son assures me that his pupils are not ignorant. They know a great deal. Like every other human group they share a tremendous amount of knowledge among themselves, much of it learned in school. The trouble is that, from the standpoint of their literacy and their ability to communicate with others in our culture, what they know is ephemeral and narrowly confined to their own generation. Many young people strikingly lack the information that writers of American books and newspapers have traditionally taken for granted among their readers from all generations. For reasons explained in this book, our children's lack of intergenerational information is a serious problem for the nation. The decline of literacy and the decline of shared knowledge are closely related, interdependent facts.

The evidence for the decline of shared knowledge is not just anecdotal. In 1978 NAEP issued a report which analyzed a large quantity of data showing that our children's knowledge of American civics had dropped significantly between 1969 and 1976.[8] The performance of thirteen-year-olds had dropped an alarming 11 percentage points. That the drop has continued since 1976 was confirmed by preliminary results from a NAEP study conducted in late 1985. It was undertaken both because of concern about declining knowledge and because of the growing evidence of a causal connection between the drop in shared information and in literacy. The Foundations of Literacy project is measuring some of the specific information about history and literature that American seventeen-year-olds possess.

Although the full report will not be published until 1987, the preliminary field tests are disturbing.[9] If these samplings hold up, and there is no reason to think they will not, then the results we will be reading in 1987 will show that two thirds of our seventeen-year-olds do not know that the Civil War occurred between 1850 and 1900. Three quarters do not know what *reconstruction* means. Half do not know the meaning of *Brown decision* and cannot identify either Stalin or Churchill. Three quarters are unfamiliar with the names of standard American and British authors. Moreover, our seventeen-year-olds have little sense of geography or the relative chronology of major events. Reports of youthful ignorance can no longer be considered merely impressionistic.[10]

My encounter in the seventies with this widening knowledge gap first caused me to recognize the connection between specific background knowledge and mature literacy. The research I was doing on the reading and writing abilities of college students made me realize two things.[11] First, we cannot assume that young people today know things that were known in the past by almost every literate person in the culture. For instance, in one experiment conducted in Richmond, Virginia, our seventeen- and eighteen-year-old subjects did not know who Grant and Lee were. Second, our results caused me to realize that we cannot treat reading and writing as empty skills, independent of specific knowledge. The reading skill of a person may vary greatly from task to task. The level of literacy exhibited in each task depends on the relevant background information that the person possesses.

The lack of wide-ranging background information among young men and women now in their twenties and thirties is an important cause of the illiteracy that large corporations are finding in their middle-level executives. In former days, when business people wrote and spoke to one another, they could be confident that they and their colleagues had studied many similar things in school. They could talk to one another with an efficiency similar to that of native Bostonians who speak to each other in the streets of Cambridge. But today's high school graduates do not reliably share much common information, even when they graduate from the same school. If young people meet as strangers, their communications resemble the uncertain, rudimentary explanations recorded in the second part of the Cambridge experiment.

My father used to write business letters that alluded to Shakespeare. These allusions were effective for conveying complex messages to his associates, because, in his day, business people could make such allusions with every expectation of being understood. For instance, in my father's commodity business, the timing of sales and purchases was all-important, and he would sometimes write or say to his colleagues, "There is a tide," without further elaboration. Those four words carried not only a lot of complex information, but also the persuasive force of a proverb. In addition to the basic practical meaning, "Act now!" what came across was a lot of implicit reasons why immediate action was important.

For some of my younger readers who may not recognize the allusion, the passage from *Julius Caesar* is:

> There is a tide in the affairs of men
> Which taken at the flood leads on to fortune;
> Omitted, all the voyage of their life
> Is bound in shallows and in miseries.
> On such a full sea are we now afloat,
> And we must take the current when it serves,
> Or lose our ventures.

To say "There is a tide" is better than saying "Buy (or sell) now and you'll cover expenses for the whole year, but if you fail to act right away, you may regret it the rest of your life." That would be twenty-seven words instead of four, and while the bare message of the longer statement would be conveyed, the persuasive force wouldn't. Think of the demands of such a business communication. To persuade somebody that your recommendation is wise and well-founded, you have to give lots of reasons and cite known examples and authorities. My father accomplished that and more in four words, which made quoting Shakespeare as effective as any efficiency consultant could wish. The moral of this tale is not that reading Shakespeare will help one rise in the business world. My point is a broader one. The fact that middle-level executives no longer share literate background knowledge is a chief cause of their inability to communicate effectively.

THE NATURE AND USE OF CULTURAL LITERACY

The documented decline in shared knowledge carries implications that go far beyond the shortcomings of executives and extend to larger questions of educational policy and social justice in our country. Mina Shaughnessy was a great English teacher who devoted her professional life to helping disadvantaged students become literate. At the 1980 conference dedicated to her memory, one of the speakers who followed me to the podium was the Harvard historian and sociologist Orlando Patterson. To my delight he departed from his prepared talk to mention mine. He seconded my argument that shared information is a necessary background to true literacy. Then he extended and deepened the ideas I had presented. Here is what Professor Patterson said, as recorded in the *Proceedings* of the conference.

> Industrialized civilization [imposes] a growing cultural and structural complexity which requires persons to have a broad grasp of what Professor Hirsch has called cultural literacy: a deep understanding of mainstream culture, which no longer has much to do with white Anglo-Saxon Protestants, but with the imperatives of industrial civilization. It is the need for cultural literacy, a profound conception of the whole civilization, which is often neglected in talk about literacy.

Patterson continued by drawing a connection between background information and the ability to hold positions of responsibility and power. He was particularly concerned with the importance for blacks and other minorities of possessing this information, which is essential for improving their social and economic status.

> The people who run society at the macro-level must be literate in this culture. For this reason, it is dangerous to overem-

> phasize the problems of basic literacy or the relevancy of literacy to specific tasks, and more constructive to emphasize that blacks will be condemned in perpetuity to oversimplified, low-level tasks and will never gain their rightful place in controlling the levers of power unless they also acquire literacy in this wider cultural sense.

Although Patterson focused his remarks on the importance of cultural literacy for minorities, his observations hold for every culturally illiterate person in our nation. Indeed, as he observed, cultural literacy is not the property of any group or class.

> To assume that this wider culture is static is an error; in fact it is not. It's not a WASP culture; it doesn't belong to any group. It is essentially and constantly changing, and it is open. What is needed is recognition that the accurate metaphor or model for this wider literacy is not domination, but dialectic; each group participates and contributes, transforms and is transformed, as much as any other group. . . . The English language no longer belongs to any single group or nation. The same goes for any other area of the wider culture.[12]

As Professor Patterson suggested, being taught to decode elementary reading materials and specific, job-related texts cannot constitute true literacy. Such basic training does not make a person literate with respect to newspapers or other writings addressed to a general public. Moreover, a directly practical drawback of such narrow training is that it does not prepare anyone for technological change. Narrow vocational training in one state of a technology will not enable a person to read manuals that explain new developments in the same technology. In modern life we need general knowledge that enables us to deal with new ideas, events, and challenges. In today's world, general cultural literacy is more useful than what Professor Patterson terms "literacy to a specific task," because general literate information is the basis for many changing tasks.

Cultural literacy is even more important in the social sphere. The aim of universal literacy has never been a socially neutral mission in our country. Our traditional social goals were unforgettably renewed for us by Martin Luther King, Jr., in his "I Have a Dream" speech. King envisioned a country where the children of former slaves sit down at the table of equality with the children of former slave owners, where men and women deal with each other as equals and judge each other on their characters and achievements rather than their origins. Like Thomas Jefferson, he had a dream of a society founded not on race or class but on personal merit.

In the present day, that dream depends on mature literacy. No modern society can hope to become a just society without a high level of universal literacy. Putting aside for the moment the practical arguments about the economic uses of literacy, we can contemplate the even more basic principle that underlies our national system of education in the first place — that people in a democracy can be entrusted to decide all important matters for themselves because they can deliberate and communicate with one another. Universal literacy is inseparable from democracy and is the canvas for Martin Luther King's picture as well as for Thomas Jefferson's.

Both of these leaders understood that just having the right to vote is meaningless if a citizen is disenfranchised by illiteracy or semiliteracy. Illiterate and semiliterate Americans are condemned not only to poverty, but also to the powerlessness of incomprehension. Knowing that they do not understand the issues, and feeling prey to manipulative oversimplifications, they do not trust the system of which they are supposed to be the masters. They do not feel themselves to be active participants in our republic, and they often do not turn out to vote. The civic importance of cultural literacy lies in the fact that true enfranchisement depends upon knowledge, knowledge upon literacy, and literacy upon cultural literacy.

To be truly literate, citizens must be able to grasp the meaning of any piece of writing addressed to the general reader. All citizens should be able, for instance, to read newspapers of substance, about which Jefferson made the following famous remark:

> Were it left to me to decide whether we should have a government without newspapers, or newspapers without a government, I should not hesitate a moment to prefer the latter.

> But I should mean that every man should receive those papers and be capable of reading them.[13]

Jefferson's last comment is often omitted when the passage is quoted, but it's the crucial one.

Books and newspapers assume a "common reader," that is, a person who knows the things known by other literate persons in the culture. Obviously, such assumptions are never identical from writer to writer, but they show a remarkable consistency. Those who write for a mass public are always making judgments about what their readers can be assumed to know, and the judgments are closely similar. Any reader who doesn't possess the knowledge assumed in a piece he or she reads will in fact be illiterate with respect to that particular piece of writing.

Here, for instance, is a rather typical excerpt from the *Washington Post* of December 29, 1983.

> A federal appeals panel today upheld an order barring foreclosure on a Missouri farm, saying that U.S. Agriculture Secretary John R. Block has reneged on his responsibilities to some debt ridden farmers. The appeals panel directed the USDA to create a system of processing loan deferments and of publicizing them as it said Congress had intended. The panel said that it is the responsibility of the agriculture secretary to carry out this intent "not as a private banker, but as a public broker."

Imagine that item being read by people who are well trained in phonics, word recognition, and other decoding skills but are culturally illiterate. They might know words like *foreclosure*, but they would not understand what the piece means. Who gave the order that the federal panel upheld? What is a federal appeals panel? Where is Missouri, and what about Missouri is relevant to the issue? Why are many farmers debt ridden? What is the USDA? What is a public broker? Even if culturally illiterate readers bothered to look up individual words, they would have little idea of the reality being referred to. The explicit words are just surface pointers to textual meaning in reading and writing. The comprehending reader must bring to the text appropriate background information that includes knowledge not only about the topic but also the shared attitudes and conventions that color a piece of writing.

Our children can learn this information only by being taught it. Shared literate information is deliberately sustained by national systems of education in many countries because they recognize the importance of giving their children a common basis for communication. Some decades ago a charming book called *1066 and All That* appeared in Britain.[14] It dealt with facts of British history that all educated Britons had been taught as children but remembered only dimly as adults. The book caricatured those recollections, purposely getting the "facts" just wrong enough to make them ridiculous on their face. Readers instantly recognized that the book was mistaken in its theory about what Ethelred-the-Unready was unready for, but, on the other hand, they couldn't say precisely what he *was* unready for. The book was hilarious to literate Britons as a satire of their own vague and confused memories. But even if their schoolchild knowledge had become vague with the passage of time, it was still functional, because the information essential to literacy is rarely detailed or precise.

This haziness is a key characteristic of literacy and cultural literacy. To understand the *Washington Post* extract literate readers have to know only vaguely, in the backs of their minds, that the American legal system permits a court decision to be reversed by a higher court. They would need to know only that a judge is empowered to tell the executive branch what it can or cannot do to farmers and other citizens. (The secretary of agriculture was barred from foreclosing a Missouri farm.) Readers would need to know only vaguely what and where Missouri is, and how the department and the secretary of agriculture fit into the scheme of things. None of this knowledge would have to be precise. Readers wouldn't have to know whether an appeals panel is the final judicial level before the U.S. Supreme Court. Any practiced writer who feels it is important for a reader to know such details always provides them.

Much in verbal communication is necessarily vague, whether we are conversing or reading. What counts is our ability to grasp the general shape of what we are reading and to tie it to what we already know. If we need details, we rely on the writer or speaker to develop them. Or if we intend to ponder matters in detail for ourselves, we do so later, at our leisure. For instance, it is probably true that many people do not know what a beanball is in baseball. So in an article on the subject the author conveniently sets forth as much as the culturally literate reader must know.

> Described variously as the knockdown pitch, the beanball, the duster and the purpose pitch — the Pentagon would call it the peacekeeper — this delightful stratagem has graced the scene for most of the 109 years the major leagues have existed. It starts fights. It creates lingering grudges. It sends people to the hospital. . . . "You put my guy in the dirt, I put your guy in the dirt."[15]

To understand this text, we don't have to know much about the particular topic in advance, but we do require quite a lot of vague knowledge about baseball to give us a sense of the whole meaning, whether our knowledge happens to be vague or precise.

The superficiality of the knowledge we need for reading and writing may be unwelcome news to those who deplore superficial learning and praise critical thinking over mere information. But one of the sharpest critical thinkers of our day, Dr. Hilary Putnam, a Harvard philosopher, has provided us with a profound insight into the importance of vague knowledge in verbal communication.[16]

> Suppose you are like me and cannot tell an elm from a beech tree. . . . [I can nonetheless use the word "elm" because] *there is a division of linguistic labor*. . . . It is not at all necessary or efficient that everyone who wears a gold ring (or a gold cufflink, etc.) be able to tell with any reliability whether or not something is really gold. . . . Everyone to whom the word "gold" is important for any reason has to *acquire* the word "gold"; but he does not have to acquire the *method of recognizing* if something is or is not gold.

Putnam does acknowledge a limit on the degrees of ignorance and vagueness that are acceptable in discourse. "Significant communication," he observes, "requires that people know something of what they are talking about." Nonetheless, what is required for communication is often so vague and superficial that we can properly understand and use the word *elm* without being able to distinguish an elm tree from a beech tree. What we need to know in order to use and understand a word is an initial stereotype that has a few vague traits.

> Speakers are *required* to know something about (stereotypic) tigers in order to count as having acquired the word "tiger"; something about elm trees (or anyway about the stereotype thereof) to count as having acquired the word "elm," etc. . . . The nature of the required minimum level of competence depends heavily upon both the culture and the topic, however. In our culture speakers are not . . . required to know the fine details (such as leaf shape) of what an elm tree looks like. English speakers are *required by their linguistic community* to be able to tell tigers from leopards; they are not required to be able to tell beech trees from elm trees.

When Putnam says that Americans can be depended on to distinguish tigers and leopards but not elms and beeches, he assumes that his readers will agree with him because they are culturally literate. He takes for granted that one literate person knows approximately the same things as another and is aware of the probable limits of the other person's knowledge. That second level of awareness — knowing what others probably know — is crucial for effective communication. In order to speak effectively to people we must have a reliable sense of what they do and do not know. For instance, if Putnam is right in his example, we should not have to tell a stranger that a leopard has spots or a tiger stripes, but we would have to explain that an elm has rough bark and a beech smooth bark if we wanted that particular piece of information conveyed. To know what educated people know about tigers but don't know about elm trees is the sort of cultural knowledge, limited in extent but possessed by all literate people, that must be brought into the open and taught to our children.

Besides being limited in extent, cultural literacy has another trait that it is important for educational policy — its national character. It's true that literate English is an international language, but only so long as the topics it deals with are international. The background knowledge of people from other English-speaking nations is often inadequate for complex and subtle communications within our nation. The knowledge required for national literacy differs from country to country, even when their national language is the same. It is no doubt true that one layer of cultural literacy is the same for all English-speaking nations. Australians, South Africans, Britons, and Americans share a lot of knowledge by virtue of their common language. But much of the knowledge required for literacy in, say, Australia is specific to that country, just as much of ours is specific to the United States.

For instance, a literate Australian can typically understand American newspaper articles on international events or the weather but not one on a federal appeals panel. The same holds true for Americans who read Australian newspapers. Many of us have heard "Waltzing Matilda," a song known to every Australian, but few Americans understand or need to understand what the words mean.

> Once a jolly swagman camped beside a billabong,
> Under the shade of a coolibah tree,
> And he sang as he sat and waited while his billy boiled,
> "You'll come a'waltzing Matilda, with me."

Waltzing Matilda doesn't mean dancing with a girl; it means walking with a kind of knapsack. A *swagman* is a hobo, a *billabong* is a pond, a *coolibah* is a eucalyptus, and a *billy* is a can for making tea.

The national character of the knowledge needed in reading and writing was strikingly revealed in an experiment conducted by Richard C. Anderson and others at the Center for the Study of Reading at the University of Illinois. They assembled two paired groups of readers, all highly similar in sexual balance, educational background, age, and social class.[17] The only difference between the groups was that one was in India, the other in the United States. Both were given the same two letters to read. The texts were similar in overall length, word-frequency distribution, sentence length and complexity, and number of explicit propositions. Both letters were on the same topic, a wedding, but one described an Indian wedding, the other an American wedding. The reading performances of the two groups — their speed and accuracy of comprehension — split along national lines. The Indians performed well in reading about the Indian wedding but poorly in reading about the American one, and the Americans did the opposite. This experiment not only reconfirmed the dependence of reading skill on cultural literacy, it also demonstrated its national character.

Although nationalism may be regrettable in some of its worldwide political effects, a mastery of national culture is essential to mastery of the standard language in every modern nation. This point is important for educational policy, because educators often stress the virtues of multicultural education. Such study is indeed valuable in itself; it inculcates tolerance and provides a perspective on our own traditions and values. But however laudable it is, it should not be the primary focus of national education. It should not be allowed to supplant or interfere with our schools' responsibility to ensure our children's mastery of American literate culture. The acculturative responsibility of the schools is primary and fundamental. To teach the ways of one's own community has always been and still remains the essence of the education of our children, who enter neither a narrow tribal culture nor a transcendent world culture but a national literate culture. For profound historical reasons, this is the way of the modern world.[18] It will not change soon, and it will certainly not be changed by educational policy alone.

THE DECLINE OF TEACHING CULTURAL LITERACY

Why have our schools failed to fulfill their fundamental acculturative responsibility? In view of the immense importance of cultural literacy for speaking, listening, reading, and writing, why has the need for a definite, shared body of information been so rarely mentioned in discussions of education? In the educational writings of the past decade, I find almost nothing on this topic, which is not arcane. People who are introduced to the subject quickly understand why oral or written communication requires a lot of shared background knowledge. It's not the difficulty or novelty of the idea that has caused it to receive so little attention.

Let me hazard a guess about one reason for our neglect of the subject. We have ignored cultural literacy in thinking about education — certainly I as a researcher also ignored it until recently — precisely because it was something we have been able to take for granted. We ignore the air we breathe until it is thin or foul. Cultural literacy is the oxygen of social intercourse. Only when we run into cultural illiteracy are we shocked into recognizing the importance of the information that we had unconsciously assumed.

To be sure, a minimal level of information is possessed by any normal person who lives in the United States and speaks elementary English. Amost everybody knows what is meant by *dollar* and that cars must travel on the right-hand side of the road. But this elementary level of information is not sufficient for a modern democracy. It isn't sufficient to allow us to read newspapers (a sin against Jeffersonian democracy), and it isn't sufficient to achieve economic fairness and high productivity. Cultural literacy lies *above* the everyday levels of knowledge that everyone possesses and *below* the expert level known only to specialists. It is that middle ground of cultural knowledge possessed by the "common reader." It includes information that we have traditionally expected our children to receive in school, but which they no longer do.

During recent decades Americans have hesitated to make a decision about the specific knowledge that children need to learn in school. Our elementary schools are not only dominated by the content-neutral ideas of Rousseau and Dewey, they are also governed by approximately sixteen thousand independent school districts. We have viewed this dispersion of educational authority as an insurmountable obstacle to altering the fragmentation of the school curriculum even when we have questioned that fragmentation. We have permitted school policies that have shrunk the body of information that Americans share, and these policies have caused our national literacy to decline.

At the same time we have searched with some eagerness for causes such as television that lie outside the schools. But we should direct our attention undeviatingly toward what the schools teach rather than toward family structure, social class, or TV programming. No doubt, reforms outside the schools are important, but they are harder to accomplish. Moreover, we have accumulated a great deal of evidence that faulty policy in the schools is the chief cause of deficient literacy. Researchers who have studied the factors influencing educational outcomes have found that the school curriculum is the most important controllable influence on what our children know and don't know about our literate culture.[19]

It will not do to blame television for the state of our literacy. Television watching does reduce reading and often encroaches on homework. Much of it is admittedly the intellectual equivalent of junk food. But in some respects, such as its use of standard written English, television watching is acculturative.[20] Moreover, as Herbert Walberg points out, the schools themselves must be held partly responsible for excessive television watching, because they have not firmly insisted that students complete significant amounts of homework, an obvious way to increase time spent on reading and writing.[21] Nor should our schools be excused by an appeal to the effects of the decline of the family or the vicious circle of poverty, important as these factors are. Schools have, or should have, children for six or seven hours a day, five days a week, nine months a year, for thirteen years or more. To assert that they are powerless to make a significant impact on what their students learn would be to make a claim about American education that few parents, teachers, or students would find it easy to accept.

Just how fragmented the American public school curriculum has become is described in *The Shopping Mall High School*, a report on five years of firsthand study inside public and private secondary schools. The authors report that our high schools offer courses of so many kinds that "the word 'curriculum' does not do justice to this astonishing variety." The offerings include not only academic courses of great diversity, but also courses in sports and hobbies and a "services curriculum" addressing emotional or social problems. All these courses are deemed "educationally valid" and carry course credit. Moreover, among academic offerings are numerous versions of each subject, corresponding to different levels of student interest and ability. Needless to say, the material covered in these "content area" courses is highly varied.[22]

Cafeteria-style education, combined with the unwillingness of our schools to place demands on students, has resulted in a steady diminishment of commonly shared information between generations and between young people themselves. Those who graduate from the same school have often studied different subjects, and those who graduate from different schools have often studied different material even when their courses have carried the same titles. The inevitable consequence of the shopping mall high school is a lack of shared knowledge across and within schools. It would be hard to invent a more effective recipe for cultural fragmentation.

The formalistic educational theory behind the shopping mall school (the theory that any suitable content will inculcate reading, writing, and thinking skills) has had certain political advantages for school administrators. It has allowed them to stay scrupulously neutral with regard to content.[23] Educational formalism enables them to regard the indiscriminate variety of school offerings as a positive virtue, on the grounds that such variety can accommodate the different interests and abilities of different students. Educational formalism has also conveniently allowed school administrators to meet objections to the traditional literate materials that used to be taught in the schools. Objectors have said that traditional materials are class-bound, white, Anglo-Saxon, and Protestant, not to mention racist, sexist, and excessively Western. Our schools have tried to offer enough diversity to meet these objections from liberals and enough Shakespeare to satisfy conservatives. Caught between ideological parties, the schools have been attracted irresistibly to a quantitative and formal approach to curriculum making rather than one based on sound judgments about what should be taught.

Some have objected that teaching the traditional literate culture means teaching conservative material. Orlando Patterson answered that objection when he pointed out that mainstream culture is not the province of any single social group and is constantly changing by assimilating new elements and expelling old ones.[24] Although mainstream culture is tied to the written word and may therefore seem more formal and elitist than other elements of culture, that is an illusion. Literate culture is the most democratic culture in our land: it excludes nobody; it cuts across generations and social groups and classes; it is not usually one's first culture, but it should be everyone's second, existing as it does beyond the narrow spheres of family, neighborhood, and region.

As the universal second culture, literate culture has become the common currency for social and economic exchange in our democracy, and the only available ticket to full citizenship. Getting one's membership card is not tied to class or race. Membership is automatic if one learns the background information and the linguistic conventions that are needed to read, write, and speak effectively. Although everyone is literate in some local, regional, or ethnic culture, the connection between mainstream culture and the national written language justifies calling mainstream culture *the* basic culture of the nation.

The claim that universal cultural literacy would have the effect of preserving the political and social status quo is paradoxical because in fact the traditional forms of literate culture are precisely the most effective instruments for political and social change. All political discourse at the national level must use the stable forms of the national language and its associated culture. Take the example of *The Black Panther*, a radical and revolutionary newspaper if ever this country had one. Yet the *Panther* was highly conservative in its language and cultural assumptions, as it had to be in order to communicate effectively. What could be more radical in sentiment but more conservative in language and assumed knowledge than the following passages from that paper?

> The present period reveals the criminal growth of bourgeois democracy since the betrayal of those who died that this nation might live "free and indivisible." It exposes through the trial of the Chicago Seven, and its law and order edicts, its desperate turn toward the establishment of a police state. (January 17, 1970)

> In this land of "milk and honey," the "almighty dollar" rules supreme and is being upheld by the faithful troops who move without question in the name of "law and order." Only in this garden of hypocrisy and inequality can a murderer not be considered a murderer — only here can innocent people be charged with a crime and be taken to court with the confessed criminal testifying against them. Incredible? (March 28, 1970)

> In the United States, the world's most technologically advanced country, one million youths from 12 to 17 years of age are illiterate — unable to read as well as the average fourth grader, says a new government report. Why so much illiteracy in a land of so much knowledge? The answer is because there is racism. Blacks and other Nonwhites receive the worst education. (May 18, 1974)

The last item of the Black Panther Party platform, issued March 29, 1972, begins

> 10. WE WANT LAND, BREAD, HOUSING, EDUCATION, CLOTHING, JUSTICE, PEACE AND PEOPLE'S CONTROL OF MODERN TECHNOLOGY.
>
> When in the course of human events it becomes necessary for one people to dissolve the political bands which have connected them with another, and to assume among the powers of the earth the separate and equal station to which the laws of nature and nature's God entitle them, a decent respect to the opinions of mankind requires that they should declare the causes which impel them to the separation.

And so on for the first five hundred of Jefferson's words without the least hint, or need of one, that this is a verbatim repetition of an earlier revolutionary declaration. The writers for *The Black Panther* had clearly received a rigorous traditional education in American history, in the Declaration of Independence, the Pledge of Allegiance to the Flag, the Gettysburg Address, and the Bible, to mention only some of the direct quotations and allusions in these passages. They also received rigorous traditional instruction in reading, writing, and spelling. I have not found a single misspelled word in the many pages of radical sentiment I have examined in that newspaper. Radicalism in politics, but conservatism in literate knowledge and spelling: to be a conservative in the *means* of communication is the road to effectiveness in modern life, in whatever direction one wishes to be effective.

To withhold traditional culture from the school curriculum, and therefore from students, in the name of progressive ideas is in fact an unprogressive action that helps preserve the political and economic status quo. Middle-class children acquire mainstream literate culture by daily encounters with other literate persons. But less privileged children are denied consistent interchanges with literate persons and fail to receive this information in school. The most straightforward antidote to their deprivation is to make the essential information more readily available inside the schools.

Providing our children with traditional information by no means indoctrinates them in a conservative point of view. Conservatives who wish to preserve traditional values will find that these are not necessarily inculcated by a traditional education, which can in fact be subversive of the status quo. As a child of eleven, I turned against the conservative views of my family and the Southern community in which I grew up, precisely because I had been given a traditional education and was therefore literate enough to read Gunnar Myrdal's *An American Dilemma*, an epoch-making book in my life.

Although teaching children national mainstream culture doesn't mean forcing them to accept its values uncritically, it does enable them to understand those values in order to predict the typical attitudes of other Americans. The writers for *The Black Panther* clearly understood this when they quoted the Declaration of Independence. George Washington, for instance, is a name in our received culture that we associate with the truthfulness of the hero of the story of the cherry tree. Americans should be taught that value association, whether or not they believe the story. Far from accepting the cherry-tree tale or its implications, Oscar Wilde in "The Decay of Lying" used it ironically, in a way that is probably funnier to Americans than to the British audience he was addressing.

> [Truth telling is] vulgarizing mankind. The crude commercialism of America, its materializing spirit, its indifference to the poetical side of things, and its lack of imagination and of high unattainable ideals, are entirely due to that country having adopted for its national hero a man who, according to his own confession, was incapable of telling a lie, and it is not

> too much to say that the story of George Washington and the cherry tree has done more harm, and in a shorter space of time, than any other moral tale in the whole of literature. . . . And the amusing part of the whole thing is that the story of the cherry tree is an absolute myth.[25]

For us no less than for Wilde, the values affirmed in traditional literate culture can serve a whole spectrum of value attitudes. Unquestionably, decisions about techniques of conveying traditions to our children are among the most sensitive and important decisions of a pluralistic nation. But the complex problem of how to teach values in American schools mustn't distract attention from our fundamental duty to teach shared content.

The failure of our schools to create a literate society is sometimes excused on the grounds that the schools have been asked to do too much. They are asked, for example, to pay due regard to the demands of both local and national acculturation. They are asked to teach not only American history but also state and city history, driving, cardiopulmonary resuscitation, consumerism, carpentry, cooking, and other special subjects. They are given the task of teaching information that is sometimes too rudimentary and sometimes too specialized. If the schools did not undertake this instruction, much of the information so provided would no doubt go unlearned. In some of our national moods we would like the schools to teach everything, but they cannot. There is a pressing need for clarity about our educational priorities.

As an example of the priorities we need to set, consider the teaching of local history in the Commonwealth of Virginia. Suppose Virginians had to choose between learning about its native son Jeb Stuart and Abraham Lincoln. The example is arbitrary, but since choices have to be made in education, we might consider the two names emblematic of the kind of priority decision that has to be made. Educational policy always involves choices between degrees of worthiness.

The concept of cultural literacy helps us to make such decisions because it places a higher value on national than on local information. We want to make our children competent to communicate with Americans throughout the land. Therefore, if Virginians did have to decide between Stuart and Lincoln they ought to favor the man from Illinois over the one from Virginia. All literate Americans know traditional information about Abraham Lincoln but relatively few know about Jeb Stuart. To become literate it's therefore more important to know about Lincoln than about Stuart. The priority has nothing to do with inherent merit, only with the accidents of culture. Stuart certainly had more merit than Benedict Arnold did, but Arnold also should be given educational priority over Stuart. Why? Because Benedict Arnold is as much a part of our national language as is, say, Judas.

To describe Benedict Arnold and Abraham Lincoln as belonging to the national language discloses another way of conceiving cultural literacy — as a vocabulary that we are able to use throughout the land because we share associations with others in our society. A universally shared national vocabulary is analogous to a universal currency like the dollar. Of course the vocabulary consists of more than just words. *Benedict Arnold* is part of national cultural literacy; *eggs Benedict* isn't.

THE CRITICAL IMPORTANCE OF EARLY SCHOOLING

Once we become aware of the inherent connection between literacy and cultural literacy, we have a duty to those who lack cultural literacy to determine and disclose its contents. To someone who is unaware of the things a literate person is expected to know, a writer's assumption that readers possess cultural literacy could appear to be a conspiracy of the literate against the illiterate, for the purpose of keeping them out of the club. But there is no conspiracy. Writers *must* make assumptions about the body of information their readers know. Unfortunately for the disadvantaged, no one ever spells out what that information is. But, as the Appendix illustrates, the total quantity of commonly shared information that the schools need to impart is less daunting than one might think, for the crucial background knowledge possessed by literate people is, as I have pointed out, telegraphic, vague, and limited in extent.

Preschool is not too early for starting earnest instruction in literate national culture. Fifth grade is almost too late. Tenth grade usually *is* too late. Anyone who is skeptical of this assertion should take a look at a heterogeneous class of fifth-graders engaged in summarizing a piece they have read. There are predictable differences between the summaries given by children with culturally adequate backgrounds and those given by children without. Although disadvantaged children often show an acceptable ability to decode and pronounce individual words, they are frequently unable to gain an integrated sense of a piece as a whole. They miss central implications and associations because they don't possess the background knowledge necessary to put the text in context. Hearing they hear not, and seeing they do not understand.[26]

Yet if you observe a kindergarten or first-grade class in which pupils have the same diversity of family background, you will *not* find a similar spread in the reading performances of pupils from different social classes. Disadvantaged first-graders do as well as middle class ones in sounding out letters and simple words.[27] What happens between first grade and fifth grade to change the equality of performance? The impression that something significant has occurred or has failed to occur in these early grades is confirmed by international comparisons of reading attainment at early ages in different countries. Before grade three, when reading skills are more mechanical than interpretive, the United States stands in the top group of countries. Later, when reading requires an understanding of more complex content, our comparative ranking drops.[28] Although our schools do comparatively well in teaching elementary decoding skills, they do less well than schools of some other countries in teaching the background knowledge that pupils must possess to succeed at mature reading tasks.

The importance of this evidence for improving our national literacy can scarcely be overemphasized. If in the early grades our children were taught texts with cultural content rather than "developmental" texts that develop abstract skills, much of the specific knowledge deficit of disadvantaged children could be overcome. For it is clear that one critical difference in the reading performances of disadvantaged fifth-graders as compared with advantaged pupils is the difference in their cultural knowledge. Background knowledge does not take care of itself. Reading and writing are cumulative skills; the more we read the more necessary knowledge we gain for further reading.

Around grade four, those who lack the initial knowledge required for significant reading begin to be left behind permanently. Having all too slowly built up their cultural knowledge, they find reading and learning increasingly toilsome, unproductive, and humiliating. It follows that teaching cultural information in the early grades would do more than just improve the reading performance of all our children. By removing one of the causes of failure, it would especially enhance the motivation, self-esteem, and performance of disadvantaged children.

Really effective reforms in the teaching of cultural literacy must therefore begin with the earliest grades. Every improvement made in teaching very young children literate background information will have a multiplier effect on later learning, not just by virtue of the information they will gain but also by virtue of the greater motivation for reading and learning they will feel when they actually understand what they have read.

Young children enjoy absorbing formulaic knowledge. Even if they did not, our society would still find it essential to teach them all sorts of traditions and facts. Critical thinking and basic skills, two areas of current focus in education, do not enable children to create out of their own imaginations the essential names and concepts that have arisen by historical accident. The Rio Grande, the Mason-Dixon line, "The Night Before Christmas," and *Star Wars* are not products of basic skills or critical thought. Many items of literate culture are arbitrary, but that does not make them dispensable. Facts are essential components of the basic skills that a child entering a culture must have.

I'm not suggesting that we teach our children exactly what our grandparents learned. We should teach children current mainstream culture. It's obvious that the content of cultural literacy changes over the years. Today the term "Brown decision" belongs to cultural literacy, but in 1945 there hadn't been any Brown decision. The name Harold Ickes was current in 1945 but no longer is. Such mutability is the fate of most names and events of recent history. Other changes come through the contributions of various subnational cultures. Ethnic words (like *pizza*) and art forms (like *jazz*) are constantly entering and departing from mainstream culture. Other subnational cultures, including those of science and technology, also cause changes in the mainstream culture. DNA and quarks, now part of cultural literacy, were unknown in 1945. In short, terms that literate people know in the 1980s are different from those they knew in 1945, and forty years hence the literate culture will again be different.

The flux in mainstream culture is obvious to all. But stability, not change, is the chief characteristic of cultural literacy. Although historical and technical terms may follow the ebb and flow of events, the more stable elements of our national vocabulary, like George Washington, the tooth fairy, the Gettysburg Address, Hamlet, and the Declaration of Independence, have persisted for a long time. These stable elements of the national vocabulary are at the core of cultural literacy, and for that reason are the most important contents of schooling. Although the terms that ebb and flow are tremendously important at a given time, they belong, from an educational standpoint, at the periphery of literate culture. The persistent, stable elements belong at the educational core.

Let me give some concrete examples of the kinds of core information I mean. American readers are assumed to have a general knowledge of the following people (I give just the beginning of a list): John Adams, Susan B. Anthony, Benedict Arnold, Daniel Boone, John Brown, Aaron Burr, John C. Calhoun, Henry Clay, James Fenimore Cooper, Lord Cornwallis, Davy Crockett, Emily Dickinson, Stephen A. Douglas, Frederick Douglass, Jonathan Edwards, Ralph Waldo Emerson, Benjamin Franklin, Robert Fulton, Ulysses S. Grant, Alexander Hamilton, and Nathaniel Hawthorne. Most of us know rather little about these people, but that little is of crucial importance, because it enables writers and speakers to assume a starting point from which they can treat in detail what they wish to focus on.

Here is another alphabetical list that no course in critical thinking skills, however masterful, could ever generate: Antarctic Ocean, Arctic Ocean, Atlantic Ocean, Baltic Sea, Black Sea, Caribbean Sea, Gulf of Mexico, North Sea, Pacific Ocean, Red Sea. It has a companion list: Alps, Appalachians, Himalayas, Matterhorn, Mount Everest, Mount Vesuvius, Rocky Mountains. Because literate people mention such names in passing, usually without explanation, children should acquire them as part of their intellectual equipment.

Children also need to understand elements of our literary and mythic heritage that are often alluded to without explanation, for example, Adam and Eve, Cain and Abel, Noah and the Flood, David and Goliath, the Twenty-third Psalm, Humpty Dumpty, Jack Sprat, Jack and Jill, Little Jack Horner, Cinderella, Jack and the Beanstalk, Mary had a little lamb, Peter Pan, and Pinocchio. Also Achilles, Adonis, Aeneas, Agamemnon, Antigone, and Apollo, as well as Robin Hood, Paul Bunyan, Satan, Sleeping Beauty, Sodom and Gomorrah, the Ten Commandments, and Tweedledum and Tweedledee.

Our current distaste for memorization is more pious than realistic. At an early age when their memories are most retentive, children have an almost instinctive urge to learn specific tribal traditions. At that age they seem to be fascinated by catalogues of information and are eager to master the materials that authenticate their membership in adult society. Observe for example how they memorize the rather complex materials of football, baseball, and basketball, even without benefit of formal avenues by which that information is inculcated.

The weight of human tradition across many cultures supports the view that basic acculturation should largely be completed by age thirteen. At that age Catholics are confirmed, Jews bar or bat mitzvahed, and tribal boys and girls undergo the rites of passage into the tribe. According to the anthropological record, all cultures whose educational methods have been reported in the *Human Relations Area Files* (a standard source for anthropological data) have used early memorization to carry on their traditions.[29]

In Korea, "numerous books must be memorized, including the five *Kyung*, and the four *Su*." In Tibet, "from eight to ten years of age, the boy spends most of his time reading aloud and memorizing the scriptures." In Chile, the Araucanian Indians use the memorization of songs as an educational technique to teach "the subtleties of the native tongue, and an insight into the customs and traditions of their tribe." In southern Africa, the children of the Kung bushmen listen for hours to discussions of which they understand very little until they "know the history of every object, every exchange between their families, before they are ten or twelve years old." In Indonesia, "memorization is the method commonly used." In Thailand, children "repeat their lessons until they know them by heart." In Arizona, the Papago Indians take children through the lengthy rituals "as many times as needed for the learner to say it all through, which may take a year."[30]

The new kind of teaching espoused by Rousseau and Dewey, which avoids rote learning and encourages the natural development of the child on analogy with the development of an acorn into an oak, has one virtue certainly: it encourages independence of mind. But the theory also has its drawbacks, one of which is that a child is not in fact like an acorn. Left to itself, a child will not grow into a thriving creature; Tarzan is pure fantasy. To thrive, a child needs to learn the traditions of the particular human society and culture it is born into.[31] Like children everywhere, American children need traditional information at a very early age.

A great deal is at stake in understanding and acting on this essential perception as soon as possible. The opportunity of acquiring cultural literacy, once lost in the early grades is usually lost for good. That is most likely to be true for children of parents who were not themselves taught the literate national culture.

In the technological age, Washington and the cherry tree, Scrooge and Christmas, the fights historical, the oceans geographical, the "beings animalculus," and all the other shared materials of literate culture have become more, not less, important. The more computers we have, the more we need shared fairy tales, Greek myths, historical images, and so on. That is not really the paradox it seems to be. The more specialized and technical our civilization becomes, the harder it is for nonspecialists to participate in the decisions that deeply affect their lives. If we do not achieve a literate society, the technicians, with their arcane specialties, will not be able to communicate with us nor we with them. That would contradict the basic principles of democracy and must not be allowed to happen.

The antidote to growing specialization is to reinvigorate the unspecialized domain of literate discourse, where all can meet on common ground. That this ideal *can* be achieved is proved by such admirable writers as Theodore H. White, John Kenneth Galbraith, Lewis Thomas, Peter Medawar, and Richard Feynman, who are able to communicate their complex expertise to a wide audience of educated people. We will be able to achieve a just and prosperous society only when our schools ensure that everyone commands enough shared background knowledge to be able to communicate effectively with everyone else.

CHAPTER II

The Discovery of the Schema

RESEARCH ON BACKGROUND KNOWLEDGE IN READING

In 1985, Dr. Robert Glaser, president of the National Academy of Education, wrote in the foreword to a national report on reading that the past two decades of scientific research "have produced an array of information which is unparalleled in its understanding of the underlying processes in the comprehension of language."[1] What so impressed Glaser and his distinguished copanelists on the National Commission on Reading? For one thing, new research has shown that reading doesn't follow an orderly pattern, as used to be thought. We don't first identify words, then word meanings, next combine word meanings to get the meanings of sentences, and finally combine sentence meanings to get the meaning of a whole text. This model isn't wrong in all respects, but we know that it is so oversimplified and incomplete that it presents a highly misleading picture of the way we understand texts.

The new picture that is emerging from language research is more complicated and more useful. It brings to the fore the highly active mind of the reader, who is now discovered to be not only a decoder of what is written down but also a supplier of much essential information that is not written down. The reader's mind is constantly inferring meanings that are not directly stated by the words of a text but are nonetheless part of its essential content. The explicit meanings of a piece of writing are the tip of an iceberg of meaning; the larger part lies below the surface of the text and is composed of the reader's own relevant knowledge. The past two decades of research have shown that such background knowledge is a far more important ingredient in the reading process than earlier theoretical accounts had supposed.

The best introduction to the new research is a psychological insight that goes back some thirty years to George Miller's path-breaking work on short-term memory, which is a special function of our minds that lasts just a matter of milliseconds.[2] It is distinguished from long-term memory (what most of us think of as memory), which lasts from a few seconds to a lifetime. Miller noticed that our capacity for remembering briefly presented disconnected items is severely limited. The mind cannot reliably hold in short-term memory more than about four to seven separate items, whether numbers, letters, points on the body, degrees of loudness, degrees of warmth, and so on. Miller's observation holds true for discrete items in every domain of experience, not just those presented in language. His discovery of this universal constraint has fostered a number of further insights into the way we perceive the world and understand language.

If you want to test Miller's discovery about the limits of short-term memory you can quickly do so with a series of numbers or letters, or indeed with any array of items. You will not reliably remember more than four to seven discrete items presented once without rehearsal, a limit on memory experts as well as ordinary people. Memory experts have worked out indirect tricks to circumvent this universal limitation, but they can never directly overcome it, because the constraint is hard-wired into our systems. Whenever we try to perform a task that consistently forces us to exceed the capacity of short-term memory, we fail to perform it reliably.

One device that memory experts have developed to resist this built-in limitation is "chunking." We can remember telephone numbers and other series of discrete items if we chunk the disparate items into a smaller number of groupings. The number 8-0-3-2-9-6-2-6-3-2 is hard to memorize, but it becomes much easier when it is treated as 803-296-26-32. What is true of numbers is also true of letters. After just one reading you can remember a short sentence like "The cat is on the mat," and later you can recall in correct order all the sixteen individual letters that compose the sentence. But after just one brief presentation, without the chunking provided by the word groupings, you would not be able to remember sixteen separate letters.

These observations are connected with the new insights about language processing referred to by Dr. Glaser. Consider just one implication of the constraints of short-term memory. How did I remember "The cat is on the mat?" I could manage it for subtler reasons than the length of the sentence — fewer than seven words. I can also remember "The cat is on the road to Mandalay" and "The cat is on the verge of a severe nervous breakdown." None of this exceeds my memory capacity. Why? Because I am able to chunk words into phrasal units and apply my long-term memory capacities as well. How do I manage this?

Short-term memory is the mind's vestibule where incoming items enjoy a brief equality lasting just long enough for the mind to give them a structure. Short-term memory holds in momentary suspension items that have come in one after another, thus enabling us to convert them into a stable structure. Amidst the temporal flow of language, short-term memory allows us to form a few words into nontemporal structures. Then we transfer those structures to long-term memory, leaving short-term memory free to deal again with the temporal flow of incoming words.

The limitation imposed by short-term memory accounts for the fact that all languages must form brief bursts of words into clauses. Every known language divides its sentences into semicomplete clausal units that are small enough to be structured within the limitations of short-term memory. As the psycholinguist T. G. Bever explains: "(1) The clause is the primary perceptual unit; (2) within each clause we assign semantic relations within major phrases; (3) after each clause is processed, it is recoded into relatively abstract form, thereby leaving short-term memory available for processing the next clause."[3]

This picture of the way we interpret language provides an answer to the question, How do we remember the meanings of whole conversations and books if short-term memory is so fleeting? Obviously we manage to remember what we have heard or read and are able to connect past moments with what we are now hearing or reading. But if short-term memories are so limited, how do we manage to remember meaning? Bever's explanation is strongly supported by the current evidence. Bever says that language is transferred from short-term memory into long-term memory not as a literal recollection of words but as a shorthand recoding of their gist, which normally erases from memory many of the individual words. On the basis of this account, we could predict that our memories for the literal words of sentences should be poor, whereas our long-term memories for their gist should be quite reliable. That is indeed the case, and this fact has fundamental implications for understanding the nature of reading.

From an evolutionary standpoint it is much more desirable that we forget the literal words we encounter and remember their meanings than that we have an absolute memory for both words and meanings. If we remembered all the surface details of our experiences, including all the words we ever heard or read, the floppy disks in our minds would quickly fill to capacity, and we would have to erase them periodically. Instead, without cluttering our memories with detail, we are nonetheless able to recall and recognize meanings with quite remarkable subtlety and accuracy. Readers can probably recognize or recall the meaning of the previous two sentences of this paragraph, but not their precise form. Memory of surface form is lost very quickly.

In fact, experimenters have found that surface forms of sentences are lost to memory within a few seconds. In 1967 Jacqueline Sachs reported a demonstration of this phenomenon.[4] She read her subjects narratives that were one paragraph long. Each paragraph contained a target sentence. Shortly after hearing the target sentence, subjects were presented either of two incorrect test sentences, to discover if they had accurately remembered the precise words of the original. A typical original sentence was "He sent a letter about it to Galileo, the great Italian scientist." The two test sentences for this original were "A letter about it was sent to Galileo, the great Italian scientist" and "Galileo, the great Italian scientist, sent him a letter about it."

Half the subjects were given one incorrect recognition probe and half the other. Those who were given the first probe responded that it was the very sentence they had heard. Subjects given the second responded that it was not the sentence they had heard. Sachs inferred from these results, and later experimentation has amply confirmed her inference, that the original form of a sentence is rapidly lost to memory, whereas an accurate memory for its meaning is retained.

In 1966 S. Fillenbaum showed that subjects don't notice that a synonym has been substituted in a test sentence.[5] In one experiment, subjects were given a number of original sentences, including "The window is not closed," and were then given multiple-choice recognition tests, including this one:

a. The window is not closed. [correct]
b. The window is closed.
c. The window is not open.
d. The window is open. [preserves the gist]

Subjects selected (d) far more often than any other incorrect choice, showing that they had indeed preserved an accurate memory for meaning. But although they were fooled by a substitution like *open* for *not closed* they were not fooled by a substitution like *cold* for *not hot*, presumably because *not hot* doesn't necessarily imply *cold*. Similarly, when the original sentence was "The man was not tall," subjects did not assume they had heard "The man was short," presumably because they realized that a man who is not tall isn't necessarily short. Most remarkable of all, it was discovered about a decade later that inferences regarding *open* versus *not closed* and *short* versus *not tall* are made at the time a sentence is understood, not later in recognition or recall.[6]

Other tests of synonym substitution were made in 1975 by W. F. Brewer, who found it to be a robust phenomenon. His subjects changed surface forms but preserved meaning in tests of both recognition and recall.[7] And in 1974 Eric Wanner showed that listeners had already lost the exact wording of a sentence when only sixteen syllables intervened between the sentence and the test.[8] Other discussions and experiments regarding memory for meaning and loss of memory for surface forms of language abound in the experimental literature.[9] The two allied phenomena are now firmly established: it is known that accurate memory of surface form normally disappears in a few seconds, while accurate memory for gist is quite persistent.

The implications of such phenomena became a focus of psycholinguistic research within a few years after the Fillenbaum and Sachs papers of 1966 and 1967. The next phase of work started in 1972 with an important paper by J. R. Barclay, J. D. Bransford, and J. J. Franks.[10] In a series of experiments they found that our initial understanding of a text depends on our applying relevant background knowledge that is not given in the text itself. Dividing their subjects into two paired groups, they conducted a series of recognition tests in which each group was given one of two slightly different sentences. One of these sentence pairs was as follows:

1. Three turtles rested *beside* a floating log, and a fish swam beneath them.
2. Three turtles rested *on* a floating log, and a fish swam beneath them.

Notice one difference in these sentences. In sentence 1, we do not necessarily infer that the fish swam under the log, and in fact it may not have done so. But in sentence 2, we can infer from our knowledge of logs, fish, and swimming that the fish *did* swim under the log. Subjects were later asked whether they recognized test sentences, of which this was one:

3. Three turtles rested (*beside/on*) a floating log, and a fish swam beneath *it*.

The (*beside/on*) notation means that if subjects had been given the *beside* version of the original, they got the *beside* version of the recognition test, and if they had been given the *on* original, they got the *on* recognition test.

At stake for the experimenters was a choice between two conflicting hypotheses about the way we understand language. According to one theory, we interpret the meanings of clauses and sentences and store them in long-term memory. But according to the other theory, we construct an elaborated model of what the words *imply* and store that. Under this second theory, we always go beyond a text's literal meanings to supply important implications that were not explicitly stated by the words of the text. We then store the fuller model of the text's meaning in long-term memory. This constructive hypothesis predicts that subjects who had been read the sentence which said that turtles rested *beside* a log wouldn't mistakenly think the original had said that the fish swam under the log. By contrast, subjects who originally heard the sentence which said that turtles rested *on* a log would think the original sentence explicitly said that a fish swam under the log, even though the sentence didn't mention a relation between the fish and the log. Subjects consistently made this mistake about the explicit words of the sentence. The constructive hypothesis, in other words, proved to be correct.

The result was not altogether surprising in light of Sachs's demonstration that we have bad memory for words but good memory for meaning. In the *on*-the-log pair of sentences, the meaning of the probe sentence that substitutes *it* for *them* is the same as that of the original, if we assume that verbal meaning includes inferences based on our prior knowledge of turtles, water, fish, logs, and so on. If all these inferences belong to the basic meaning of the sentence, the meanings of the two different sentences, the original and the probe, would indeed be the same. But this conception of meaning is exactly what was at issue. Is our background knowledge itself part of the meaning of a text? Are all these extralinguistic inferences part of the meaning we initially understand? The answer given by this and other experiments is "Yes, that is the nature of verbal meaning: inferences based on prior knowledge are part of meaning from the very beginning." This constructive hypothesis of verbal meaning has been closely studied and reconfirmed many times in the past several years. According to R. J. Spiro, "The study by Bransford, Barclay and Franks served as a prototype for what was to become a near avalanche of demonstrations that inferential elaborations are a part of the process of understanding prose."[11]

From this finding we can predict that there will be mutual influences between the mental models we have in our minds on the basis of prior knowledge and the words of the text as we read them. To make sense of what we read, we must use relevant prior knowledge to form a model of how sentence meanings hang together. The model constructed from our prior knowledge and the words of the text in turn helps us make sense of further words and sentences in the text. The idea was quickly tested by Bransford and his associates in 1972.[12] They used a passage written in language so general and vague that, in the absence of a context, it was difficult to construct a mental model from it. But if the passage was given a title that invoked relevant prior knowledge, subjects constructed a mental model that enabled them to understand and remember the sentences. The passage began:

> The procedure is actually quite simple. First you arrange the items in different groups. Of course one pile may be sufficient depending on how much there is to do. If you have to go somewhere else due to lack of facilities that is the next step; otherwise you are pretty well set.

Some subjects were given the title "Washing Clothes" before they read the passage, some were given it after, and some were not given it at all. Only the group who had been given the title before they started to read could recognize sentences from the passage. The title enabled them to integrate the sentences into a mental model that they constructed from prior knowledge about washing clothes. This model gave the sentences meaning, and the sentences in turn adjusted the model of the passage that was finally stored in memory. Apparently such an integrated model is essential to understanding and remembering discourse. Bransford and his associates conducted further experiments, using pictures instead of titles to provide the appropriate model, and the effect on reading was the same.[13]

It's easy to imagine variations on these Bransford experiments that would illustrate the connection between background knowledge and literacy. Persons who lack cultural knowledge are in just the position of the subjects who were given the clothes-washing passage without benefit of a title to form a context for the sentences. Informationally deprived people constantly run across passages that look like the Bransford one, because the texts contain important referential clues they can't understand. Although they can read the individual sentences, they can't make sense out of the whole.

Some less formal examples will corroborate the point. In 1978 community college students were given a prose selection to read, part of which follows.

GRANT AND LEE

When Ulysses S. Grant and Robert E. Lee met in the parlor of a modest house at Appomattox Courthouse, Virginia, on April 9, 1865, to work out the terms for the surrender of Lee's army of Northern Virginia, a great chapter in American life came to a close, and a great new chapter began.

These men were bringing the Civil War to its virtual finish. To be sure, other armies had yet to surrender, and for a few days the fugitive Confederate government would struggle desperately and vainly, trying to find some way to go on living now that its chief support was gone. But in effect it was all over when Grant and Lee signed the papers. And the little room where they wrote out the terms was the scene of one of the poignant, dramatic contrasts in American history.

They were two strong men, these oddly different generals, and they represented strengths of two conflicting currents that, through them, had come into final collision.

Lee was Tidewater Virginia; he embodied a way of life that had come down through the age of knighthood and the English country squire. . . .

Grant, the son of a tanner on the western frontier, was everything Lee was not. He had come up the hard way and embodied nothing in particular except the eternal toughness and sinewy fiber of the men who grew up beyond the mountains.[14]

The community college test population found this passage difficult to understand because they were, surprisingly, ignorant of the identities of Grant and Lee. They were not stumped by the vocabulary of the text in the ordinary sense of that term. For instance, they easily understood *burdensome, reliability, availability*, and *reassurance* in the following passage, which they read with perfect facility and accurate recall.

A GOOD FRIEND IS HARD TO FIND

Troubles always seem less burdensome and joys more pleasant when a good friend is present to share them. What makes a person a good friend? The qualities are numerous and hard to define; but two traits, availability and reliability, are essential. When I say that good friends are "available," I mean they are always nearby, ready to lend a hand. When I say that they are "reliable," I mean that they stand by their friends no matter what happens.

Good friends are always interested in their companions' day-to-day activities, always able to give reassurance. We never know what surprises the day may bring, and this uncertainty makes us nervous. When the telephone rings, our anxiety increases. Then we hear our friend's familiar greeting; and as the warm and cheery voice dispels our tension, our fears subside.

A person often finds himself in family predicaments that call for an outsider's help.[15]

These two passages were part of some large-scale experiments that my coworkers and I conducted in 1978.[16] In the course of them we developed a technique for testing large numbers of subjects (more than 700) for variations in reading skill that can be attributed to variations in relevant background knowledge. Dividing our audiences in half, we used two versions of the same text, one well written, the other stylistically impaired according to definite principles. As long as both versions of a text concerned a subject familiar to the readers, their performances showed a definite sensitivity to the stylistic superiority of one version over the other. When the topic was familiar, the group reading the better version understood it more efficiently; when it was unfamiliar, the performances of the two groups were nearly the same.

The following is a graph of the result we obtained with a pair of texts written on a familiar topic. The dotted line represents the performance of the group that was given the superior text, the solid line the performance of the group given the stylistically degraded version.[17] (These are called quintile graphs because the audience is divided into five groups according to reading rate, with the slowest fifth of readers labeled 1 along the base of the graph, the next fastest fifth labeled 2, and so on. The vertical line marks off reading rates in words per minute. The points through which the two lines are drawn are the average rates for each quintile taken as a group. Comprehension tests determined that all subjects had understood the passages, making reading rate an informative variable.)

QUINTILE GRAPH: "*TIME* VS. *NEWSWEEK*"

Reading Rates of Group A Compared With Rates of Group B When Reading Student Paper (A) and Stylistically Improved Version (B).

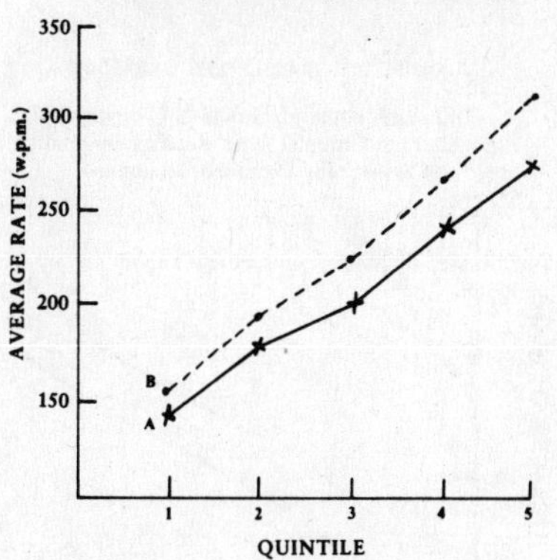

We were able to determine beforehand that our two groups were well matched, because we got the result shown in the next graph when each group was given the same text.

QUINTILE GRAPH: CONTROL ESSAY

Reading Rates of Group A Compared With Rates of Group B When Reading the Same Control Essay.

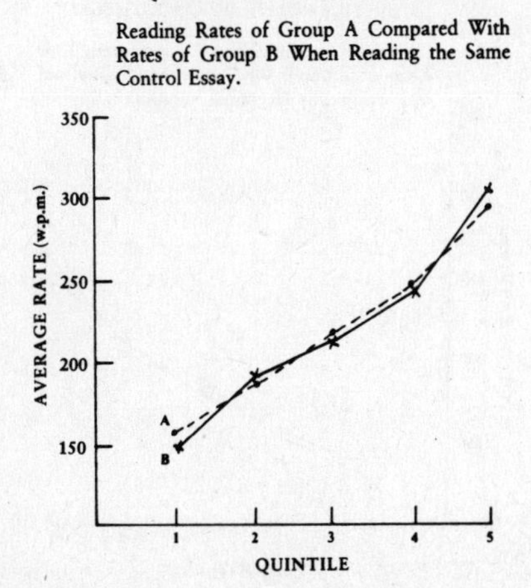

Then, some distance into our experiments, we noticed an interesting effect when we started using texts that addressed unfamiliar topics. Lack of familiarity not only debased the reading rates of our audiences, it also erased the differential effects of good and bad style. Below are two results from texts taken from *The History of Civilization* by Will and Ariel Durant. The style of the Durants' prose is of course clear and nontechnical, and the procedure we

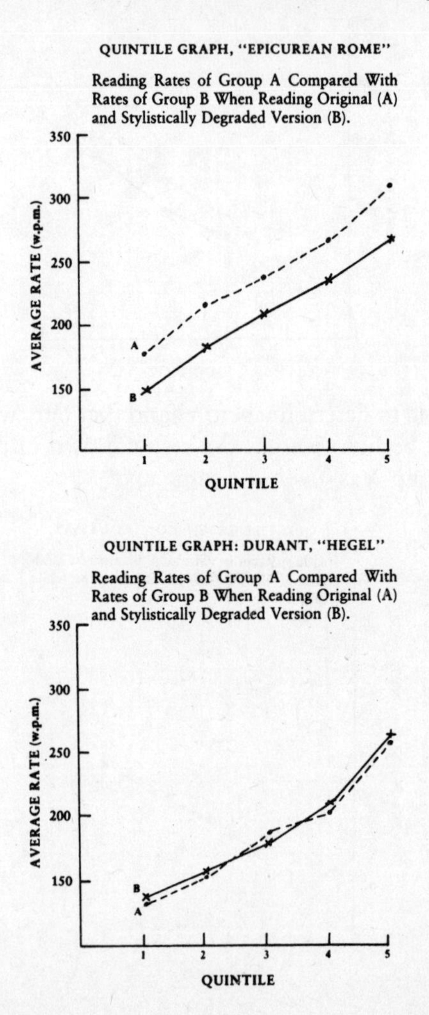

used for impairing their prose style was exactly the same in all cases. The text for the Epicurean Rome graph focused on the public baths of ancient Rome; the other graph was for an explanation of Hegel's conception of logic as metaphysics, a topic unfamiliar to our audience.

This effect was duplicated every time we tested it. We had unwittingly discovered a way to measure the variations in reading skill attributable to variations in the relevant background knowledge of audiences. Later, when we compared the results of our university presentations with the results we obtained at a community college, the contrasts were striking. The comparative results for the essay on Grant and Lee, one version of which had been stylistically impaired, are shown below.

QUINTILE GRAPH:
CATTON, "GRANT AND LEE"
UNIVERSITY AUDIENCE

Reading Rates of Group A Compared With Rates of Group B When Reading Original (A) and Stylistically Degraded Version (B).

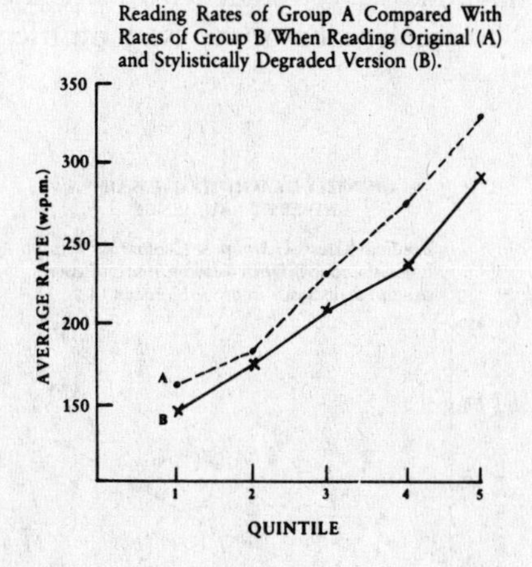

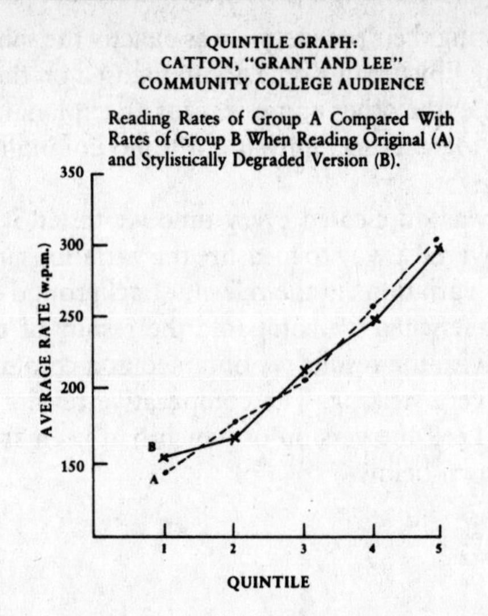

But such comparisons did not always reflect badly on the reading skills of the community college students. Here is a comparison of the two groups' comprehension of the essay on friendship.

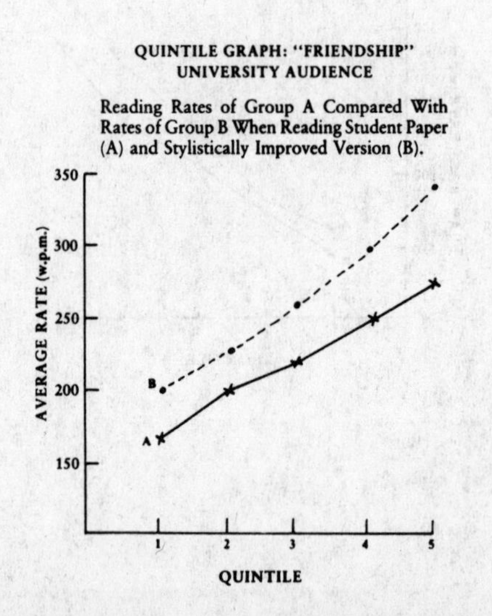

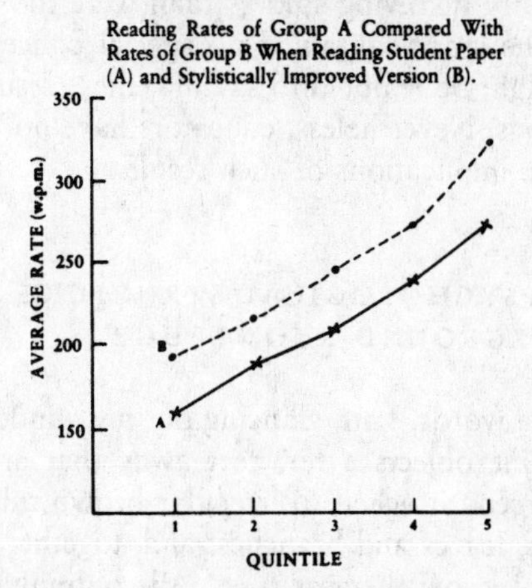

To those who know how to read them, these graphs tell a sad yet promising story — sad because the results with "Grant and Lee" show that the community college students lacked the background information needed for general literacy, but promising because the results with "Friendship" show that background information was really all they were lacking. Their memory capacities, eye movements, basic vocabularies, and reading strategies — in short, their reading skills — were all up to par. What they were missing was background information about Grant, Lee, and the Civil War (and, it can be inferred, much else that writers take for granted in their readers).

In experiments with children, researchers have drawn significant conclusions about the importance of background knowledge for general reading ability. T. Trabasso and his colleagues discovered that differences in reading ability between five-year-olds and eight-year-olds are caused primarily by the older children's possessing more knowledge, not by differences in their memory capacities, reasoning abilities, or control of eye movements.[18]

Similar work by P. D. Pearson and his associates has shown that, among seven-year-olds who score the same on reading and IQ tests, those who have greater knowledge relevant to the text at hand show superior reading skills. In one experiment, equally talented second-graders were tested to find out how much they knew about spiders.[19] Those who knew a little about them were much better readers of a story involving spiders than were the other children, even though the story contained no special concepts or difficult words. One might be tempted to say that these results are predictable and obvious. Nevertheless, educators have not acknowledged or acted on the implications of such results.

THE PSYCHOLOGICAL STRUCTURE OF BACKGROUND KNOWLEDGE

As I write these words, I am glancing out my window. My view is blocked by some objects a few feet away that are flat, roughly oblong, and green, attached to irregular brown tubes of different sizes. These are leaves and branches, and, together with the roots beneath them, I know them as trees. All continuing experience is partial and fragmented like my view of those trees. Our cognitive life takes place through a small window of attention that is framed by short-term memory. We use past knowledge to interpret this window of experience, to place its momentary fragments within larger wholes that give them a function and a place. The raw data of visual or linguistic perception come in bits and pieces, and they will remain meaningless if they continue to be nothing but colored flecks or mere sequences of letters or words. In our minds these transitory fragments can acquire meaning only by being placed within larger, not presently visible wholes that are based on past knowledge.

When I ask people what they see out of my window, they invariably answer trees. They don't respond that they are seeing the out-of-doors or nature or woods. Those categories are apparently too broad. At the other extreme, they don't say that they see some ends of branches with oak leaves, although that is all they see directly. Without being able to view a single tree trunk or top or bottom, they nonetheless say that they see trees. In structural terms, this response parallels the perception by the subjects who read that a fish swam under a log, even though the sentence didn't explicitly say that. The unseen trunks and roots are parts of what we "see," just as the fish that swam under the log is part of what we understand from a sentence saying the fish swam under turtles resting on a log. We "see" trees when we see only ends of branches, because we know from past experience that the branches are part of unseen structures beyond the edge of perception.

But why should people interpret what they see from my windows as trees rather than branches or the out-of-doors, since those categories are also valid interpretations based on past knowledge? The answer is that, if no other constraints are at work, people tend to interpret their experiences through middle categories, that is, through classifications that are neither specific, like oak leaves, nor general, like flora. We normally interpret experience through the categories that have been most useful to us in the past. We try them out initially as the most efficient instruments for perceiving the world and acting in it. Research has shown that middle-level categories are the ones children learn first in acquiring language; they learn *tree* before *oak*, and they learn *dog* before *animal*.[20]

Eleanor Rosch has called these middle categories basic-level terms. We owe much of our recent insight into their primacy to work done by her and her associates. In a number of papers she has argued that middle-level categories are the basic furniture of our conceptual world.[21] She has demonstrated that, in the absence of any special context or constraint, people understand the world in terms of basic classifications. Furthermore, people understand these normal classifications through commonly encountered examples. For instance, a typical association of the category tree for North Americans is leaves, rather than fronds.

In one experiment Rosch asked her subjects to arrange some specific names under the categories *fruit, furniture, bird,* and *clothing,* ranking the names from the most to the least typical.[22] The results were quite consistent from person to person. For instance, under *fruit,* the subjects agreed on the following order of typicality:

apple	fig
plum	prune
cherry	coconut
watermelon	olive

Under *furniture,* Rosch found the following ranking:

chair
dresser
davenport
footstool
lamp
cupboard
radio
ashtray

And under *bird* she got:

robin
swallow
eagle
crow
pheasant
goose
chicken
penguin

If people in our culture tend to agree that a robin is more typical than a pheasant in the bird category, it is likely that, other things being equal, they will think of a robin-sort-of-creature when they hear the word *bird*. With this in mind, Rosch asked subjects to compose isolated sentences using *bird*, and they produced sentences like

I heard a bird twittering outside my window.
Three birds sat on the branch of a tree.
A bird flew down and began eating.

Then Rosch replaced the class name *bird* with various specific members of the class (e.g., *robin, ostrich, chicken*), asking other subjects to judge whether the sentences of the type shown above made good sense. She found that if you replace *bird* with *robin* in each of the above sentences, subjects always say that the sentences make sense, but if you replace *bird* with *ostrich* or *chicken*, subjects say that the sentences don't make sense. Chickens don't act the way the birds in the sentences do — they don't twitter, sit on branches, or fly. In isolated sentences, when an untypical member of a class is substituted for the class name, sentences that previously sounded reasonable often fall into absurdity.

These two findings fit together neatly — people agree about typical examples of a class and the isolated sentences they make with class names work best with typical examples. The more typical an example is for its class, the more it accords with an isolated sentence that uses the class term. This finding suggests that we hold in our minds typical exemplars or prototypes of the category words we use and that these prototypes constitute the usual furniture of our minds. They are the classifications of things we use every day and keep at the ready in perception, conversation, reading, and writing. Rosch and others have shown that such prototypes are processed much faster than atypical examples in verifying the truth or falsity of isolated sentences. For instance, it takes a subject much longer to say true or false to the sentence "A chicken is a bird" than to "A robin is a bird."[23]

Reseachers have concluded that our usual prototypes for terms like *bird, tree,* and so on, contain definite features that we match up when we verify sentences like "A chicken is a bird." Since a chicken isn't like the usual prototype, we take rather long to compare features of birds and chickens before reaching a decision. But we can make an instant decision about robins. The consistent difference in the time it takes to reply true or false to typical and untypical examples suggests that part of our mental representation of a category is a prototype, e.g., for a bird the prototype is a vaguely robinlike creature.

Knowing about prototypes is essential for understanding how we apply past knowledge to the comprehension of speech. These mental models are the same as Hilary Putnam's "stereotypes."[24] We are able to make our present experiences take on meaning by assimilating them to prototypes formed from our past experiences.[25] Psychologists have been investigating these prototypes intensively and have given them various names such as frames, theories, concepts, models, and scripts. Researchers who have been relating these mental entities to reading, particularly R. C. Anderson and his associates, have chosen the word *schema* for them, and it is the term I use to refer to the phenomena. *Schema* and its plural *schemata* correctly suggest somewhat abstract mental entities rather than concrete images.[26]

If Rosch had tested her subjects in Australia, her results would probably have been different, and she would have found the typical bird schema to be unlike a robin in many respects. The creature nearest the Australian schema would be large and colorful, like a parakeet or a galah, with bright scarlet, green, and blue plumage, for those are the brilliant colors of the everyday birds one sees in one's garden in Australia. It would be odd indeed if the basis for an Australian bird schema were as drab a specimen as a robin. With this kind of qualification in mind, psychologists have amplified Rosch's work in one important respect. They have found that the schemata under which we create and interpret isolated sentences are not necessarily the initial schemata we apply in other contexts. Demonstrations of this variability have been conducted with the words *cup, eat, red,* and *held.*[27] It is clear that Rosch's work must be further generalized so that it reflects the context sensitivity of our initial schemata.

The research with the word list just referred to has shown that our minds have a remarkable ability to change initial schemata according to the situations in which we find ourselves. Such adjustments are largely unconscious, but one can perceive the pattern of the quick adjustments we make even with isolated sentences, as Anderson has suggested in the following passage:

> 1. The punter kicked the ball.
> 2. The baby kicked the ball.
> 3. The golfer kicked the ball.
>
> A different sort of ball is, loosely speaking, implied by each sentence. The punter is kicking a football, and the golfer a golfball. Although a baby could be kicking either of these kinds of ball, this is not the inference that will be drawn by most readers. Instead, a ball a baby is likely to kick will be hypothecated — perhaps a brightly colored, inflated, plastic ball. *Kick* has different senses in the three sentences. Compare the smooth powerful kick of a punter with the hesitant, uncoordinated, possibly accidental kick of a baby. Golfers do not ordinarily kick their balls; this fact leads to the supposition that this one was angry or maybe cheating.[28]

Anderson and others have thus made an important adjustment to the principle that we interpret the world through a basic set of schemata. We are in fact much more flexible. In reading, for example, we adjust our initial schemata to the specific text. In a story about a Thanksgiving feast, our initial schema for *bird* is *turkey,* not *robin.*[29] Two-way traffic takes place between our schemata and the words we read. We apply past schemata to make sense of the incoming words, but these words and other contextual clues affect our initial choices of schemata and our continuing adjustment of them.

In light of what has been described so far, we can say in general how a reader actively brings past schemata to bear upon what he or she is reading. According to the picture sketched by recent research, the reader is confined to a rather narrow window of attention that is limited by short-term memory. Through this window, the reader constantly connects a few words into clauses that have meaning and the clauses to appropriate schemata based on past experience. Thus, the reader is not just passively receiving meaning but is actively selecting the most appropriate schemata for making sense of the incoming words. Then the reader actively adjusts those schemata to the incoming words until a good fit is achieved. This process can work efficiently only if the reader has quick access to appropriate schemata. When the appropriate schemata are not quickly available, and the reader is forced to do a lot of pondering to construct them at the time of reading, the limits of short-term memory are quickly reached, and the process has to be painfully restarted and restarted.[30]

The immediately needed schemata go far beyond birds and cups to include the wider knowledge of cultural literacy. Consider, as a brief example of what is required, the opening words of the Grant and Lee passage that caused community college students so much trouble.

> When Ulysses S. Grant and Robert E. Lee met in the parlor of a modest house at Appomattox Courthouse, Virginia, on April 9, 1865, to work out the terms for the surrender of Lee's army of Northern Virginia, a great chapter in American life came to a close, and a great new chapter began. These men were bringing the Civil War to its virtual finish.

These words are like the leaves outside my window. If I do not know how they connect with larger schemata, I cannot make sense of them. On the other hand, the schemata I need are rather abstract entities that do not require profound knowledge. Consider how little detail there is in the schematic information needed to read the passage.

1. America fought a Civil War.
2. The two sides were the Union and the Confederacy.
3. Grant was the chief general for the Union.
4. Lee was the chief general for the Confederacy.
5. The Union won.

These ideas do not take the form of such a list in our minds but probably exist as a schematic model.[31] Clearly, these five propositions don't exhaust the schematic information one needs to read the passage, but, on the other hand, the necessary further schemata are much more elementary and were certainly known to the community college students. More specialized information is provided explicitly by the text.

We know that, in reading, our short-term memories allow us to attend only to a few salient features of word meanings — just those that are needed to make the meanings fit together. In the quoted passage, a reader could be attending to only a few surface ideas like Lee surrenders to Grant. Nonetheless, those meanings are connected to a lot of subsurface information, just as leaves are connected to information about trunks and roots of trees. One must integrate the passage on Grant and Lee with schematic background information about what a general is, what Civil War entails, what surrender means, and so on, although one does not pay direct attention to the implications.

The salient surface meanings that we pay attention to in reading thus *stand for* a whole world of relationships that we are not paying conscious attention to. When we really comprehend what we are reading, we are able to supply those implied background relationships. A schema functions as a unified system of background relationships whose visible parts stand for the rest of the schema. Because our narrow windows of attention confine us to just a few elements at a time, the technique of using surface elements to stand for larger wholes is an essential feature of our mental life.[32] Schemata are our necessary instruments for making the surfaces of what we read connect significantly with the background knowledge that is withheld from immediate consciousness by the limits of short-term memory.

To pursue the practical importance of this fact, let us examine more closely how these schemata work. The evidence that schemata function roughly as described so far goes back many years. As long ago as 1922, the German psychologist Franz Wulf observed that we have a tendency to "schematize" the details of what we remember about pictures and events so that, with a lapse of time, the details we remember become more and more like the average or typical things of our experience.[33] F. C. Bartlett, in his famous book *Remembering,* showed that our memories are freshly constructed from our habitual schemata, not just reproduced from actual memory traces. Our memories are always introducing elements from our normal schemata that weren't in an original event, and, by the same token, they are always suppressing some elements of the original event that don't exist in our normal schemata.[34] Thus, according to Bartlett, memory is active and constructive rather than passive and reconstructive.

> An individual does not normally take a situation detail by detail and meticulously build up the whole. In all ordinary instances he has an overmastering tendency simply to get a general impression of the whole; and on the basis of this, he constructs the probable detail. Very little of his construction is literally observed. But it is the sort of construction which serves to justify his general impression.[35]

Bartlett backed up his observation by testing subjects' memories of an American Indian folktale. His subjects' recollections of the story were distorted in the direction of their habitual schemata. All this is evidence that schemata are essential instruments of our cognitive lives.

Further strong evidence for the importance of schemata in our understanding of language was provided by B. H. Ross and G. H. Bower in 1981.[36] They set up their experiments on this reasoning: if we understand language through schemata, then any important element in a schema ought to call to mind other important schematic elements. If we are presented the term "U. S. Grant," it should call to mind the term "Civil War." If schemata do indeed govern our associations, then our tendency to associate words that are schematically connected ought to be greater than would be expected merely from the frequency of their co-occurrence in our past experience, which is the prediction of traditional learning theory and associationism. Ross and Bower gave subjects eighty sets of four words to study. Some had schematic associations, as in the case of *driver, trap, rough,* and *handicap,* all of which belong to the schema golf. When one word from this set (or from any other schematic set) was later given as a cue, subjects showed a strong tendency to recall the other three words belonging to the schema. Their performance was much better than had been predicted by stimulus-response theory or associationism. This is strong evidence that schemata function powerfully in both comprehension and memory.

Although we know in a general way what schemata are and how they function, psychologists do not understand many details. The latest view (that of Johnson-Laird, for instance) is that we use at least two radically different types of schemata, one analogous to static pictures and another to scripts or procedures.[37] In addition, we have not only general schemata of categories like birds but also memory traces of occasions when we perceived or read about birds.[38] We know that schemata overlap and get embedded in other schemata, that we treat them as provisional theories open to revision, and so forth. Indications are that an accurate modeling of our use of schemata would be very complex indeed. But we do not have to know the fine detail of the process to make intelligent practical advances in the teaching of literacy. We need to know how to put the principles of schemata to work to improve the performance of semiliterate people. What do we know about schemata that will enable us to do that?

We know that schemata perform two essential functions that are relevant to literacy. The first is storing knowledge in retrievable form; the second is organizing knowledge in more and more efficient ways, so that it can be applied rapidly and efficiently. Without appropriate background knowledge, people cannot adequately understand written or spoken language. And unless that knowledge is organized for rapid and efficient deployment, people cannot perform reading tasks of any complexity. Although there are sizable variations in reading rates among good readers, no good reader is a very slow reader. Slowness of reading beyond a certain point makes assimilation of complex meaning impossible. The limits of short-term memory do not allow the integration of "unchunked" material, and so crucial parts of meaning are lost to memory while other parts are being painstakingly worked out.

The evidence has shown that schemata are useful as a kind of mental shorthand that helps us work within the limits of short-term memory. One element of a schema represents many other subterranean elements, allowing us to deploy that one surface element as though the whole complex schema were a single item. In other words, a well-developed schema not only helps us make sense of incoming data but also helps us to manipulate and connect information rapidly. In this process, speed of comprehension is equivalent to quality of comprehension, because without the speed and the shorthand provided by well-organized schemata our circuits get overloaded. We can't perform the necessary manipulations before we run out of memory, and we continually have to start over again.

Since use of schemata is of course common to literate and illiterate alike, we need to ask two specific questions. What sorts of schemata must people acquire to be really literate? And how can these particular schemata be made efficient enough to create good readers? A. M. Collins and M. R. Quillian published an important piece of work on this subject in 1969.[39] Their theory is that the knowledge most often needed is also the most directly available and is, so to speak, right at the surface of the schema. Other parts of the schema are "deeper" and take longer to retrieve. One of their examples also concerns a bird. They reasoned that general information about birds would be farthest from the surface and that specific information (e.g., direct information about robins or canaries) would be most often used and closest to the surface.

They posited the following schematic network for canaries, starting with the most available information provided by a mention of the word *canary* and going down to the least available and most general level.

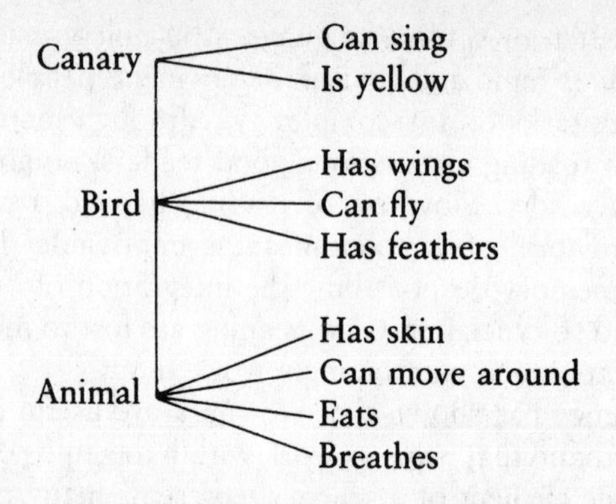

Starting from the top of the vertical line, there is an increasingly long path from bird traits to animal traits. The prediction is that, if knowledge is organized in this kind of pattern, the decision whether sentences are true or false will take longer the farther down the vertical path the sentences require us to go. Collins and Quillian gave subjects the following sentences:

Canaries are yellow.
Canaries lay eggs.
Canaries can breathe.

Subjects did in fact take longer to decide the truth of sentences the farther down the conjectured schematic path they had to go. This kind of result has been confirmed many times by researchers.[40]

What does this experimentation tell us about the rapid deployment of background information in reading? Collins and Quillian's observations suggest that the top portion of a schema is the important part to know. The schema canary can yield an indefinite number of facts and association by remote inference from knowledge of the world: canaries have backbones; canaries have their own special pattern of DNA; canaries are descended from reptiles; canaries must drink water; canaries mate; canaries die. One could go on this way for a long time, with specifications not only from biological but from physical knowledge: canaries obey the law of gravity and the laws of motion, and so on. But this secondary information about canaries is not important in communicating with fellow human beings. What is functional in reading, writing, and conversing is the distinctive system of traits in the schemata we use — the traits that differentiate canaries from other birds: their smallness, yellowness, ability to sing, use in human culture, being kept in cages, and so on. We need to know the primary traits commonly associated with canary in our culture in order to deploy the associations rapidly when we encounter the word *canary* in reading.

There is no substitute for simply knowing these primary associations. They must be called up with lightning speed in the course of reading and conversing. We do not have the luxury of figuring out such associations one at a time. We may do this with one or two words in a paragraph — that is the way we learn new words — but we cannot pause over many words at a time. When we encounter U. S. Grant, the primary associations must be available to us in milliseconds: that he was an important Union general, that he became president, that he drank. These are some of the implicit associations needed to make meaningful what is explicitly written about Grant.

Research into the importance of primary associations thus introduces a subject of profound significance for teaching reading and writing. Successful communication depends upon shared associations. To participate in the literate national culture is to have acquired a sense of the information that is shared in that culture. No adult-level discourse retreats to the rudiments of knowledge. If assumptions about rudiments could not be made, ordinary discourse would be so lengthy and intricate as to obscure its own point.

Educators in the Rousseau-Dewey tradition, who favor less emphasis on mere fact and more emphasis on the intensive study of a few cases, encourage us to believe that students will thereby understand general principles and learn how to think critically.[41] But literacy requires us to have both intensive knowledge of relationships and extensive knowledge of specifics. We need not only a general understanding of the principles of biology (which would enable us to infer that canaries breathe and lay eggs) but also specific knowledge of facts about canaries. We need to know not only the broad social and historical significance of the American Civil War but also who U. S. Grant was, and what the word *Appomattox* signifies. It is not enough to say that students can look these facts up. The research reviewed above shows that in order for readers to integrate phrases into comprehensible meanings, they must already possess specific, quickly available schemata. When readers constantly lack crucial information, dictionaries and encyclopedias become quite impractical tools. A consistent lack of necessary information can make the reading process so laborious and uncommunicative that it fails to convey meaning.

SKILL AS KNOWLEDGE AND KNOWLEDGE AS SKILL

Researchers in cognitive psychology and the area of computer science known as artificial intelligence (AI) have come to strikingly similar conclusions about the knowledge-bound character of *all* cognitive skills. AI research demonstrates that the ability of humans to exercise a skill depends on their possession of specific schemata that are sufficiently numerous and detailed to handle the many varieties of the tasks they are called on to perform. It is more accurate to speak of "reading *skills*" than of "reading skill." The graphs showing the community college students' high degree of skill in reading the essay on friendship but their lack of skill in reading about Grant and Lee accord with the recent discovery of AI and cognitive psychology that a skill is not a unified system of intellectual muscles that can be developed by calisthenics into a vigorous all-purpose ability.

Dr. Herbert A. Simon, a leading figure in AI research, once wryly remarked that saying an expert performance is caused by a "skill" is like Molière's doctor saying that the sleep-inducing properties of opium are caused by its "dormative power."[42] Simon, a Nobel laureate, has been working since the 1950s on the detailed structure of cognitive skills. The discoveries that he and his coworkers have made should induce a deep skepticism toward the belief that our schools can teach reading, writing, and critical thinking as all-purpose general skills applicable to novel problems. Simon and his colleagues have cast doubt on the idea that there are *any* general or transferable cognitive skills. All cognitive skills depend on procedural and substantive schemata that are highly specific to the task at hand.

Once the relevant knowledge has been acquired, the skill follows.[43] General programs contrived to teach general skills are ineffective. AI research shows that experts perform better than novices not because they have more powerful and better oiled intellectual machinery but because they have more relevant and quickly available information. What distinguishes good readers from poor ones is simply the possession of a lot of diverse, task-specific information.

Probably the most dramatic illustrations of the knowledge-bound character of human skills came from some remarkable experiments conducted by Adriaan de Groot, a Dutch psychologist, who described his findings in a book entitled *Het Denken van den Schaker* (literally, "the thinking of chess players").[44] De Groot discovered that chess masters are astonishingly skilled at remembering and reproducing chess positions after a very brief exposure to them. The subjects in his experiments were players of various abilities, as indicated by their official chess rankings. In one experiment, de Groot displayed for five to ten seconds a chess position from an actual game in which twenty-five pieces were left on the board. The subjects were asked to reproduce the position from memory. Grand masters performed this feat with 100 percent accuracy, masters with 90 percent accuracy. Weaker players were lucky if they could correctly place five or six pieces.

Then de Groot varied the conditions of his experiment in one respect. Instead of placing the twenty-five pieces in positions from an actual game, he placed them on the board randomly. The results were unexpected. All his subjects — grand masters, masters, class A players, and class B players — performed the same as novices did, placing only five or six pieces correctly. This experiment has been duplicated in several different laboratories, and structurally in several other fields, including algebra, physics, and medicine, always with the same striking results.[45,46]

When the configuration of a task is significantly changed, past skills are not transferred to the new problem.[47] In normal circumstances, of course, elements from past problems appear in present ones, and experts perform well with duplicated elements. But beyond similar or analogous circumstances, skill is not transferred.

Since the 1950s, when Simon introduced de Groot's work to the American research community, no convincing counterarguments or experiments have challenged these results. Researchers have consistently found that people do not develop general, transferable skills in problem solving, critical thinking, or in any other field.[48]

What are the reasons for these astonishing results? The fullest explanations have come from those engaged in making computer models of skilled and unskilled performances. AI scientists have formulated programs that conform extremely well to actual human performances and to the models currently inferred by cognitive psychologists. The convergence of the accounts from both AI and empirical psychology increases one's confidence in their correctness.[49]

There is another reason why the AI research results should be taken seriously. AI models actually work. You can play chess against a computer program and lose. An up-to-date chess program behaves like a skilled player, not because the computer is directed to zip through every possible variation — it could not possibly do that in the few seconds it takes to respond — but because in some ways, though not in all, it imitates the knowledge-based procedures of experts.

I said that models from research in artificial intelligence and from experimental psychology are converging. Both approaches show that expert performance depends on the quick deployment of schemata. In the case of de Groot's chess experiments, the currently accepted models would explain the results as follows. When de Groot's subjects were exposed to a chessboard for about six seconds, the limits of short-term memory were quickly reached. The constraint of short-term memory explains, of course, why novices could manage to place only about six pieces — the range predicted by research. There's no difficulty, then, in explaining the poor performance of the novices. But what explains the superb performances of the experts?

In his second experiment de Groot proved that expert chess players have no better memories or general skills than novices. Like everyone else, they can remember only five or six pieces from a random pattern. But when they are asked to survey a position that is not random, they quickly match the observed patterns with specific schemata already stored in memory. That process instantly facilitates the cognitive task. Consider the arithmetic of the situation. If expert schemata for chess patterns average five or six pieces per schema, that would remove the burden of remembering twenty-five individual items. Think of the experts as perceiving the positions of five or six pieces all at once, as words rather than individual letters. Because they already possess positional schemata, experts would need to remember only four or five chunked items — well within the range of short-term memory.

It is probable that the grand masters in de Groot's experiment quickly focused on one or two variations from known patterns, and that those one or two variations were all they needed to remember. They were in the masterful position we would be in if we were asked to spell out the sixteen letters of "The cat is on the mat" after an exposure of only six seconds. Our performance would be made possible by our possession of spelling schemata for the words. When de Groot's chess masters were asked to reproduce the original position, they needed only to recall two or three variations and were able to reconstruct the rest from the schemata they already possessed.

Skill in reading is like skill in chess in many respects. Good reading, like good chess, requires the rapid deployment of schemata that have already been acquired and do not have to be worked out on the spot. Good readers, like good chess players, quickly recognize typical patterns, and, since they can ignore many small-scale features of the text, they have space in short-term memory to take in an overall structure of meaning. They are able to do all of this because, like expert chess players, they have ready access to a large number of relevant schemata. By contrast, unskilled readers lack this large store of relevant schemata and must therefore work out many small-scale meaning relationships while they are reading. These demanding tasks quickly overload their short-term memories, making their performance slow, arduous, and ineffective.

How large is the "large number of schemata" that skilled persons have acquired? It has been estimated that a chess master can recognize about 50,000 positional patterns.[50] Interestingly, that is the approximate number of words and idioms in the vocabulary of a literate person. Is there any significance in this coincidence of numbers? Probably, according to Simon and Barenfeld.[51] A schema for a chess pattern is the functional equivalent of a schema for a word or idiom. There must be an upper limit to the number of schemata that we can effectively utilize, because we must have immediate access to them if they are to be effective. Apparently, a number in the range of 50,000 marks the upper limit of items to which we can have rapid access in any domain of activity. Using a significantly greater number of items would cause the process of search and retrieval to occupy too much time.

There are, of course, many more than 50,000 items stored in the full text of long-term memory. A basic vocabulary of 50,000 schemata serves merely as a quickly accessible index to a much larger volume of knowledge.[52] Any of the 50,000 schemata can be related to others, and the further relationships can be stored in long-term memory. A useful illustration of the way one schema can serve as a mental shorthand for enormous complexes of associated schemata is the field of mathematics, where many decades of mathematical labor can be reduced to a single symbol that can be manipulated as though it were a mere digit like the number 5. The term "Civil War" represents not just its own schema, but also whole ranges of further, associated schemata that can be applied when needed but do not obtrude into the window of the mind unless they are called forth. As we have seen, the most effective system for the mind, whether in chess or in reading, is to keep most of its indexed schemata at a medium level of generality.[53]

But although parallels between skill in reading and skill in chess are informative, the two kinds of expertise are structurally different in one respect. Chess players do not have to communicate their stored patterns to anyone else and can organize their schemata in whatever way they like. But when we use verbal schemata, we have less freedom. The patterns of association in the verbal schemata of one person must approximate those of another, otherwise we could not use surface meanings to represent larger systems of subsurface associations. Words and idioms therefore represent systems of association that belong not just to the individual mind but to the language community as a whole. Words, idioms, and grammatical systems represent shared systems of association[54] — cultural literacy.

The last piece of research that I shall describe brings some of these strands together and proves the importance of cultural literacy in a striking way. The work was conducted and reported by R. M. Krauss and S. Glucksberg.[55] Imagine an experiment in which some of the special constraints of reading and writing are acted out physically in the laboratory. One constraint of reading is that author and reader cannot converse with each other. Only the author is the source of the words; the reader has no access to an author's gestures or facial expressions. To reproduce this constraint, we erect a physical barrier between two people so that only one of the subjects can be heard and neither can see the other. Then we give these two subjects a communication task to perform. The speaker must explain to the listener the order in which the six following unfamiliar shapes must be listed.

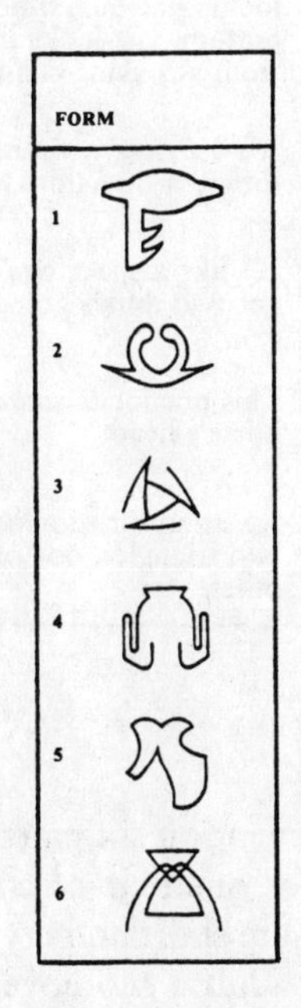

Charts on pages 65–67 from R. M. Krauss and S. Glucksberg, "Social and Nonsocial Speech."

To establish a standard of performance, we run the experiment with pairs of literate adults, who find the task almost ridiculously easy. They make virtually no errors on their first attempt. Here is a typical set of descriptions by a literate adult playing the role of author:

FORM	
1 	Looks like a motor from a motorboat. It has a thing hanging down with two teeth.
2 	It looks like two worms or snakes looking at each other. The bottom part looks like the rocker from a rocking chair.
3 	It's a zigzag with lines going in all different directions.
4 	It's like a spaceman's helmet; it's got two things going up the sides.
5 	This one looks something like a horse's head.
6 	It's an upside-down cup. It's got two triangles, one on top of the other.

Now we try the experiment on six pairs of young children from four to five years old. Not one pair of children completes a trial correctly. Their messages are short and cryptic rather than full and elaborated like those of adults. Moreover, the messages depend upon associations that are not widely shared in the speech community.[56] A summary chart of some results with young children is on the next page.

FORM	CHILD				
	1	2	3	4	5
1 	Man's legs	Airplane	Drape-holder	Zebra	Flying saucer
2 	Mother's hat	Ring	Keyhold	Lion	Snake
3 	Somebody running	Eagle	Throwing sticks	Strip-stripe	Wire
4 	Daddy's shirt	Milk jug	Shoe hold	Coffeepot	Dog
5 	Another Daddy's shirt	Bird	Dress hold	Dress	Knife
6 	Mother's dress	Ideal	Digger hold	Caterpillar	Ghost

Later the experimenters tested older children from kindergarten through fifth grade. Krauss and Glucksberg give the following account of what they found:

> The results were somewhat surprising. Kindergartners performed no better than nursery school children, and displayed the same lack of improvement with practice. Considering that adults made virtually no errors on the very first trial, the performance of children in the first, third, and fifth grades is even more surprising: they were no better than kindergartners on the first trial. The older children did show marked improvement with practice, but it seemed clear that even the fifth-graders (who were about 10 years old) did not approach the adult level. . . . We proceeded to test children from grades three through nine in the Princeton school system. . . . We were again surprised at the generally low level of performance. . . . Ninth-graders, although they showed dramatic improvement in suc-

cessive trials, still did not attain the virtually perfect accuracy that adults displayed from the very first trial.[57]

Krauss and Glucksberg inferred from this — correctly, I believe — that the older children performed poorly not because of their insufficient cognitive development but because of their lack of information.[58] They had not acquired an easy sense of the degree to which their schemata were shared with strangers in the speech community. Their lack of information strained their cognitive capacities when they tried to carry out the task.

> When the demands of the task are relatively light, children do engage in social, nonegocentric speech, and they communicate rather successfully. As the demands become heavier children may still attempt to employ social-communication strategies, but they do so less effectively than adults. Finally, when the demands of the task become heavy enough, children may not have the opportunity to bring into play the social-communication skills they possess.[59]

The performance of the young children in this experiment is like the performance of poor readers. Both are ineffective because of cognitive overload. A semiliterate person reading or a young child describing strange shapes has to figure out too many things at one time. In effective reading, one must not only call up one's own schematic associations but also monitor whether they are appropriate ones shared by the wider speech community. Literate adults have internalized these shared schemata and have made them second nature. As the Krauss-Glucksberg experiments indicate, literate adults have a sure instinct for what will and will not be shared by others in the wider culture. Young children and other semiliterates do not confidently know what other members of the speech community can be expected to know. Thus, besides their lack of substantive information, young children and semiliterates also lack something equally important: readily accessible information about what is shared by others. In reading and writing, as in communicating shapes across a physical barrier, it is essential to know the other person's unspoken systems of association.

Such cultural knowledge is not entirely a function of age. Some children acquire it rather early, and illiterate adults never acquire it fully. Experiments reported by Basil Bernstein suggest that the performances of children attempting tasks similar to those in the Krauss-Glucksberg experiments vary according to the children's degree of literacy, and their performances therefore have, under present circumstances, a strong correlation with social class.[60] In Bernstein's experiments, the most important variable was whether the children were used to talking with literate strangers and had thereby gained a sense of the wider speech community. The shared schemata necessary for reading and writing are always those of the wider community. Bernstein's experiments reconfirmed that literacy is a function of a national rather than a local culture.

CHAPTER III

National Language and National Culture

THE FORMATION OF MODERN NATIONAL LANGUAGES

Historical research into the origins of national languages and cultures directly reinforces the psychological research I have just traced. History explains from a quite different vantage point why the level of one's literacy depends upon the breadth of one's acquaintance with a national culture. History also shows why the connection between literacy and national culture is a general principle of modern times, one that holds true for all modern nations.

If you drive in the French Riviera and stop at the town of Menton, you can find small children speaking rapidly in excellent French. Their easy mastery of French grammar and pronunciation will seem charming and enviable. If you then drive east from Menton for just a few minutes and pass over a line painted across the road, you will come to the town of Ventimiglia. There you can find small children speaking charming, enviable Italian. To the children on both sides of the painted line, and perhaps to you, it all seems quite normal: the easy mastery of French or Italian, the arbitrariness of the border, and the fact that the painted line determines which language the children speak. We have come to accept such arrangements as being natural, but from a linguistic point of view they are not. French and Italian, as well as English and all the other national languages, were just as consciously and politically constructed as the national borders that separate them. These standardized national languages were fixed in essentially their present forms by seventeenth-, eighteenth-, and (in some countries) nineteenth-century language normalizers who made their decisions, more often than not, at the direction of a central national government. National languages and national borders are codependent artifices. Taken together they have generated one of the most important features of the modern world — the huge, linguistically homogeneous populations of the industrial nations.[1]

That small children should speak Hungarian inside the borders of Hungary (or Polish inside the borders of Poland), and that the language spoken in one place in Hungary should be the same as that spoken in another, is a situation that can exist with such precision only because it is carefully sustained by the Hungarian system of education. Inside a national border, education helps to keep the national language stable by holding it to standards that are set forth in national dictionaries, spelling books, pronunciation guides, and grammars. In the modern world we therefore find linguistic diversity among the nations but, with a few exceptions, linguistic uniformity inside the nations. This pattern did not arise by chance; it is a self-conscious political and educational arrangement.

Consider the languages of Europe in their natural earlier state, before they were standardized into national literary languages. In the Middle Ages it often happened that only closely neighboring dialects were dependably intelligible to one another. If you traveled four villages away instead of three you might not be able to understand what people were saying. A dialect map for the fourteenth century would show isoglosses marking off domains of mutual unintelligibility between speakers.[2] No linguistic lines were painted across the road; the shifting linguistic borders could be drawn differently, depending on which dialect was used as a base. What's more, these languages changed radically over time. A fourteenth-century Rip Van Winkle waking from a sleep of a hundred — rather than twenty — years might find it hard to understand the speech of his children's grandchildren. The natural law of oral languages is constant change, but that law has been amended by the development of national written languages sustained by national systems of education.

A little more than a hundred years ago, in the 1870s, Henry

Sweet, the distinguished linguist who was the model for Henry Higgins in *My Fair Lady,* predicted that in a hundred years the English, Australians, and Americans would be speaking mutually incomprehensible languages because of their great distance and isolation from each other.[3] Sweet was one of the most knowledgeable linguists of his day, and his prediction was one that other scholars of the time would have agreed with. Up to Sweet's time, languages had followed the universal law of constant change. Whenever people who spoke the same oral dialect divided from each other geographically, their languages also came to diverge. That is why, judging by previous linguistic history, Sweet's prediction seemed sound. Before the spread of literacy in the nineteenth century, speakers had neither an external standard nor an internal gyroscope to keep their languages stable. Thus, in the eighteenth century Alexander Pope wrote:

> Our sons their fathers' failing language see,
> And such as Chaucer is, shall Dryden be.[4]

But Pope and Sweet were wrong. We not only understand the British and Australians today and they us, but we are able to read Pope and Dryden, and most American schoolchildren can read *Gulliver's Travels* by Pope's contemporary Jonathan Swift. The modern English language has turned out to be far more stable than anyone in those days could have predicted. The same has been true of other European languages.

The monolingual nation as we know it developed alongside a new kind of social and economic organization — the industrial nation state. In earlier, agrarian times, when economies were local, one's occupation and position in the community were fixed. Because the economic unit was confined to a small area, an oral dialect sufficed, and the mutual unintelligibility of different dialects within a large region was no serious handicap to economic and social life. When foreign travelers and traders of those times needed a language beyond the local dialects, they could use an international language like the lingua franca or the koine. These were the earlier equivalents of the great modern national languages, each of which now functions as a lingua franca within a nation.

After the industrial revolution, that is, some time in the eighteenth century, economic arrangements required a different political and linguistic system. Economic units became larger, and economic advance became perpetual. The water wheel gave way to the steam engine, the steam engine to the internal combustion engine, and so on. The worker had constantly to adapt to new, more efficient methods. Because of the continually changing occupations that were increasingly demanded by large industrial societies, people had to communicate with a wider economic and social community. Achieving wider communication required literacy and a common language. At the same time, the political system had to become correspondingly bigger, requiring wider circles of communication to carry out laws and provide centralized authority.

The correlation of modern nationhood and the needs of industrial society is a thesis that Ernest Gellner develops brilliantly in his *Nations and Nationalism.*[5] The formation of the modern nation makes possible complex communication on a large scale, which makes possible, in turn, the specializations of modern industrial society.[6] To meet the needs of the wider economy, the modern industrial nation requires widespread literacy. At the heart of modern nationhood is the teaching of literacy and a common culture through a national system of education.

"Nationalism," Gellner writes, "is rooted in a certain kind of division of labor, one which is complex, and persistently, cumulatively changing." Consequently, what is needed is a general education in a common culture. Gellner goes on to observe:

> The major part of training in industrial society is *generic* training . . . Industrial society may by most criteria be the most highly specialized society ever; but its educational system is the *least* specialized, the most universally standardized that has ever existed . . . It is assumed or hoped that every properly trained recruit can be retrained from one specialism to another without too much loss of time.[7]

Because of modern economic needs, the goals of language standardization and universal literacy become ever more urgent. Gellner describes education in cultural literacy as *the* central requirement of industrial society:

> Universal literacy and a high level of numerical, technical and general sophistication are among [industrial society's] functional prerequisites. Its members . . . must be able to communicate by means of written, impersonal, context-free, to-whom-it-may-concern-type messages. Hence these communications must be in the same shared and standardized linguistic medium and script.[8]

Gellner's analysis explains the underlying reasons for the development of standardized languages and modern national economies and also explains why enormously expensive systems of education are universal in the modern nations. Totalitarian nations may pay only lip service to such ideals as free speech and free elections. But their guarantee of universal education is, as Gellner says, "an ideal more honored in the observance than the breach. In this it is virtually unique among modern ideals, and this calls for an explanation." The explanation lies in the weighty consequences that proceed from education in our society.

> The employability, dignity, security, and self-respect of individuals, typically, and for the majority of men now hinges on their *education* . . . A man's education is by far his most precious investment, and in effect confers his identity on him. Modern man is not loyal to a monarch, or a land, or a faith, whatever he may say, but to a culture . . . [This] school-transmitted culture, not a folk-transmitted one, alone confers usability and dignity and self-respect on industrial man.[9]

To be sure, large-scale social and cultural unification based on general education and a standard written language were effects whose causes were sometimes obscure to the societies that produced them. But the manufacturer of textile goods certainly realized that he had to communicate in writing with his distant shippers, customers, and suppliers. The bureaucrat engaged in army raising or tax raising realized that he had to communicate with officials and citizens thoughout the land. The new economy with its multiple specialties, and the new nation with its bureaucratic structures, required an ever broader use of the written word, and people became increasingly aware of the need for universal literacy and a common language. Everywhere sentiment grew to "improve" and "ascertain" — that is, to stabilize — the national languages.[10]

The economic and technical forces that first led to language standardization and mass literacy have continued to gain momentum. Now that economic relationships are instantaneous and global, national vocabularies have grown still larger in scope. Our national vocabulary has three distinct domains. The first is international. Basic literacy in the contemporary world requires knowledge of certain terms known by literate people everywhere in the world, no matter what language they speak. This core lexicon of modern education includes basic words from world history, world cultures, geography, and the physical and biological sciences. Taught in all national educational systems, and not confined to any particular national language, it is the most broadly shared literate vocabulary in the world.

Lying beyond the core is the sphere of vocabulary needed for literacy in English, no matter in what country the language is used. Words like *Achilles* and *Scrooge* and *Falstaff* and *Cinderella* belong to cultural literacy in all nations where English is spoken, even if they were founded recently. This broad knowledge belongs to transnational cultural literacy in English, a sphere that is shared by literate Britons, Indians, South Africans, Americans, and Australians. Despite grumblings in all these countries about the foreign, all-too-English character of these traditional elements, they are probably here to stay, because they form a useful basis for international exchanges in English.

But in addition to broadly shared, international spheres of knowledge, every literate person today has to possess information and vocabulary that is special to his or her own country. A literate Briton has to know more about the game of cricket and the Corn Laws than an American. An American has to know more about baseball and the Bill of Rights than a Briton. Textbooks containing a national vocabulary have always been developed in evolving nations.[11] In the early days of development, this dimension of cultural literacy is usually standardized along with the standard version of the national language. To explain the character and significance of this historical development, it is helpful to contrast Europe with China. Why did linguistic and national standardization arise in Europe in the eighteenth century but not in China?

By the seventeenth century, China had printing presses and a stable written language. But even after the arrival of printing, the oral Chinese language did not become standardized throughout the country. To this very day, China is a polyglot nation of mutually unintelligible dialects. And in the early years of the twentieth century China presented a cautionary picture of what can happen in the modern world to a populous nation that lacks language unification and standardization. In the absence of a standard tongue China was not able to function successfully as a modern industrial and economic unit.

What kept China from achieving language standardization? Part of the answer is simple and direct. European languages use an alphabetic system of writing that connects writing and speaking. The written spellings are stable, and because of the alphabetic — that is, semiphonetic — system of writing, the standardized spellings have a definite connection with spoken sounds. Widespread schooling in spelling and pronunciation keeps the sounds of the language from straying very far. Schoolteachers in Australia use basically the same standards of pronunciation and spelling as schoolteachers in Britain and America.[12] The written language as taught in school thus stabilizes the spoken. This is why Sweet's 1877 prediction went wrong. If you are able to read and write English you can make yourself understood when speaking to another person who can read and write English. But if you are able to read and write Chinese you will not necessarily be able to speak to another person who can read and write Chinese, for the Chinese written symbol is not phonetic. Although the meaning of a written symbol is the same for every Chinese dialect, it represents different sounds in different dialects. The chief dialects of China are in fact mutually unintelligible, and the only way speakers of different dialects can communicate is by writing notes to one another.

Thus the standardization of writing and the spread of reading did not have the same stabilizing effect on language in China as it had in Europe. On the other hand, the example of modern Japan shows that effective standardization of the spoken language is possible without alphabetic script, as long as a national system of education enforces common standards for pronunciation and grammar. Nonetheless, the easiest way to standardize and stabilize a language is to follow the European pattern: fix upon a single dialectal norm, freeze its grammar at a particular time, fix standard spellings, and fix pronunciations that are reasonably well represented by the spellings. Conscious of this, China recently attempted the transcription of Chinese into Western alphabetic script and has set up a single dialect — the Mandarin — as the basis for the national language. The size, labor, expense, and dislocation of this undertaking were breathtaking, and that China was willing to undertake it showed an appreciation of the importance to a modern nation of fixing a common national language in both spoken and written forms.[13]

From the standpoint of cultural literacy, the interventionist character of eighteenth-century language standardizing in Europe is useful for illustrating the need for self-conscious planning in national education. Fixed national languages are deliberate constructs. In France the process began as early as 1635, when the king issued royal letters patent to the French Academy, instructing it to "labor with all care and diligence to give certain rules to our language, and to render it pure, eloquent, and capable of treating the arts and sciences." Thus the French Academy marched under the banner of "purifying" the language, and, indeed, purification was the usual ideology or metaphor under which the dictionary-making process was carried out. But the real job of the French Academy and other dictionary-making groups elsewhere was to fix the usage, grammar, and spelling of the national language. They were to establish one form of spelling and pronunciation as the norm, to promulgate it in authoritative dictionaries and grammars, and, in consequence, to eliminate all other dialects, spellings, and pronunciations in order to create a single standard language.

As it was in France, so was it in Spain. Because of the importance of Spanish on the current U.S. scene, it's worth mentioning that the language now spoken by Hispanics in our country was developed by exactly this same deliberate process. Spanish is no more an "ethnic" language than French. By the time of the conquistadores, efforts to standardize written Spanish had made headway, but the final consolidation came in the early eighteenth century, when the newly formed Spanish Academy, under the duke of d'Escalona, was given the task of purifying and improving the Spanish language under royal authority. The academy, called the Real (Royal) Academia de la Lengua, was to issue a dictionary that distinguished correct words from "low, obsolete or barbarous" ones. In practical fact, court Castilian was set up as the dialect base of the Spanish national language — and forever after the Castilian-based *Diccionario* of the academy has been the permanent basis for school instruction wherever Spanish is taught and spoken.[14]

The standardization of English achieved the same result, but by more indirect means. Although England did not establish a national academy, prominent intellectuals in the seventeenth and eighteenth centuries, including Daniel Defoe and Jonathan Swift, proposed one, and others agitated to purify and ascertain the language in dictionaries and grammars. The famous authoritative dictionary issued by Samuel Johnson in 1755 was the most important member of this series. Webster's dictionary (1806) was based on Johnson's, but it added well-known, minor changes in spelling (as in dropping *u* in *honour* and in *theater* instead of *theatre*). With few exceptions since Johnson's day, English spelling, grammar, and punctuation, as well as the main features of usage, have remained stable. The only deviations from current forms that I find in the Declaration of Independence are *hath* for *has* and *compleat* for *complete*. Surprisingly, Jefferson and Hancock followed earlier dictionaries, not the Tory Johnson, in their spellings of *public* and *honor,* making their document seem all the more up to date to us.[15]

The most striking characteristic of language standardizing is its initial arbitrariness, which is similar to that of setting up almost any common standard. Early grammarians and the makers of spelling books and dictionaries were often forced to choose from among several accepted possibilities, and in all cases had to freeze the then current form of the language, thus inhibiting further grammatical or phonetic evolution. When a group of scientists met in Paris in 1795 to decide on the length of the standard meter bar, they had an elaborate justification for the particular length they chose, just as Samuel Johnson offered justifications for his decisions about spelling.[16] But that justification was irrelevant to the utility of the meter as a common standard for measuring length. Any usable length would have served the purpose equally well. Language normalizers have always offered justifications for their choices from among current forms. But beyond helping to give the decisions a socially persuasive force, little hinges on such justifications. The fact of a common standard is much more important than the intrinsic character of the standard chosen.

The meter bar, like the French language itself, was established by a central authority in Paris. By contrast, the British system of language standardizing was less imperious, less obviously imposed from above. But the British system achieved the same final result as the French. Both approaches to standardization always achieve the same result. But an important difference between establishing the meter as a standard of measurement and establishing a standard written language is that the language must be constructed on less rational principles. The choice of forms and conventions of word order and grammar must all be taken from currently accepted forms, whether or not these have any inherent symmetry or efficiency. One form must be chosen from among several candidates and declared to be the pure or correct one.[17]

Take, as an example of this process, what happened to the verb in standard written English. Long before the eighteenth century, the present tenses of verbs had begun to lose special endings, because English had largely dispensed with such inflections. Modern English indicates the grammatical relationships between words by the relative positions of the words. (Some of the special inflected forms we retain are the *s* to denote plural nouns and the final *d* to denote past tense in verbs.) But in modern English the special forms of verbs that denote first, second, and third person are no longer necessary. Nonetheless, despite the usual absence of inflection in the verb we still say:

I run	We run
You run	You run
He/she/it run*s*	They run

All the forms in the present tense are uniform except for the *s* in he, she, or it run*s*. The *s* is a special ending to denote the third person and distinguish it from first and second persons. But in modern English it is quite pointless to distinguish the person by a special ending. We don't say "runs" to mean "he runs," as the Italians do. (If we did, it would make sense to use different verb forms for the different persons.) But since we always say "*he* runs," the *s* doesn't tell us anything about who is doing the running that we don't already know.

Hence the form "he run," used in some oral dialects, would not only be sufficient, it would make the verb entirely regular. People would need to learn just one form for the present tense. That arrangement would not only be more rational, it would represent a more advanced stage in the development of a syntactic language, as the linguist Jespersen has argued.[18] It is a pattern that English would surely have reached if it had remained an oral language and been allowed to evolve further.[19] In fact, as a dialectal form, "he run" has evolved independently in many different isolated places, in both America and Britain. If plain *run* is good enough for *I, you, we, they,* why isn't it good enough for *he, she, it*? Because we have no choice in the matter. The decision was made by those who fixed our grammar at a certain stage of its evolution, and their decision will probably stand forever.

Even more pointless linguistically is the standardized form of the verb *to be,* where the related forms don't even sound related.

I am	We are
You are	You are
He/she/it is	They are

Contrast this model, from the standpoint of simplicity and efficiency, with the more advanced pattern developed in many oral dialects of English:

I be	We be
You be	You be
He/she/it be	They be

That is a far more effective and rational pattern. It, too, has developed independently in many different isolated oral dialects.[20] But for all its virtues, this superior pattern is highly unlikely to replace the arbitrarily fixed national standard.

Before Samuel Johnson's day, the first language normalizers of Britain were not content merely to fix certain illogical patterns of grammar, they were also illogical pedants in the matter of spelling, having left us some very peculiar spellings that, on the evidence, were never sounded as the letters indicate. The word *doubt,* for instance, never had a *b* sound in English.[21] Why then spell it with a *b*? Because schoolmasters chose to show a connection between the English word *doubt* and the Latin word *dubito,* an unwise decision that created a tension between the standard spelling and pronunciation of the word. But it would be even more unwise to tamper with established spellings that are now recognized by everyone in hundreds of thousands of books. It is much better to stick to them, whatever their intrinsic drawbacks.[22]

These examples show that national languages are essentially different from oral dialects.[23] Even linguists have been known to miss the distinction between unconsciously evolving oral dialects and consciously created written languages. They have been corrected as follows by Dr. M. M. Guxman, a Soviet specialist in national languages:

> One should not separate the formation of a written language from the activity of normative theoreticians, from the creation of normative grammars and first dictionaries, or from the activity of language societies, academies, etc. The negative sides of this normalization in the history of individual languages are widely known. . . . The normalization of the language in 16th- and 17th-century Italy or France was of interest undoubtedly, to a relatively narrow social stratum. However the formation of a new type of written language is impossible without conscious normalization, without theoretical comprehension of the norm, and codification of definite rules of pronunciation, usage, and inflection. As material taken from the histories of various languages shows, the formation process of the written norm of a national language is so complex, the regularities of the process so specific in contrast to the life of a regional dialect that the written norm is never in fact the simple codification of a system of dialect characteristics of any one region.[24]

The process of creating a national language could hardly be other than what Dr. Guxman describes, and her views are seconded by the American specialist Einar Haugen.[25] An oral dialect cannot be transposed directly into a standard written language. The conventions of oral dialects evolved from using language in face-to-face situations, whereas written languages, which Haugen calls *grapholects,* must be adapted to anonymous situations in which the writer cannot be sure who the reader will be. Oral dialects have no settled conventions for sustaining long sentences, so these have to be invented. Oral dialects lack the vocabulary needed to serve the new economic, scientific, and administrative functions of the nation. Since the required words do not exist, they have to be specially invented for the national language.

The self-conscious, artificial element in national written languages shouldn't make us misconceive them as purely artificial constructs like Esperanto. They are living organisms. Once their grammar and spelling are fixed, national languages always evolve the means to deal with changing circumstances, just as oral dialects do. Written languages even exhibit occasional changes in grammar and spelling of great interest to lexicographers. But these events are comparatively rare and occur with glacial slowness, because of the conservatism of writing. But standard languages are not conservative in evolving vocabulary. New words are constantly coming into use, and old ones are constantly disappearing. In short, though standard languages were created artificially, they continue to evolve naturally.

But in many other respects national languages are distinct from oral dialects. Among several distinctive features that make them unique linguistic phenomena, Dr. Guxman has stressed one that is especially significant for the subject of this book: every national language is a conscious construct that transcends any particular dialect, region, or social class.[26]

❧ THE FORMATION OF MODERN NATIONAL CULTURES

What may be less obvious is that every national culture is similarly contrived. It also transcends dialect, region, and social class and is partly a conscious construct. National cultures were formed on many of the same principles as national languages, and for many of the same reasons, as Ernest Gellner observes:

> The cultural shreds and patches used by nationalism are often arbitrary historical inventions. Any old shred or patch would have served as well. But in no way does it follow that the principle of nationalism itself, as opposed to the avatars it happens to pick up for its incarnations, is in the least contingent and accidental. Nothing could be further from the truth than such a supposition. Nationalism is not what it seems, and above all, not what it seems to itself. The cultures it claims to defend and revive are often its own inventions, or are modified out of all recognition.[27]

Gellner shows that nation builders use a patchwork of scholarly folk materials, old songs, obscure dances, and historical legends, all apparently quaint and local, but in reality selected and reinterpreted by intellectuals to create a culture upon which the life of the nation can rest.

> If the nationalism prospers it eliminates the alien high culture, but it does not then replace it by the old local low culture; it revives, or invents, a local high (literate, specialist-transmitted) culture of its own, though admittedly one which will have some links with the earlier folk styles and dialects. But it was the great ladies at the Budapest Opera who really went to town in peasant dresses, or dresses claimed to be such.[28]

Because language making has been studied more than culture making, the historical process of creating a national culture is perhaps less well understood. But the need for a culture in building a nation is really just another dimension of the need for a language. A nation's language can be regarded as a part of its culture, or conversely, its culture can be regarded as the totality of its language. The American legend about Lincoln in his log cabin can be conceived either as part of our culture, or, with equal justification, as part of our shared language. Americans need to learn not just the grammar of their language but also their national vocabulary. They need to learn not just the associations of such words as *to run* but also the associations of such terms as *Teddy Roosevelt, DNA,* and *Hamlet.*

For nation builders, fixing the vocabulary of a national culture is analogous to fixing a standard grammar, spelling, and pronunciation. When culture makers begin their task in the early days of a nation, they are limited, as are language normalizers, by the range of materials that history has made available to them, but the choices made from those possibilities are not always inevitable.[29] Abraham Lincoln was certain to become a central figure in our culture, but Betsy Ross was not. The candidates for her position of legendary Revolutionary War heroine were potentially many. But Martha Crabtree, Sarah Smith, and Janet Blair were weighed in the balance and found wanting. Such choices are no more inevitable than the spelling *monk* instead of *munk.*[30]

In addition to using dictionaries that transmit the national language to all parts of the nation, national systems of education use textbooks and readers that carry the national culture to outlying provinces. After Napoleon's time, it used to be said that on a particular day in France each child in the fifth grade would be reading the same page of the same textbook. The British, like the Americans, used more subtle means for achieving the same uniformity. Textbooks were not prepared by the central government but by the provinces. The effect, however, was the same.

The story of one such provincial textbook, Blair's *Rhetoric,* is instructive. In 1762, seven years after the publication of Johnson's dictionary, the first professorship of English was established, and significantly, it was created in the provinces — in Scotland — where instruction in English national culture was felt to be needed. The new chair was the Regius Professorship of Rhetoric and Belles Lettres (i.e., composition and literature) at the University of Edinburgh. The first holder of the chair, Hugh Blair, was a Scot. In 1783 he delivered the fruit of twenty years of teaching, his *Lectures on Rhetoric and Belles Lettres,* to an eager public that had already been using pirated versions of his *Rhetoric* based on notes from his university lectures.

Blair's book became one of the most influential textbooks ever issued in Great Britain or the United States. Between 1783 and 1911 it went through 130 editions.[31] Throughout the nineteenth century the *Rhetoric* remained in the college and school curriculum on both sides of the Atlantic. Its authority in the United States persisted long after the Civil War. Designed as a college text, it was condensed and adapted for use in schools, and it influenced the contents of other school readers and spellers.

What did Blair's book contain? Its index includes not one mention of a Scottish poet, despite the distinction of Blair's fellow Scotsmen William Dunbar and Robert Henryson. Blair and his public implicitly understood that his job was to introduce his students and readers to the specific tradition that they needed to know if they were to read and write well in English. He was thus an early, perhaps the first, definer of cultural literacy for the English national language. He gathered and codified for the Scots materials that literate Englishmen had absorbed through the pores. The clarity and authority of his book made it nearly as influential in fixing the cultural content of the language as Johnson's dictionary was in fixing its forms. Blair created, in effect, a dictionary of cultural literacy for those who had not been born to English literate culture, for use by provincials like the Scots and colonials like the Americans. His book would later be used to educate native-born Englishmen as well.

The literate tradition that Blair thus rendered explicit, which largely persists to the present day, was by no means simply English in its origins. It contained material from Greece and Rome and from Europe. The index to his *Rhetoric* reads like a sampling from the pre-nineteenth-century part of a current index to American cultural literacy. Some items are:

Achilles
Adam
Addison
Aeneid
Aeschylus
Aetna
Arabian Nights
Aristophanes

Aristotle
Bacon
Berkeley
Caesar
Cicero
Corneille
King David
Dido

Dryden
Euripedes
Eve
Fielding
Job
Helen
Herodotus
Homer
Horace
Iliad
Isaiah
Jeremiah
Dr. Johnson
Juvenal
Livy
Locke
Longinus
Lucretius
Machiavelli
Milton
Molière
Odyssey
Oedipus
Paradise Lost
Pericles
Pindar
Plato
Pope
Racine
Robinson Crusoe
Rousseau
Satan
Shakespeare
Solomon
Sophocles
Swift
Tacitus
Thucydides
Virgil
Voltaire

For each of these items, and for many more, Blair conveyed the attitudes and associations that make up the lore of the literate tradition. For example, this is how he gave his readers the traditional range of views about Achilles:

> Homer has been blamed for making his hero Achilles of too brutal and inamiable a character. But I am inclined to think that injustice is commonly done to Achilles, upon the credit of two lines of Horace, who has certainly overloaded his character.
>
> Impiger, iracundus, inexorabilis, acer,
> Jura negat sibi nata; nihil non arrogat armis.
>
> [Energetic, angry, inexorable, fierce, / He spurns the law, and respects only arms.]
>
> Achilles is passionate indeed to a great degree; but he is far from being a contemner of laws and justice . . . Besides his

> wonderful bravery and contempt of death, he has several other qualities of a Hero. He is open and sincere. He loves his subjects and respects the Gods. He is distinguished by strong friendships and attachments.[32]

And so on through two volumes and more than a thousand pages, each sentence of which conveyed commonly shared information that aspiring readers, writers, and speakers would do well to remember.

By the early twentieth century Blair was obsolete, not because of any defect in his presentation but because essential new elements not found in his book had come into literate culture during the nineteenth century, and some names had drifted into oblivion. Dickens and Hawthorne came in, Fenelon and Dr. Pitcairn went out. A reconstituted Blair could have served anywhere English was written and read. Yet no one in the United States created a revised Blair, because such a book would still have lacked the national dimension of cultural literacy.

In the nineteenth century we began to replace Blair with textbooks that attempted to create and transmit the mythology and values of the new country. In a study of American school materials of the nineteenth century, Ruth Miller Elson found an almost complete unanimity of values and emphases in our schoolbooks from 1790 to 1900.[33] They consistently contrasted virtuous and natural Americans with corrupt and decadent Europeans; they unanimously stressed love of country, love of God, obedience to parents, thrift, honesty, and hard work; and they continually insisted upon the perfection of the United States, the guardian of liberty and the destined redeemer of a sinful Europe.

Among the militant and self-conscious writers of these schoolbooks, the jingoistic Noah Webster was as typical as he was important. But although his spellers, readers, and dictionaries enjoyed uniquely large sales, they were not unique in any other respect. In fact, as Elson has shown, the contents of American schoolbooks of the nineteenth century were so similar and interchangeable that their creators might seem to have participated in a conspiracy to indoctrinate young Americans with commonly shared attitudes, including a fierce national loyalty and pride.[34]

One American culture maker who was driven by the aim of doing well by doing good was Mason Weems, the author of numerous popular works, including an edition of Franklin's *Autobiography* expanded by anecdotes, a "romanticized" life of General Francis Marion, and many popular tracts in support of virtuous living, early marriage, and the avoidance of strong drink. His chef-d'oeuvre and main contribution to the American tradition was his biography of George Washington, wherein could be found the original legend of the cherry tree.

We have more significant stories about Washington — for instance, the winter at Valley Forge — and more important traditions of national life. But the story of the cherry tree is a useful illustration of the way our national culture was formed. What were Weems's motivations in creating that durable piece of American folklore? His letters suggest that he was not consciously helping to form part of the tradition needed to weld Americans into a nation. He assumed that George Washington had already become part of American lore by virtue of the great offices he had held. He had been glorified unceasingly up and down the land in many a published oration and eulogy. Weems felt that these outpourings of official praise had turned Washington into an intimidating, distant personage, because they presented his life entirely in terms of generalship and statesmanship. No ordinary boy or girl could identify with such a demigod.

But since Americans had an infinite appetite for Washingtonian hagiography, and since no one had yet humanized Washington, Weems detected a market opportunity. As an itinerant book salesman, he knew that the public wanted a Washington who, while still mythic, was nonetheless human and private. Weems deduced that the public needed a domesticated Everyman whose life would serve as a model for American youth. He confided as much in the first pages of his biography.

> However glorious, I say, all this [bravery and statesmanship] may have been to himself, or instructive to future generals and presidents, yet does it but *little* concern our *children*. For who among us can hope that his son shall ever be called, like Washington, to direct the storm of war, or to ravish the ears of deeply listening Senates? . . . Oh no! give us his *private* virtues!

> In *these* every youth is interested, because in these every youth may become a Washington — a Washington in piety and patriotism, — in industry and honour — and consequently a Washington in what alone deserves the name, SELF ESTEEM and UNIVERSAL RESPECT.[35]

Characteristically, some of the most persistent elements of our national lore owe their longevity to human universality rather than conscious political design: Lincoln in his log cabin, Washington in his father's garden. The stories of Weems have outlived those of Webster. There could hardly be a more attractive tale than the one which portrays for the delight of children a parent who happily forgives a wayward child (for what child does not feel wayward?) and for parents a model who, in the most charming possible way, persuades young people to tell the truth.

> *George,* said his father, *do you know who killed that beautiful little cherry-tree yonder in the garden?* This was a *tough question;* and George staggered under it for a moment; but quickly recovered himself: and looking at his father, with the sweet face of youth brightened with the inexpressible charm of all-conquering truth, he bravely cried out, *I can't tell a lie, Pa; you know I can't tell a lie. I did cut it with my hatchet.*[36]

If this legend had been left to languish in Weems's book, it might have been forgotten. For the sober later biographers of Washington, anxious to discriminate between fact and what Weems openly called romance, were successful in discrediting Weems's book, the popularity of which waned greatly in the later nineteenth century. But with a sure instinct, the compilers of textbooks took up the Weems stories. McGuffey included a sterner version of the cherry-tree episode in his *Second Eclectic Reader* and thus assured it a place in many other readers, and in our permanent lore.

Abraham Lincoln relates in his *Autobiography* how he educated himself by carefully reading and rereading a few books . . . Weems's *Life of Washington,* the Bible, *Robinson Crusoe, Pilgrim's Progress,* the *Autobiography* of Benjamin Franklin (possibly the expanded version by Weems), Paine's *Age of Reason,* and Volney's *Ruins.*[37]

This typical frontier education itself became part of American national mythology after Lincoln's assassination. In the Lincoln story, as narrated inside and outside the school, Americans continued an ideal of a peculiarly American education, in which the reading of a few central books could yield virtue, patriotism, and prudence. As Lawrence A. Cremin notes,

> The Lincoln of folklore had a significance even beyond the Lincoln of actuality. For the Lincoln of folklore embodied what ordinary inarticulate Americans cherished as ideals. Put otherwise, if the Lincoln of actuality imbibed the American *paideia* [i.e., our traditional scheme of education], the Lincoln of folklore personified it, and in reflecting it back on education writ large, helped transmit it to successive generations of Americans.[38]

The Washington and Lincoln legends might have developed differently, just as the spelling of the word *doubt* might have. In the early stages of a nation's life, its traditions are in flux. But with the passage of time, traditions that have been recorded in a nation's printed books and transmitted in its education system become fixed in the national memory. They become known by so many people over so long a time that they enter the oral and written tradition, where they tend to remain through generations. Consequently, these early traditions are not easy to change. Important legends, names, and events become fixed by constant usage, just as spellings do.

But the analogy with spelling and grammar is only partial. Our national culture resembles a vocabulary more than a system of grammar and spelling. And the vocabulary of a culture, like that of a language, is open to change. All languages are linguistically progressive. That is, they tend to shorten words that are used frequently. For instance, *TV* will probably slowly supplant *television,* and *phone, telephone.*[39] Coinages come into the cultural lexicon, and old words drop out or get expelled. Sometimes entirely new objects or events must be named. Occasionally it is possible to change our vocabulary by acts of common will, as we are changing it to remove racism and sexism in language.

But the occurrence, and more rarely the introduction, of specific change into our vocabulary has led some to believe, erroneously, that our culture can be remade on a large scale by an act of common will. This is a false and damaging myth. Rapid, large-scale change is no more possible in the sphere of national culture than in the sphere of national language. It is no more desirable or practicable to drop biblical and legendary allusions from our culture than to drop the letter *s* from the third person singular.

The traditional materials of national culture can be learned by all citizens only if the materials are taught in a nation's schools. But to teach them, the schools must have access to books that explain them — dictionaries like Johnson's and indexes to cultural literacy like Blair's. Because such compendia help outsiders enter mainstream literate culture, works like Blair's and Johnson's are socially progressive instruments, despite the fact that they contain traditional materials. Like everything that helps to spread literate language and culture, a nation's dictionaries, including those of cultural literacy, have helped to overcome class distinctions and barriers to opportunity. Historically, they have had a liberalizing and democratic effect.

But these benefits of national literate culture will be lost if we take our cultural traditions and national language too much for granted. It is all too easy for us to make this mistake, because of our history. When our nation began, we did not experience the bloody animosities and social dislocations that followed the imposition of national languages in France, Spain, and Britain and that are now following the same process in Russia. Fortunately, we inherited a standard written language that by 1776 had become normalized in grammar, spelling, and pronunciation. Our ancient charters, the Declaration of Independence and the Constitution, were written in a language that is current more than two hundred years later — a remarkable fact that we too easily take for granted when we read them. We remain happily unaware of the political struggles that usually accompanied the establishment of a national language. The Scots and Irish and Welsh did not begin to speak English because they believed it to be superior to their own language. The work of standardizing our language had been done for us long ago in such bloody, faraway battles as Flodden, Worcester, and Drogheda and in numerous decades of work by English scholars and schoolmasters.

Our only experience of civil strife over the language was a tempest in a teapot called the war of the dictionaries. Joseph Worcester of Massachusetts and Noah Webster of Connecticut argued over such towering questions as whether the *a* in *grass* should be pronounced like the "*grahs* of a British lawn or the *grass* of the boundless prairies," or whether the word for honest work should be spelled *labour* as in Britain or *labor* as befits the land of opportunity and equality. Worcester, the conservative, wanted to follow British practice in everything. Webster, representing the spirit of national pride and independence, wanted to introduce an American flavor into pronunciation and spelling. Worcester's loyalty to Britain in these matters was unpopular and found acceptance only in a few places, notably Harvard and the University of Virginia; elsewhere in the land, Noah Webster's dictionary was victorious.[40]

Our fortunate inexperience of bloodshed over language may explain why some of us look with equanimity upon recent proposals favoring multilingualism in our country. Defenders of linguistic pluralism invite us to look to Switzerland, not realizing that Switzerland has achieved multi*literacy* (as distinct from multilingualism) through a small, intensive, centralized educational system that, coupled with universal military service, enables the Swiss to communicate with one another despite their linguistic handicaps. Moreover, they have achieved this only after hundreds of years of bloody conflict between the Swiss cantons. In fact, there are good reasons why no large nation has been able to imitate Switzerland. The examples of Belgium and Canada are not encouraging.

In America the reality is that we have not yet properly achieved *mono*literacy, much less multiliteracy.[41] Because of the demands created by technology we need effective monoliteracy more than ever. Linguistic pluralism would make sense for us only on the questionable assumption that our civil peace and national effectiveness could survive multilingualism. But in fact, multilingualism enormously increases cultural fragmentation, civil antagonism, illiteracy, and economic-technological ineffectualness. These are the very disabilities the Chinese are attempting to overcome.

National languages are not ethnic media. Each one is an elaborate composite contrived to overcome local and ethnic dialectal variations inside a large nation.[42] It is contrary to the purpose and essence of a national language, whether English or German or Spanish or French, that a modern nation should deliberately encourage more than one to flourish within its borders. Once a national language is permanently fixed in grammars, schoolbooks, and dictionaries, and used in millions of books, magazines, and newspapers, it becomes, except for its vocabulary, an immovable, almost unchanging substance. When two great standard literate languages like English and Spanish, or English and French, coexist inside a nation, neither can yield to the other except by strife or vigorous intervention in the educational system.

In considering bilingualism in America, we should therefore understand that well-meaning linguistic pluralism, which would encourage rather than discourage competing languages within our borders, is much different from Jeffersonian pluralism, which has encouraged a diversity of traditions, values, and opinions. Toleration of diversity is at the root of our society, but encouragement of multilingualism is contrary to our traditions and extremely unrealistic. Defenders of multilingualism should not assume that our Union has been preserved once and for all by the Civil War, and that we can afford to disdain the cultural and educational vigilance exercised by other modern nations. To think so complacently is to show a fundamental misunderstanding of the role of national literacy in creating and sustaining modern civilization.

This book is not, of course, directly concerned with the question of bilingualism. But I know that well-meaning bilingualism could unwittingly erect serious barriers to cultural literacy among our young people and therefore create serious barriers to universal literacy at a mature level. I am opposed neither to bi*literacy* nor to the learning of foreign languages. I am strongly in favor of both. In the best of worlds, all Americans would be multiliterate. But surely the first step in that direction must be for all of us to become literate in our own national language and culture.

CHAPTER IV

American Diversity and Public Discourse

OUR TRADITIONS OF DIVERSITY AND UNITY

The first chapter of this book cites evidence that our literacy has been declining and that the long-range remedy for restoring and improving American literacy must be to institute a policy of imparting common information in our schools.[1] But before we can agree on such a radical change in school policy, we must deal clearly with some of the usual disputes about intervention in the school curriculum. Such conflicts have been, but need not be, divisive, slogan-ridden, and confused. Some of the old disputes may very well be moderated by our new knowledge of literacy. Some choices regarding the contents of the school curriculum are more purely technical than they have been assumed to be.

But technical research cannot provide a neutral, scientific answer to the problem. The illusory hope for such a formal solution has only encouraged evasion and fragmentation. To deal effectively with the school curriculum, we must consider more than technical goals: we must also consider specific contents. But in a diverse society, who has the right to define nationwide requirements? In the American context, the tradition of pluralism in education is so important that the subject deserves a chapter of its own.

Although the structure of a solution to the problem of declining literacy is straightforward, our tradition ensures that the political accomplishment of the solution cannot be correspondingly simple. The reader may already have inferred that I am committed to pluralism and local control in education. It is my belief that we can work within those traditions and still achieve a far higher level of national literacy than we now have. I hope that the schools themselves will act on the implications of the new findings about literacy and independently recognize our need to teach more shared information on a national scale.[2]

Because our country started out with a powerful commitment to religious toleration, we developed habits of cultural tolerance to go with it. Since the nineteenth century, when we managed to accommodate a tremendous influx of new citizens from many different nations and cultures, pluralism and tolerance have been part of our self-portrait. We believe that our diversity brings us a special strength and vitality. Paralleling our cultural diversity, and in fact preceding it, has been our tradition of political diversity, which developed out of the balance of powers between the states and the federal government.

But cultural pluralism has always been a moderate tradition in this country. We do not seethe with cultural animosities like warring Serbs and Croats. Our discussions have produced few influential defenses of cultural separatism. The dominant model of American pluralism has been that of the "hyphenated American": the Italo-American, the Polish-American, the Afro-American, the Asian-American, and so forth. Moreover, even the emotion-ridden arguments between cultural pluralists and cultural assimilationists have been about the most appropriate degrees of diversity within a basically moderate framework. The arguments revolve around such questions as: Shall we aim for the gradual assimilation of all into one national culture, or shall we honor and preserve the diverse cultures implicit in our hyphenations? Shall we slow down the pace of new immigration in order to retain the present amalgam of cultures or shall we continue to respect the tradition of America as a refuge for all groups?

In the context of these traditional arguments, we must set aside as a completely different issue the current debate over linguistic pluralism or separatism. Our most ardent proponents of cultural pluralism did not support linguistic pluralism. The great American apostles of pluralism — William James and Horace Kallen chief among them — assumed that our diversity would develop in a context of a common language. They assumed that although we might act and think very differently, we would talk and argue with each other as members of a single language community, peacefully and in literate English. Our diversity has been represented by the motto on all our coins — E PLURIBUS UNUM, "out of many one." Our debate has been over whether to stress the *many* or the *one*.

If we *had* to make a choice between the *one* and the *many*, most Americans would choose the principle of unity, since we cannot function as a nation without it. Indeed, we have already fought a civil war over that question. Few of us accept the extreme and impractical idea that our unity can be a purely legal umbrella, which formally contains but does not integrate our diversity. On the other side, the specific content of our larger national culture is not and must not be detailed, unchanging, or coercive, because that would impinge on our equally fundamental principles of diversity, localism, and toleration. A balanced, moderate position is the only workable American position, and it is bound to be the one that will prevail.

If our system had not encouraged localism and diversity, we would in any case have developed them. If our diversity had not arisen from immigration, local accident, and other historical causes, we would have evolved local differences anyway. Localism is constantly being reinvented all over the world, since the large, modern national state does not and cannot lend enough social glue or emotional meaning to satisfy the human desire for community. Among the democracies, France, that supposed model of cultural homogeneity, continues to preserve local and even contranational traditions of the most diverse kinds. In his absorbing book *Peasants into Frenchmen,* Eugen Weber shows that, contrary to common opinion, a truly shared French national culture did not really come into being until well into the twentieth century and even then did not supplant local traditions as thoroughly as many have thought.[3]

The worlds of the private and the familial and of the group — the neighborhood, the professional association, the club — are the worlds in which we mainly live. Erving Goffman and other social psychologists have shown that all of us inhabit numerous local cultures and adopt hundreds of small-scale cultural roles within the large-scale culture.[4] Moreover, the American tradition encourages the development of all these local cultures and associations as a matter of fundamental legal and ethical principle, with the result that our nation has a deliberately contranational element built into it. Our code is designed to protect local and individual interests against the wider nation, just as it is designed to protect minorities against majorities.

This tradition was encapsulated for me in a moment during the television drama of the Watergate hearings. Senator Sam Ervin, in the full glory of his local twang, decided to remind us that what had become an amorphous spectacle called Watergate had in fact to do with a basic principle: our protection of the local against the national, of the private against the public, the individual against the state. Ervin's words had nothing to do with the abstract breaking of this or that statute but with the deliberately built-in limits of state authority. The words he quoted were spoken by that great defender of the American colonists, William Pitt the Elder, and they became permanently etched in my mind in a Southern drawl that rang like poetry:[5]

> The poorest man may in his cottage
> bid defiance to all the force of the Crown.
> It may be frail;
> its roof may shake;
> the wind may blow through it;
> the storms may enter,
> the rain may enter, —
> but the King of England cannot enter.

I can still hear Ervin saying, "But thuh King of Inglun kennawd ennuh."

It is fortunate that such life-enhancing localism has been part of our tradition, because the brute fact of history in every modern nation has been the increasing dominance of the national culture over local and ethnic cultures. Studies of the demographic structures of American cities during the nineteenth and twentieth centuries show the continuing dispersion of ethnic groups away from separate neighborhoods and into the broader city.[6] People have gradually located themselves according to economic status rather than cultural background. This pattern of cultural assimilation and increasing homogeneity has been reinforced by the growth of regional and national over purely local economic arrangements. Under these circumstances local flavor may sometimes take on a self-conscious, desperate character — one reason for there being so much talk about pluralism these days. When we had more of it, we talked about it less.

To acknowledge the importance of minority and local cultures of all sorts, to insist on their protection and nurture, to give them demonstrations of respect in the public sphere are traditional aims that should be stressed even when one is concerned, as I am, with national culture and literacy. But this book is not, and no single book could be, an inquiry into the multifarious local and ethnic traditions that are found in the United States. It is for the Amish to decide what Amish traditions are, but it is for all of us to decide collectively what our American traditions are, to decide what "American" means on the other side of the hyphen in Italo-American or Asian-American. What national values and traditions really belong to national cultural literacy?

The larger national culture must be extremely capacious and somewhat vague. That is the case in a large monocultural country like France, and it is even more emphatically so in a deliberately diversified one like our own. What is common to our broad culture? Besides the English language and the national legal codes, American culture possesses first of all a civil religion that underlies our civil ethos.[7] Our civil ethos treasures patriotism and loyalty as high, though perhaps not ultimate, ideals and fosters the belief that the conduct of the nation is guided by a vaguely defined God. Our tradition places importance on carrying out the rites and ceremonies of our civil ethos and religion through the national flag, the national holidays, and the national anthem (which means "national hymn"), and supports the morality of tolerance and benevolence, of the Golden Rule, and communal cooperation. We believe in altruism and self-help, in equality, freedom, truth telling, and respect for the national law.

Besides these vague principles, American culture fosters such myths about itself as its practicality, ingenuity, inventiveness, and independent-mindedness, its connection with the frontier, and its beneficence in the world (even when its leaders do not always follow beneficent policies). It acknowledges that Americans have the right to disagree with the traditional values but nonetheless acquiesce in the dominant civil ethos to the point of accepting imprisonment as the ultimate means of expressing dissent.

Although these principles have not been immune to internal attack in American history, they have nonetheless proved durable. Our national culture was created at the start of the modern age, when dogmatic, sectarian religion had already come under the devastating criticism of the Enlightenment, and when American civil religion, in the vague form in which our founders created it, began to accommodate itself to the secularism of the modern age. This civil religion, "big-tented and tolerant," as Charles Krauthammer calls it, lends coherence to the larger American public culture and is the basic source of American values.[8]

Although some modern secularists do not accept public religious expressions of any sort, and do not regard them as the necessary source of social bonding and civic virtue, their position has not been sustained by history. The American civil religion, as expressed in our national rites and symbols, is in fact a central source of coherence in American public culture, holding together various and even contradictory elements of its tradition. Secularists who deplore any public references to God, and regard benevolent social ideas as ultimate civic principles, are, in the end, just another species of hyphenated Americans — secularist-Americans — who form a large class but acquiesce in the second side of the American hyphen like most of us who sing the national hymn, pledge allegiance ("under God") to the flag, know that all are "endowed by their Creator" with inalienable rights.

When George Washington in his Farewell Address said that "religion and morality are indispensable supports" of the American commonwealth, these sentiments were by no means peculiar to him. Those who collaborated in writing his address included Alexander

Hamilton, James Madison, and John Jay, and their sentiments represented ideas expressed elsewhere by other founders, including Jefferson.[9] The American founders were well aware of the paradox that precisely because established sectarian religion must be forbidden, a nonsectarian civil "religion" must be put in its stead to secure a good and harmonious democracy. Since the people are to govern themselves, they must govern on high, broadly religious principle for the larger public good as well as for their own private good.

Such religious sentiments must have expression in rituals and sacred texts. The civil religion honors the values of tolerance, equality, freedom, patriotism, duty, and cooperation; it has symbols and rites like the flag, public oaths, and the holidays. It also has its own bible, a knowledge of which is at the heart of cultural literacy. That bible was not decided upon by a synod once and for all. No doubt some of its "books" — the Declaration of Independence, the Gettysburg Address, some parts of the Bible itself — will always belong in it, but our consensual form of civil religion is much like our legal system in that it allows for change and amendment.

I am not the first to make this observation about our civil bible. Horace Kallen, that enthusiast for cultural pluralism, proposes that the following make up its canon:

> Its book of Genesis would of course be the Declaration of Independence, which is also the simplest, clearest, most comprehensive yet briefest telling of the American Idea. It sets the theme and whatever follows is a variation upon it.

Kallen lists his preferences for additional sacred texts.

> George Washington's letter to the Jewish Congregation at Newport; Jefferson's First and Second Inaugurals; his Virginia Bill of Religious Liberty; his letters to John Adams on Natural Aristocracy; certain articles from the *Federalist;* the Constitution; certain decisions and statements of John Marshall's. The Bible might include James Madison's "Memorial and Remonstrance"; James Monroe's promulgation of the Monroe Doctrine; the Constitution of the American Anti-Slavery So-

> ciety; Horace Mann's Twelfth Report to the Massachusetts Board of Education; the Seneca Falls Declaration on Women's Rights; Abraham Lincoln's "House Divided" speech; John Brown's speech to the Court that sentenced him . . .[10]

And so on for a couple of paragraphs, through the Truman Doctrine and the reports of Truman's Commission on Higher Education and on Civil Rights.

Kallen's list is dated, too long, and too narrowly based in his own values. It takes too little account of the distinction between what is broadly and consensually established among Americans over the generations and what he thinks it would be good to throw in. But Kallen rightly includes contemporary documents because the American bible is constantly being brought up to date through new additions, as is the American Constitution through new interpretations. Cultural revision is one of our best traditions.

There is, of course, a very good reason why the principle of cultural revision should parallel our principle of legal change and constitutional reinterpretation. They are fundamentally similar. The Constitution has biblical status for the nation, but it is understood to be amendable because it serves a principle more ultimate than itself — that of the sovereignty of the people. The bible of the American civil religion is based on fundamental principles of justice, freedom, and equality that permit progress and change.

One recent addition to the current American bible is the "I Have a Dream" speech by Martin Luther King, Jr., which self-consciously draws on earlier texts of the American bible to make its new contribution, just as the writers of the New Testament deliberately reappropriated the words of the Old. I have placed in italics King's quotations from and allusions to documents that belong to the cultural literacy of every American.

> I have a dream that one day this nation will rise up and live out the true meaning of its creed: *We hold these truths to be self-evident; that all men are created equal.* . . . I have a dream that one day *every valley shall be exalted, every hill and mountain shall be made low, the rough places will be made plains, and the crooked places will be made straight, and the glory*

of the Lord shall be revealed, and all flesh shall see it together. . . . This will be the day when *all of God's children* will be able to sing with new meaning, *My country 'tis of thee, sweet land of liberty, of thee I sing. Land where my fathers died, land of the pilgrims' pride, from every mountainside, let freedom ring. . . .* When we let freedom ring, when we let it ring from every village and every hamlet, from every state and every city, we will be able to speed up that day when all of God's children, black men and white men, Jews and Gentiles, Protestants and Catholics, will be able to join hands and sing in the words of that old Negro spiritual, *Free at last! Free at last! Thank God Almighty, we are free at last!*

THE VOCABULARY OF A PLURALISTIC NATION

Civil religion gives American culture its direction and defines its fundamental values, but it does not determine the diversified contents of American national culture. American national culture is neither coherent nor monolithic, and no convincing attempt fully to define its character has ever appeared — not even Alexis de Tocqueville's brilliant sketches of 1835. The national culture, as contrasted with the national civil religion, depends on a highly diverse vocabulary of communication rather than a coherent system of fundamental values and principles. Like the bible of the civil religion, the national vocabulary changes with the consent of those who use it, but because of its use in communication, it is fundamentally conservative and its core contents change very slowly.

Suppose we think of American public culture as existing in three segments. At one end is our civil religion, which is laden with definitive value traditions. Here we have absolute commitments to freedom, patriotism, equality, self-government, and so on. At the other end of the spectrum is the *vocabulary* of our national discourse, by no means empty of content but nonetheless value-neutral in the sense that it is used to support all the conflicting values that arise in public discourse. This vocabulary is hospitable to God and mammon, pornography and prudery, Catholicism and Zen. It is our medium for engaging in argument and agreement about highly diverse political and cultural issues. Between these two extremes lies the vast middle domain of culture proper. Here are the concrete politics, customs, technologies, and legends that define and determine our current attitudes and actions and our institutions. Here we find constant change, growth, conflict. This realm determines the texture of our national life.

Although it is in some respects more important than the other two, the middle realm lacks the stability of either our national religion or vocabulary. It shifts more with the times than our other two domains. The lines between these three realms cannot be firmly drawn; each influences the others and is influenced by them. But the middle domain is the only one whose contents are worth arguing about.

Because the middle domain is so significant, contentious, and value-laden, we must be all the more solicitous for the integrity of the vocabulary of public discourse itself. There is no point in arguing about either our civil religion or our vocabulary. They are our national givens, our starting points. Our civil religion defines our broadly shared values as a society, and our national vocabulary functions, or should function, as our broadly shared instrument of communication. Only through a capacious and widely shared vocabulary can our democracy deal effectively with the contentious issues of the middle domain.

If our civil religion is "big-tented and tolerant," how much more capacious and tolerant is our national vocabulary. (Again, I mean something very broad by the word *vocabulary;* I mean cultural literacy — the whole system of widely shared information and associations.) This everyday vocabulary is much more pragmatic and tolerant of diversity than even the civil religion. What counts in the sphere of public discourse is simply being able to use the language of culture in order to communicate *any* point of view effectively.

Some have objected that to publish the contents of our national vocabulary would have the effect of promoting the culture of the dominant class at the expense of minority cultures. But historically, the publication of vocabularies and dictionaries has not fixed the vocabulary of any national language. Nor does the national vocabulary reflect a coherent culture of a dominant class or other group in the same way that a local dialect does. It is primarily an instrument of communication among diverse cultures rather than a cultural or class instrument in its own right. In fact, one of the main uses of a national vocabulary is to enable effective and harmonious exchange despite personal, cultural, and class differences. This was well understood by David Hume.

> Men of the most confined knowledge are able to remark a difference of taste in the narrow circle of their acquaintance, even when the persons have been educated under the same government, and have early imbibed the same prejudices. . . . As this variety of taste is obvious to the most careless inquirer; so will it be found, on examination, to be still greater in reality than in appearance. The sentiments of men often differ . . . even while their general discourse is the same.[11]

To regard a standardized cultural instrument as a class culture is facile oversimplification. It is, as Orlando Patterson observed, bad sociology, and it is certainly an incorrect historical observation about language.[12]

To put this point in perspective, consider a historical moment remote enough from the current American scene to provide a clear and disinterested insight into the inherently classless character of cultural literacy. In the England of the fifteenth and sixteenth centuries, long before dictionary makers began a conscious effort to standardize the national language, there existed a very strong tendency toward standardization of public discourse in the great towns. The big cities of Europe and Asia were the first cultural melting pots; America has no historical monopoly on that phenomenon. Within these growing cities, neither diversity of social class nor diversity of regional dialects could inhibit the inexorable process of linguistic and cultural standardization that occurred when great numbers of people moved to town from the provinces.

This process, as it then occurred in London, is an illustration of Patterson's observation that mainstream culture is not a class culture and that outsiders and newcomers influence its forms as much as they are influenced by them. Provincial newcomers of all classes who migrated to London gradually changed the local London speech as much as they themselves were changed by it. In the documents preserved from that era, we can find, even from one decade to another, evidence that local London forms were being "driven out by forms previously only found in other districts, especially those of the North."[13] Even the place names of London — and place names are perhaps the most conservative cultural forms of any words in ordinary use — show the effects of the new eclectic speech. Isemonger Lane became Ironmonger Lane, Crepelgate became Cripplegate, and so on, all under the influence of the provincial immigrants.

Dialects rubbed up against each other in the public streets and halls of London. The great city was a meeting place for public interactions of all sorts. There, people of all types — artisans, tradespeople, and aristocrats — were attracted by the magnetism of London's money, amusement, and excitement. The need for a common medium of intercourse among all these different classes of people gradually pulled into use a common, composite speech for use in public discourse. The local London dialect actually disappeared and was gradually replaced by something that had never existed before — an amalgam that had no single identifiable parent. It did not represent the speech of any particular location, class, or ethnic group.

The old claim that this London speech, which became the basis of our standard written English, was just the upper-class dialect of the royal court is incorrect. The members of the court itself came from all parts of England and spoke different native dialects. King and courtier alike had to learn the common London speech; it formed the upper-class speech of the court, not vice versa. The dialect that formed the basis of our own national language was, in origin, the democratic speech of the marketplaces and alleyways of the big melting pot of London.

In *Mankind, Nation, and Individual from a Linguistic Point of View*, Otto Jespersen traces the same process of forming an eclectic common speech in many of the big cities of Europe.[14] The famous Italian standard of speech idealized the process memorably: *lingua toscana in bocca romana* ("Tuscan speech in Roman mouth"). The great cities forged the beginnings of the common, classless languages of all the great European nations.

Neither in origin nor in subsequent history have national languages been inherently class languages. It is true that after national dictionaries were formulated, the standard languages were more likely to be acquired by people who were rich enough to be educated than by poor people. But the distinction is one of schooling, which we have made universal, not of economic or social class. Ideological phrase dropping about the connections between cultural literacy and social class should therefore leave us unimpressed. Historically, the modern democratic nations arose at the same time as the great national literate languages, and, ever since, democracy and literate culture have been essentially connected.

It is, therefore, a very odd cliché that connects literate national culture with elitism, since it is the least elitist or exclusive culture that exists in any modern nation. Literate culture is far less exclusive, for instance, than any ethnic culture, no matter how poverty bound, or pop culture or youth culture. It has no in-group, no generational or geographical preference. It can be mastered in the country or in the city, in a shanty or a mansion, so long as the opportunity is given. But it must be given effectively by schooling that produces literacy, not by ceremonies of schooling that do not.

By accident of history, American cultural literacy has a bias toward English literate traditions. Short of revolutionary political upheaval, there is absolutely nothing that can be done about this. It is not a weakness of our literate culture that it has its origins in English traditions, for, like all the other literate traditions connected with great national languages, the English tradition is broad and heterogeneous and grows ever more so. For many centuries it has embraced a wide range of materials, as evidenced in Hugh Blair's *Rhetoric,* which contains elements from many lands and cultures. Yet Blair's book did not contain any items from his native land. Many national cultures are neglected in our national vocabulary — not just Scottish, Welsh, and Irish, but also German, French, Spanish, and Italian. Dozens of other cultures could consider themselves disenfranchised by the continued dominance in our nation of English literate culture. What have Americans to do, in any ethnic or national sense, with 1066 or Chaucer or Milton? Nonetheless, we have kept and still need to keep English culture as the dominant part of our national vocabulary for purely functional reasons.

After more than two hundred years of national life, the main elements of our vocabulary have transcended the sphere of contention and dispute. We do not argue whether Abraham Lincoln in his log cabin belongs in the vocabulary of literate Americans, any more than we argue about spelling. No matter how value-laden or partisan some of these common elements were in their origins long ago, they now exist as common materials of communication. History has decided what those elements are. They are the medium of public discourse, the instruments through which we are able to communicate our views to one another and make decisions in a democratic way.

It is cultural chauvinism and provincialism to believe that the content of our vocabulary is something either to recommend or deplore by virtue of its inherent merit. Think how well the French or Chinese have done without Shakespeare or George Washington, and how well we have done without Racine or Lao-tse. No doubt it benefits the French and Chinese to learn about Shakespeare and Washington, just as it benefits us to learn about Racine and Lao-tse. But the benefit we derive is to come to the tolerant understanding that no single national vocabulary is inherently superior or privileged above all others.

That is the virtue of broadening our horizons by encountering cultures other than our own. We discover not only that other cultures have produced other successful vocabularies for dealing with life, but also that all of the great national vocabularies, including our own, have a relativity about them. Each vocabulary would be different if history had been different — if Shakespeare had never been born, for instance, or if he had chosen not to write about Hamlet. The specific contents of the different national vocabularies are far less important than the fact of their being shared.

Any true democrat who understands this, whether liberal or conservative, will accept the necessary conservatism that exists at the core of the national vocabulary, which must serve all sorts and conditions of people from all generations. Changes at its core must occur with glacial slowness if it is to accommodate all the people and serve as our universal medium of communication.

Many Americans who have graduated from high school in the

recent past have been deprived of the cultural vocabulary that was commonly possessed by educated persons in past generations. Some repair work is necessary for them and for the members of the current school generation. They must be reintroduced to the cultural vocabulary that continues to be the foundation for literate national communication. The new illiteracy is sometimes excused by the argument that our schools are now educating larger portions of our population. The point is that we are *not* educating them. We undertook the great task of universal education precisely in order to produce a truly literate population, but we have not succeeded in that task in recent years. We must assure that new generations will continue to be enfranchised in our medium of national communication as securely as they are enfranchised at the polls.

There is a second respect in which the national vocabulary must be enhanced for the current school generation. As national and international life has come to contain an increasingly technical element, the idea of literacy has gradually come to include a larger vocabulary of shared scientific and technical knowledge. Especially today, when political decisions in our democracy have an increasingly technical element, our schools should enhance scientific and technical vocabularies. We require not only that ordinary citizens be scientifically literate but that technicians and scientists master the nonscientific literate culture. To explain the implications of their work to others, experts must be aware of the shared associations in our literate vocabulary and be able to build analogies on those associations.

Both of these proposals — bridging the generation gap in cultural literacy and enhancing its scientific component — are closely tied to basic principles of the American republic. I have in mind the Founding Fathers' idea of a literate and informed citizenry. Essential to this concept is the principle that, when desirable, the main features and implications of the most arcane specialty can be explained to literate and educated citizens. Economic issues can be discussed in public. The moral dilemmas of new medical knowledge can be weighed. The implications of technological change can become subjects of informed public discourse — not about technical details, but about the broad issues of the debate. Otherwise we are in danger of falling victim to technological intimidation.

The founders of our republic had in mind a Ciceronian ideal of education and discourse in a republic. Cicero claimed that he could explain Greek science and philosophy or anything else to his fellow Romans in ordinary Latin terms, and he did. Our founders greatly admired Cicero's aims. Thomas Jefferson used the concepts in the Declaration of Independence and constantly referred to Cicero's writings in the notebook he kept. John Adams quoted Cicero at length in his *Preface on Government* and said of him that "all the ages of the world have not produced a greater statesman and philosopher combined."[15]

The Ciceronian ideal of universal public discourse was strong in this country into the early twentieth century. In the Roman republic of Cicero's time, such discourse was chiefly oral, and the education Cicero sought was in "rhetoric" rather than "literacy." But the terms are equivalent. Literacy — reading and writing taken in a serious sense — is the rhetoric of our day, the basis of public discourse in a modern republic. The teaching of Ciceronian literacy as our founders conceived it is a primary but currently neglected reponsibility of our schools.

CHAPTER V

Cultural Literacy and the Schools

THE RISE OF THE FRAGMENTED CURRICULUM

School is the traditional place for acculturating children into our national life. Family, church, and other institutions play an important role, but school is the only institution that is susceptible to public policy control. In the modern age, the role assigned to our schools is to prepare our children for the broader activities of society and to train them in the literate public culture. Our schools have played this role less well than they should, chiefly because they have followed faulty educational ideas. The practical importance of ideas in human affairs, while not a recent revelation, is one that is too easily forgotten.

The decline of American literacy and the fragmentation of the American school curriculum have been chiefly caused by the ever growing dominance of romantic formalism in educational theory during the past half century. We have too readily blamed shortcomings in American education on social changes (the disorientation of the American family or the impact of television) or incompetent teachers or structural flaws in our school systems. But the chief blame should fall on faulty theories promulgated in our schools of education and accepted by educational policymakers.

Consider William Raspberry's comments on test results which

show that black students score 35 to 45 percent lower than white students in standardized achievement tests.

> The news hits like a series of bombshells as one suburban school district after another reveals that black children are significantly behind their white counterparts on standardized achievement tests. . . . Whose fault is it that blacks tend to get lower scores? I don't know all the answers to that one. Surely a part of it is the simple fact that those children who come to school already knowing a good deal of what the society deems important to know tend to find it easier to learn more of it. The more you know, the more you can learn.[1]

We know that Raspberry is right, not only about achievement tests but also about reading and writing "skills." "The more you know, the more you can learn." What does his judgment imply for schooling? Some children, he says, enter school already possessing the information needed to make further advances in the literate culture, while others come to school lacking that information.

Why have we failed to give them the information they lack? Chiefly because of educational formalism, which encourages us to ignore the fact that identifying and imparting the information a child is missing is most important in the earliest grades, when the task is most manageable. At age six, when a child must acquire knowledge critical for continuing development, the total quantity of missing information is not huge. As Dr. Jeanne Chall has pointed out, the technical reading skills of disadvantaged children at age six are still on a par with those of children from literate families. Yet only a year or so later, their reading skills begin to diverge according to socioeconomic status, chiefly because low-income pupils lack elementary cultural knowledge.[2] Supplying missing knowledge to children early is of tremendous importance for enhancing their motivation and intellectual self-confidence, not to mention their subsequent ability to learn new materials. Yet schools will never systematically impart missing background information as long as they continue to accept the formalistic principle that specific information is irrelevant to "language arts skills."

Educational formalism holds that reading and writing are like baseball and skating; formalism conceives of literacy as a set of techniques that can be developed by proper coaching and practice. The following definition of reading as a skill is typical of those in many education textbooks:

> Reading is a recoding and decoding process, in contrast with speaking and writing which involve encoding. One aspect of decoding is to relate the printed word to oral language meaning, which includes changing the print to sound and meaning.

(The characteristic title of this book is *Language Skills in Elementary Education.*)[3]

The skill idea becomes an oversimplification as soon as students start reading for meaning rather than for cracking the alphabetic code. If reading were just hitting the right alphabetic ball with the right phonic bat, or just learning "text strategies," it *would* be like baseball. We could teach everybody to groove their swings and watch for the seven different types of pitches. The trouble is that reading for meaning is a different sort of game entirely. It is different every time, depending on what the piece of writing is about. Every text, even the most elementary, implies information that it takes for granted and doesn't explain. Knowing such information is *the* decisive skill of reading.

Educational formalism assumes that the specific contents used to teach "language arts" do not matter so long as they are closely tied to what the child already knows, but this developmental approach ignores Raspberry's important point that different children know different things. Current schoolbooks in language arts pay little systematic attention to conveying a body of culturally significant information from grade to grade. Their "developmental" approach contrasts sharply with textbooks from earlier decades, which consciously aimed to impart cultural literacy. Texts now used to teach reading and writing are screened not for the information they convey but for their readability scores and their fit with the sequence of abstract skills that a child is expected to acquire. On this skills model, the ideal method of language arts instruction would be to adjust the reading curriculum to the interests and competencies of each child. In fact, just this formalistic approach is recommended by P. S. Anderson as the "self-selection" method of reading instruction, according to which the child selects his or her own curriculum for mastering decoding skills.

> A special method of individualizing instruction within a classroom has been identified by the terms *self-selection* and *language approach*. The self-selection program allows each child to seek whatever reading material stimulates him and work at his own rate with what he has chosen.[4]

I cannot claim to have studied all the recent textbooks intended to train teachers or educate children in the language arts, but those I have consulted represent learning to read as a neutral, technical process of skill acquisition that is better served by up-to-date "imaginative literature" than by traditional and factual material. "Reading in the content areas" is typically regarded as inferior to reading up-to-date fictions. Current language arts textbooks not only overlook the fundamental acculturative aims of our schools but go wrong even on technical grounds, for it has become clear that effective reading depends on acquiring factual and traditional schemata. By the same token, teachers are not expected to have mastered particular factual and traditional information or any special academic discipline; they are trained only to impart skills.

To miss the opportunity of teaching young (and older) children the traditional materials of literate culture is a tragically wasteful mistake that deprives them of information they would continue to find useful in later life. The inevitable effect of this fundamental educational mistake has been a gradual disintegration of cultural memory, causing a gradual decline in our ability to communicate. The mistake has therefore been a chief cause of illiteracy, which is a subcategory of the inability to communicate.

Paradoxically, some contemporary educational theorists who understand the importance of specific cultural information nevertheless consider it to be unteachable by the schools. Professors of education have accepted the view that family background is so important and so deeply ingrained in young children that the schools are powerless to make a significant difference in the academic achievements of children from educationally deprived backgrounds.

This fatalistic conception was given currency by the famous Coleman report of 1966, which found, among other things, that differences in academic achievement were more strongly correlated with students' family backgrounds than with differences in the schools they attended.[5]

The research team that wrote the report, led by James S. Coleman, then of the Johns Hopkins University, was a distinguished one. It based its conclusions on data gathered from some four thousand schools. Because the report was thorough and objective, its conclusions were widely accepted and were later backed up by reports of the Carnegie Council on Children and a book-length study, *Inequality*, by Christopher Jencks and others.[6]

That the Coleman report should have shown a strong correlation between family background and academic achievement is not surprising. Common sense predicts that children from literate households can more readily gain the literate culture necessary for reading than those from illiterate households. Moreover, we have become increasingly sensitive to subtle psychological influences that intensify this effect, such as the academic defeatism of minority children who lack models of academic achievement. Where low-income children *do* have traditions of academic achievement and literacy in another language, as do many Asian-Americans, the initial lack of American background information is less damaging. Such further evidence, added to the Coleman report, has strengthened the consensus among educators that the schools alone cannot do much to offset cultural deprivations or family inadequacies.

But the data can be interpreted differently. We might infer from them that the schools have not done much to compensate for cultural deprivations; that the significant part of our children's education has been going on outside rather than inside the schools; and finally, that this state of affairs is not inevitable.

Diane Ravitch, tracing the aftermath of the Coleman report, makes this trenchant observation:

> One commentator wrote in the *Harvard Educational Review*, "It is highly uncertain at this point what *school* policies, if any, can compensate for the inequalities in cognitive skills between rich and poor children that are apparent at the time

> they enter school." The same sentiment was expressed countless times by authors and policy makers as a demonstrated fact in the years after 1966. . . . Whether students did well or poorly in schools seemed determined for the most part by their social background, and little, if at all, by anything that teachers and schools did. Consider the consequences of this conclusion: If schools were so ineffectual in affecting the educational outcomes of their students, it becomes difficult to argue on behalf of any given curriculum, requirement, or policy.[7]

The flaw in the current view is not that the sociological observations are wrong (they have been reconfirmed many times), but that the inferences drawn from them are unwarranted. It is true that, under our present curricular arrangements, academic achievement is heavily determined by family background. But we cannot conclude from the present state of affairs that deprived children would be predestined to low achievement under a different school curriculum. This consideration suggests that there has been an oversight in the conclusions drawn from recent sociological observations. It has been silently assumed that our recently fragmented school curriculum is a permanent and necessary feature of our educational system.

Historically, as the school curriculum has become more incoherent, literacy has declined even among children from literate homes. This fact has an important corollary: family background is *not* the uniquely decisive determinant of our children's level of literacy. Specific curricula also significantly affect academic outcomes. In the computation made by Herbert Walberg and Timothy Shanahan from a huge sampling of data, it appears that the chief factor in academic achievement is the time the student spends in studying the material to be mastered.[8] All we can legitimately infer from the correlations between family background and academic achievement is that they reflect a truth about present-day public schools rather than a state of affairs inherent in the socioeconomic nature of things.

This very point was forcefully made by a new Coleman report issued in 1981. Based on a survey of almost sixty thousand sophomores and seniors from a thousand schools and on interviews with their teachers and principals, that report shows that schools have a larger effect than had been supposed. It contrasts the educational outcomes in public schools with those in private schools and finds that private schools produce better academic results for all students, even when family backgrounds are taken into account. Children from low-income families reach higher levels of achievement in private schools than they do in public schools.[9]

There are, of course, many differences between private and public schools, and we can't be sure which differences are most important. But in light of what we know about literacy, an important factor must be that curricula of private schools impart more literate information than those of public schools. Private schools offer fewer nontraditional and vocational courses and give each student proportionally more academic courses. This interpretation is supported by Walberg and Shanahan, who suggest, in commenting on the new Coleman report, that the crucial factor is "time on task."[10] In private schools, both middle-class and disadvantaged students spend more time in content courses and are exposed to more of the information that belongs to literate culture. The implication is that many more students could become highly literate if they were presented with the right sort of curriculum, particularly in their early years.

The American school curriculum is fragmented both horizontally across subjects and vertically within subjects.[11] For one student in grade nine, social studies may focus on family relations; for another, the focus may be on ancient history. In an American history course in one school, students may focus on industrial America, but in another school, the focus may be on westward expansion.[12]

How such fragmentation arose can be grasped in broad terms by looking at two decisive moments in American education represented by two historic documents, one published in 1893, the other in 1918. The earlier one is the *Report of the Committee of Ten on Secondary School Studies*; the later report is *Cardinal Principles of Secondary Education*.[13] The contrasts between them bring into clear relief the change in educational theory that occurred in the first quarter of this century.[14]

Between the 1920s and the 1970s, the history of American secondary education has been one of the increasing dominance of the *Cardinal Principles* and the corresponding decline of the principles of the Committee of Ten, which recommended a traditional humanistic curriculum.[15] The earlier report assumed that all students would take the same humanistic subjects and recommended giving a new emphasis to natural sciences. It took for granted that secondary school offerings would continue to consist of just the traditional areas that its subcommittees had been formed to consider — Latin, Greek, English, other modern languages, mathematics, physics, chemistry and astronomy, natural history, botany, zoology, physiology, history, civil government, economy, and geography.

Despite the conservatism of these subject divisions and the prominence given to Latin and Greek, the 1893 report was surprisingly modern in its conception of the various subjects. For instance, it regarded geography as we do ecology, saying that it embraced "not only a description of the surface of the earth, but also the elements of botany, zoology, astronomy and meteorology, as well as many considerations pertaining to commerce, government, and ethnology." All sections of the 1893 report stressed the importance of integrating the contents of the subjects. It was emphatic, for instance, in holding that English composition should not be conceived as a skill in isolation from subject matter, and in one passage it explicitly rejected what I have called educational formalism in English.

> The Conference doubts the wisdom of requiring for admission to college set essays . . . whose chief purpose is to test the student's ability to write English. It believes that there are serious theoretical and practical objections to estimating a student's power to write a language on the basis of a theme composed not for the sake of expounding something that he knows or thinks, but merely for the sake of *showing his ability to write*.[16]

On the other hand, the Committee of Ten was not completely averse to educational formalism when it came to defending the traditional curriculum. It subscribed to the claim that studying Latin and Greek "trains the mind" and that studying geography enhances "(1) the power of observation, (2) the powers of scientific imagination, and (3) the powers of reasoning." It is not surprising therefore that the Committee of Ten should have been lenient toward schools that were not able to teach all recommended subjects, for such schools could still "train the mind." But one shrewd member of the committee, James H. Baker, then president of the University of Colorado, sniffed out this hint of educational formalism and filed a minority report objecting to it.

> I cannot endorse expressions that appear to sanction the idea that the choice of subjects in secondary schools may be a matter of comparative indifference. . . . All such statements are based upon the theory that, for the purposes of general education, one study is as good as another, — a theory which appears to me to ignore Philosophy, Psychology, and Science of Education. It is a theory which makes education formal and does not consider the nature and the value of the content. Power comes through knowledge; we can not conceive of observation and memory in the abstract.[17]

In deliberate contrast to the 1893 report, *Cardinal Principles of Secondary Education* explicitly rejected the earlier focus on subject matter. Instead, it stressed the seven fundamental aims of education in a democracy: "1. Health. 2. Command of fundamental processes. 3. Worthy home membership. 4. Vocation. 5. Citizenship. 6. Worthy use of leisure. 7. Ethical character."[18] The shift from subject matter to social adjustment was a deliberate challenge to the 1893 report and to conservative school practices generally. American education should take a new direction. Henceforth it should stress utility and the direct application of knowledge, with the goal of producing good, productive, and happy citizens.

The origins of these new aims were European romanticism and American pragmatism as amalgamated in the educational philosophy of John Dewey, though Dewey was not the only important American source of these ideas.[19] European romantic writers like Rousseau and Wordsworth contributed an emphasis on the development of the whole child as a unique individual, under the theory that the infant has an inborn, instinctive tendency to follow its own proper development. Wordsworth captured the underlying spirit as he mused upon a six-year-old: "Thou whose exterior semblance doth belie / Thy soul's immensity."[20]

From the perspective of intellectual history, the conception of natural human growth has been the most decisive influence on American educational theory over the past six decades. Although schools of education have clothed this romantic idea in the language of developmental psychology, their basic assumptions owe more to Rousseau than to Piaget. As the originator of these ideas, John Dewey is usually given too much credit (or blame), and Jean Rousseau too little. In basic educational assumptions Dewey was a disciple of Rousseau. Of course, were there not some truth in those assumptions, they would not have endured. But half-truths, because of their plausibility, are frequently more dangerous than downright mistakes. Even today, Rousseau's principles reappear in the doctrine, straight from *Emile*, that a child's positive self-concept is the true key to learning.[21] Dewey and his followers agreed further with Rousseau and Wordsworth in scorning secondhand, bookish education. Dewey attacked the abstract, rote-learned material of literate culture, which he considered to be, as Wordsworth put it, "a weight / Heavy as frost and deep almost as life."[22]

The 1918 report implicitly accepted these ideas, to which they added Dewey's pragmatic emphasis on direct social utility as an educational goal. Thus, the most appropriate replacement for bookish, traditional culture would be material that is directly experienced and immediately useful to life in society. Said the report, "Subject values must be tested in terms of the laws of learning and the application of knowledge to the activities of life, rather than primarily in terms of the demands of any subject as a logically organized science."[23] The schools were henceforth to focus upon the needs of the child and society, as Dewey had recommended.

Not surprisingly, the 1918 report explicitly rejected the 1893 assumption that training in such subjects as Latin and Greek was important for developing "general mental discipline" — the idea to which James Baker had objected in his dissent to the 1893 report. By 1918 educational psychology, particularly the work of Edward Thorndike, had vindicated Baker's objection to the idea that skills in one area are automatically transferred to another. This finding was used to cast doubt on the entire rationale of the traditional curriculum.[24] Modern psychology, the report stated, required a "reexamination and reinterpretation of . . . teaching methods with reference to general discipline"; these "former conceptions" must be "thoroughly revised."[25]

In 1918, modern psychology was also invoked to oppose the view expressed in 1893 that everyone, college bound or not, should take the same course of study. Psychology (reinforcing the romantic emphasis on variety and individuality) had demonstrated that children possess different aptitudes and needs. The *Cardinal Principles* therefore recommended introducing a wide array of courses that would accord with children's "individual differences in capacities and aptitudes."[26]

There were two sides to the emphasis on individual differences, one high-minded, the other practical. On the high-minded side, found in Dewey, was the romantic view that each person has a unique temperament with a unique value. On the practical side, stressed by professional educators, was the venerable observation that some children are smarter than others. Both the romantic and the practical conceptions accorded well with the high value Americans placed on pluralism and tolerance. But a hidden premise was attached to the emphasis on diversity. Because every child was to be brought to an acceptable level of reading, writing, and arithmetic, which the report of 1918 called a "command of fundamental processes," the emphasis on diversity required an acceptance of educational formalism. For if all are to attain literacy and numeracy through different materials suited to their different temperaments, the "fundamental processes" of reading, writing, and arithmetic must be conceived as purely formal skills. Only under a formalistic conception can all students command the same basic processes, even though the materials by which they learn them are diversified to suit their "individual differences in capacities and aptitudes."

From the perspective of this book, one might assume that if we had only stuck to the principles of the Committee of Ten and allowed the *Cardinal Principles* to sink into oblivion, all would be well with American education. It is tempting to see the 1918 document as the moment of our educational Fall, and to conceive a return to the principles of 1893 as the beginning of our educational Redemption. But the issues are more complex than a simple pattern of Eden, Fall, and Redemption. Though the 1918 report was full of the educational half-truths of romantic formalism, it also attempted to answer pressing needs ignored by the report of 1893.

The later report tried to adjust school aims to the new situation created by immigration and a consistent doubling of the school population every ten years. By 1918, greater percentages of Americans were graduating from high school than ever before. Reflecting these demographic changes, the *Cardinal Principles* expressed a laudable commitment to educate every American through the high school level — an ideal that had been rejected as unfeasible by the Committee of Ten. In that respect, the report of 1918 evinced a more democratic point of view than that of 1893.

Yet the Committee of Ten had been highly democratic in stating that all students should receive exactly the same educational foundation as long as they could stay in school. On this score, the earlier document was more egalitarian than the later. While the *Cardinal Principles* expressed a laudable desire to put everyone through high school, it assumed that many students would be constitutionally unable to assimilate the knowledge necessary for literate culture. The stress on individual differences and on vocational training implicitly accepted a permanent stratification of economic and social positions. It's a moot question, therefore, which report was, in the end, more democratic. Certainly the 1893 idea that everyone can and should start out from the same educational foundation was an admirable democratic ideal that needs to be renewed.

From our current perspective, one great failing of the *Cardinal Principles* was its premature conclusion about the proper application of what were then new psychological theories. There is a deep paradox here, one that reaches to the heart of our current problems. The system of American education since 1918 has continued to be partly based on Thorndike's valid claim that training is not transferred from one area of learning to another. From the principle of the nontransfer of training, the 1918 report argued that if we want to prepare people for life in a modern democracy we ought to train them for the specific work they are going to do.

But the 1918 report pushed Thorndike's psychological insight too far in some areas. For example, it overstressed nontransferability when it implied that Latin cannot help students in using

English. Some things learned in Latin are directly applicable to English, and therefore no transfer in Thorndike's sense is required. Moreover, a limited degree of transfer is always going on when we undertake any new task, as Thorndike himself acknowledged.[27] The human mind operates by analogy in many of its activities, and it generalizes from individual cases. When children say *mouses* we know they are using transfer, because that is a word they have probably never heard before. The principle of nontransfer is not as absolute as the 1918 report suggested.

On the other hand, the report ignored the principle of nontransference when it said that schools should teach "the fundamental processes."[28] By this phrase was meant "reading, writing, arithmetical computations, and the elements of oral and written expression." The report assumed that reading and writing are formal skills that can be applied to different tasks, regardless of subject matter. Thus, while repudiating the idea of the transfer of training for Latin, the 1918 report unwittingly adopted it for reading and writing. With similar inconsistency, it stressed specific content for vocational courses but deemphasized content in language arts courses. These intellectual inconsistencies were to have disastrous consequences.

Nonetheless, the reorientation of the schools to practical social goals was intended as a generous and humane goal in the writings of John Dewey, Clarence D. Kingsley, William H. Kilpatrick, and other leaders of the progressive movement. They could not have been expected to foresee that, when their principles were actually put into effect in institutional settings, humaneness would be difficult to preserve. Dewey, in fact, became appalled by the neutral scientism of those American educational administrators who began to institutionalize progressive ideas.[29] Despite his opposition to book-centered instruction, Dewey assumed that children *would* become highly literate under his learning-by-doing principles of education. Although that assumption turned out to be incorrect, Dewey was in some respects on the side of traditionalists, many of whom, for their part, continue to honor his aims of pluralism and social utility.

But the ideal of accommodating individual differences by offering different types of courses became institutionalized as "tracking" and "grouping" — systems that put bright students in one class, average students in another, and poor students in a third. The principle of adjusting to diverse capacities produced, in effect, three academic castes, each of which received different kinds of information. In language arts courses, for instance, where content became an arbitrary vehicle to inculcate the "fundamental processes" of reading and writing, the tracking system led to Shakespeare for some, sports and fantasy stories for others.

The fragmentation produced by tracking reinforced the fragmentation that was being introduced by vocational courses. Schools were to be directly useful in preparing children for citizenship, work, and leisure. Girls should be taught courses in homemaking and boys courses in shop or other vocational subjects. The introduction of such courses, like the introduction of the tracking system, further multiplied the different sorts of courses offered in school, leading ultimately to the shopping mall school with its extreme horizontal fragmentation.[30]

The principles of 1918 also led to the institution of social studies courses that were supposed to inculcate directly the traditions and duties of Americans. History was seen as an indirect and inefficient means of achieving those social goals, and was transformed into social studies. Like vocational courses, social studies courses were directed "to the activities of life rather than to the demands of any subject as a logically organized science."[31] But since the applications of social studies "to the activities of life" were infinitely various, different schools came to teach different sorts of information in them, and the transformation of history into social studies led inexorably to a lack of shared historical information.

The private schools were less influenced by the new theories, and many of them continued to provide traditional content. As a consequence, their graduates were, on the whole, more literate than those who came from the public schools. Such differences exacerbated the class stratifications that the educators of 1893 had sought to avoid.

Despite these drawbacks, the new theories made steady headway. Immediately after World War II, for instance, a resolution passed by educators meeting in Washington, D.C., asserted that only 40 percent of our children were being properly educated. Twenty percent of American youth were being prepared for vocations, while another 20 percent were being prepared for college, but the remaining 60 percent, the resolution complained, would not

> receive the life adjustment training they need and to which they are entitled as American citizens — unless and until the administrators of public education with the assistance of the vocational education leaders formulate a similar program for this group.[32]

This resolution was greeted favorably by numerous regional conferences and ratified at a national conference in 1947. Professor Ravitch summarizes the results in this way:

> The conference described educationally neglected youths as coming from low-income homes with low cultural environments; as retarded in school; as making low scores on intelligence and achievement tests; as less emotionally mature than other students, with lower grades and less interest in school work. What these children needed was "life adjustment education," which consisted of guidance and education in citizenship, home and family life, use of leisure, health, tools of learning, work experience, and occupational adjustment.[33]

This view is the ground for our current practice of giving academic credit for such courses as family relations, adolescent parenting, and apartment and income property management.[34] Nor did the conference participants believe that life adjustment education should be directed only to disadvantaged students. It was regarded as a universal principle, "best suited to meet the needs of *all* American youth." The life adjustment movement of the 1940s and 1950s continued the advance of the *Cardinal Principles*. It was "indistinguishable in everything but name" from many already established versions of progressive education, going back to 1918.[35]

The "open education" of the 1960s and 1970s was more insistently romantic even than the romantic-pragmatic principles of 1918. The earlier reformers did not go as far as the sixties progressivist Charles H. Rathbone, who held that "there is no indispensable body of knowledge that every single child should know,"[36] nor as far as Roland S. Barth, who wrote in January 1970:

> In a real sense children's own experiences are the subject matter — the content of their learning. These experiences are good and bad, productive and non-productive, pleasant and unpleasant. Open educators worry less about whether a child has had a particular experience than about the quality and the meaning for him of the experiences he has had. It is for time and future experience to judge the significance of a student's experience, not for the adult to judge.[37]

Even if this was not couched in the style of 1918, its ideas were built upon the same basic principles that lay behind the 1918 report. The romantic formalism of the sixties and seventies was an extreme yet logical extension of the romantic formalism that has been the dominant theory taught in our schools of education over the past fifty years.

PRINCIPLES OF REFORM

The counterreform of the 1980s seems bent upon a return to a more traditional curriculum. This welcome course correction demonstrates the underlying good sense of the American people, who have launched a grassroots movement to advance that reform. But the movement is being greeted unenthusiastically by many educators. School administrators and senior professors in schools of education who were trained in the theories of the *Cardinal Principles* naturally resist fundamental deviations from them, fearing superficial and mindlessly reactionary effects. Indeed, if traditional facts were to be presented unimaginatively or taught ignorantly or regarded as ends in themselves, we would have much to deplore in a return to traditional education. But dry incompetence is not the necessary alternative to lively ignorance.

Pragmatists in the school of Dewey are right to say that the "higher values" traditionalists invoke are not the special property of Western culture. Higher values comprising humankind's accumulated wisdom about human nature are found in all civilized traditions, East and West, ancient and modern, popular and aristocratic. Confucius is as wise as Socrates. Pragmatists are also right to say that human values can be taught through many sorts of materials, traditional or untraditional. But in the end, given our newly gained understanding of literacy, we must be traditionalists about content. For we have learned the paradox that traditional education, which alone yields the flexible skill of mature literacy, outperforms utilitarian education even by utilitarian standards.

The flaw in utilitarianism is its lack of utility for the modern world. Narrow vocational education, adjusted to the needs of the moment, is made ever more obsolete by changing technology. Vocations have multiplied beyond the abilities of the schools to accommodate them. What is required is education for change, not for static job competencies. Aside from preparation for low-paying, simple vocations, this was already true when the *Cardinal Principles* were enunciated; it is emphatically true today.

Also unrealistic is the pragmatist emphasis on individuality, at least as the idea has been institutionalized. The best teaching does accommodate itself to individual differences in temperament, but a child's temperament does not come freighted with content. To learn a culture is natural to human beings. Children can express individuality only in relation to the traditions of their society, which they have to learn. The greatest human individuality is developed in response to a tradition, not in response to disorderly, uncertain, and fragmented education. Americans in their teens and twenties who were brought up under individualistic theories are not less conventional than their predecessors, only less literate, less able to express their individuality.

We should resist the extreme views of pragmatists and traditionalists alike. Those pragmatists who have based their doctrines upon scientific psychology are obliged to follow where psychology has led, which is back to common content. The antitraditional goals of the progressive movement have turned out to depend upon traditional information. This paradox yields a middle ground for people of good will from both camps. It opens up the possibility of a compromise — a curriculum that is traditional in content but diverse in its emphases, that is pluralistic in its materials and modes of teaching but nonetheless provides our children with a common core of cultural information.

The curriculum reform that I have in mind accords with an eloquent proposal for educational reform offered by Dr. Patricia Graham, dean of the Harvard Graduate School of Education.[38] She argues that we need both commonality and flexibility in American education and that there is no reason we cannot have both at once. Schools across our nation should share common goals, but their means for achieving those goals should be varied and adaptive.

One can think of the school curriculum as consisting of two complementary parts, which might be called the extensive curriculum and the intensive curriculum. The content of the extensive curriculum is traditional literate knowledge, the information, attitudes, and assumptions that literate Americans share — cultural literacy. Of course, this curriculum should be taught not just as a series of terms, or list of words, but as a vivid system of shared associations. The name John Brown should evoke in children's minds not just a simple identifying definition but a whole network of lively traits, the traditionally known facts and values.

The nature of this world knowledge as it exists in the minds of literate adults is typically elementary and incomplete. People reliably share just a few associations about canaries, such as yellow, sing, kept in cages, but not much more. Literate people know who Falstaff is, that he is fat, likes to eat and drink, but they can't reliably name the Shakespeare plays in which he appears. They know who Eisenhower was, and might recognize "military-industrial complex," but they can't be counted on to state anything else about Eisenhower's Farewell Address. In short, the information that literate people dependably share is extensive but limited — a characteristic central to this discussion.

Yet students' possession of that limited information is a necessary preliminary to their acquiring more detailed information. To understand the full text of Dwight D. Eisenhower's Farewell Address and the historical circumstances that gave rise to it, they have to know who Eisenhower was and what a farewell address is in the American tradition. The extensive curriculum would be designed to ensure that all our high school graduates are given the traditional information shared by other literate Americans. This extensive network of associations constitutes the part of the curriculum that has to be known by every child and must be common to all the schools of the nation.

But the extensive curriculum is not a sufficient basis for education by itself. It is simply a minimal description of elements that should be included in every child's schooling, no matter what form the schooling takes. The extensive curriculum can be taught in a highly formal traditional school or in a more informal progressive school. Any sort of school can find ways of incorporating these minimal contents in its courses, given a determination to do so and coordination among grade levels in deciding on the appropriate times for introducing particular aspects of particular subjects.

The intensive curriculum, though different, is equally essential. Intensive study encourages a fully developed understanding of a subject, making one's knowledge of it integrated and coherent. It coincides with Dewey's recommendation that children should be deeply engaged with a small number of typical concrete instances. It is also that part of the total curriculum in which great flexibility in contents and methods can prevail. The intensive curriculum is the more pluralistic element of my proposal, because it ensures that individual students, teachers, and schools can work intensively with materials that are appropriate for their diverse temperaments and aims.

The conception of a two-part curriculum avoids the idea that all children should study identical materials. It also resists the lure of a core curriculum, if that proposal is taken to mean that all high school graduates should study, say, *Romeo and Juliet*. A common extensive curriculum would ensure that students have *some* information about *Romeo and Juliet*, but in their intensive curriculum they might study *The Tempest* or *Twelfth Night* in detail. If a school decided that all its students should read two Shakespeare plays in depth, even the most convinced traditionalists would find it hard to agree on which two plays they should be. Schools can find means of imparting extensive information side by side with an approach that conveys intensive knowledge as well, without imposing an arbitrary core curriculum.

Unlike children of today, the Major-General in Gilbert and Sullivan's *Pirates of Penzance* had plenty of extensive information; it was the intensive curriculum that he had missed:

> I am the very model of a modern Major-General,
> I've information vegetable, animal, and mineral,
> I know the kings of England, and I quote the fights historical,
> From Marathon to Waterloo, in order categorical;
> I'm very well acquainted too with matters mathematical,
> I understand equations, both the simple and quadratical,
> About binomial theorem I'm teeming with a lot o' news —
> With many cheerful facts about the square of the hypotenuse.[39]

These "cheerful facts" are *all* the Major-General knows, and they were part of the intellectual baggage possessed by every literate schoolboy in nineteenth-century Britain. Everyone in Gilbert's audience knew those same facts, and this extensive information made them no better at military strategy than it made Major-General Stanley:

> When I have learnt what progress has been made in modern gunnery,
> When I know more of tactics than a novice in a nunnery:
> In short, when I've a smattering of elemental strategy,
> You'll say a better Major-Gener*al* has never *sat* a gee.

Instead of just being able to name the fights historical, if the Major-General had studied at least a battle or two in some detail — Austerlitz or Waterloo — he might have developed a coherent idea of nineteenth-century warfare. Thereafter, any new fact about battles that he encountered could be accommodated to the mental model, or schema, that he had gained from intensive study of the Battle of Waterloo. To understand how isolated facts fit together in some coherent way, we must always acquire mental models of how they cohere, and these schemata can come only from detailed, intensive study and experience.

Almost any battle will do to gain a coherent idea of battles. Any Shakespeare play will do to gain a schematic conception of Shakespeare; it doesn't matter whether the play read in ninth grade is *Macbeth* or *Julius Caesar*. Our choice of intensive curricular materials can vary with circumstances and should depend on many grounds for choice, including student and teacher interest, local community preferences, and the aims and values that predominate in particular schools or classrooms. But there *is* a limit to the flexibility of the intensive curriculum. If we want people to have a conception of Shakespearean drama, then a play by Neil Simon is not a satisfactory substitute for a play by Shakespeare.

The consciously conveyed extensive curriculum is the new part of my proposal. Some educators with whom I have talked about it have raised questions about the difficulties of putting the idea into practice. Educated people, they say, usually acquire extensive knowledge through a long process that includes not only intensive study in school but also many years of communication with other literate people. You can't expect students to remember the extensive curriculum as a mere catalogue of information. Nobody remembers information unless it is embedded in interesting material. In practice, according to such observers, you can't teach the extensive curriculum without transforming it into an intensive, core curriculum.

It is probably true that the full range of cultural literacy will be conveyed by a broad variety of experiences, inside and outside school. But school can play a central role in conveying shared information. First of all, the nature of that information can be determined, and it can be expressed as an index of cultural literacy for the use of curriculum developers and educators. Of course, we must always present material to children in an interesting way. But very young children *are* interested in extensive, limited information. In the early grades, truly intensive study is in any case difficult to pursue. The predicted difficulties of teaching the extensive curriculum simply do not apply to young children, and it's chiefly to young children that the extensive curriculum needs to be taught. They like to pick up adult information long before they can make sense of it. A special motivation for this focus in the early grades should be our understanding that if students still lack important elements of the extensive curriculum by tenth grade, they will rarely be able to make up the loss.[40]

Children may not be as intrigued by "imaginative literature" as recent curriculum makers assume. We need readers that contain a much larger proportion of nonfictional materials, as well as a larger proportion of traditional myths and stories. Textbooks should be prepared so that they systematically convey as much of the national vocabulary as possible. Young children are fascinated by straightforward information and absorb it without strain. Even untraditional schools have not found a way to avoid rote learning of the alphabet or the multiplication table or the months of the year. Children don't have to be forced to memorize facts; they do it anyway. There is little an opponent of rote learning can do to stop a child from memorization. The great oversight of a watered-down "developmental" curriculum for the early grades is that while our children are busily remembering whatever they experience in and out of school, their school materials are often transitory and unshared with others in the culture. The unconscious learning of transitory materials is the least useful kind of memorization.

A curriculum reform designed to teach young children the basics of cultural literacy will thus require radical changes in textbooks and other teaching materials. I have just mentioned some of the "new" kinds of materials I have in mind. But from a historical perspective, these would not be novel in conception. In the early nineteenth century, Charles and Mary Lamb produced *Tales from Shakespeare* and *The Adventures of Ulysses* for very young children, for just the purposes I envision. Among the most popular elementary schoolbooks in America in the early part of this century was the series *Everyday Classics* by A. H. Thorndike (a different Thorndike) and F. T. Baker, self-consciously designed to teach cultural literacy to very young children. Here is an excerpt from one of their prefaces (I have italicized a few phrases to show how fully aware they were of the need for teaching shared content in the days before the dominance of educational formalism).

> We have chosen what is common, established, almost proverbial; what has become indisputably "classic," what, in brief, *every child in the land ought to know*, because it is good, *and because other people know it*. The educational worth of such materials calls for no defense. In an age when the *need of*

> *socializing and unifying our people* is keenly felt, the value of a *common stock of knowledge*, a common set of ideals is obvious. A people is best unified by being taught in childhood the best things in its intellectual and moral heritage. Our own heritage is, like our ancestry, composite. Hebrew, Greek, Roman, English, French, and Teutonic elements are blended in our cultural past. We draw freely from all of these. An introduction to the best of this is one of our ways of making good citizens.[41]

Of course, we have now widened our recognition of the elements of our shared culture, but Baker and Thorndike's method still responds to our needs.

What Baker and Thorndike did not say was that many early materials of cultural literacy do *not* attempt to foster "a common set of ideals" or to indoctrinate us in moral values. We don't get common ideals from "Baa, Baa, Black Sheep," or moral values from "Here We Go Round the Mulberry Bush" or "Humpty Dumpty" or "Jack Sprat" or "Sing a Song of Sixpence." Nor is any value system supported by the principle that the angle of incidence of light equals the angle of reflection. Nor is Gresham's law a moral principle. Many a proverb has its opposite in the national vocabulary, so that often one discovers dueling platitudes. Too many cooks may spoil the broth, but many hands make light work. Absence makes the heart grow fonder, but out of sight, out of mind. You're never too old to learn, unless you happen to be an old dog trying to learn new tricks.

At later levels of education, where teaching is done according to subject divisions, the national vocabulary needs continued systematic attention. We should incorporate the elements of cultural literacy into the structure of textbooks, courses, and school requirements. We should teach more surveys that cover large movements of human thought and experience. Yet even now the goal of teaching shared information is under attack by the latest version of educational formalism, the "critical thinking" movement. This well-meaning educational program aims to take children beyond the minimal basic skills mandated by state guidelines and to encourage the teaching of "higher order" skills. Admirable as these goals are, the denigration of "mere facts" by the movement's proponents is a dangerous repetition of the mistakes of 1918.

Any educational movement that avoids coming to terms with the specific contents of literate education or evades the responsibility of conveying them to all citizens is committing a fundamental error. However noble its aims, any movement that deprecates facts as antiquated or irrelevant injures the cause of higher national literacy. The old prejudice that facts deaden the minds of children has a long history in the nineteenth and twentieth centuries and includes not just the disciples of Rousseau and Dewey but also Charles Dickens who, in the figure of Mr. Gradgrind in *Hard Times*, satirized the teaching of mere facts. But it isn't facts that deaden the minds of young children, who are storing facts in their minds every day with astonishing voracity. It is incoherence — our failure to ensure that a pattern of shared, vividly taught, and socially enabling knowledge will emerge from our instruction.

The polarization of educationists into facts-people versus skills-people has no basis in reason. Facts and skills are inseparable. There is no insurmountable reason why those who advocate the teaching of higher order skills and those who advocate the teaching of common traditional content should not join forces. No philosophical or practical barrier prevents them from doing so, and all who consider mature literacy to be a paramount aim of education will wish them to do so.

CHAPTER VI

The Practical Outlook

DEFINING THE CONTENTS OF CULTURAL LITERACY

Having traced the nature of cultural literacy and shown its importance to national education, I want to consider the practical implications of the ideas I have set forth.

One immediate implication is that we have an obligation to identify and publish the contents of cultural literacy. It is reasonable to think that those contents can be identified explicitly, since they are identified *implicitly* by every writer or speaker who addresses the general public. If writers did not make tacit assumptions about the knowledge they could take for granted in their audiences, their writing would be so cumbersome as to defeat the aim of communication.

It is true that the specific content of the national literate vocabulary changes from year to year, even from day to day, as striking events catch national attention. But such changes are few when compared to the words and associations that stay the same. Of course, one literate person's sense of the shared national vocabulary is not precisely identical with another's; individual experiences produce different assumptions in different people about shared knowledge. But these differences are insignificant compared to what is common in the systems of associations that we acquire by daily experiences of literate culture.

It's also true that we adapt our conjectures about what others know to particular circumstances. Obviously, the knowledge we assume when we talk to a young child is substantially different from that which we take for granted in addressing an educated adult, and we constantly make other adjustments to our audiences. But when we address a general audience we must assume that we are addressing a "common reader," that is, a literate person who shares with us a common body of knowledge and associations. Since we so frequently have to posit a common reader in writing or public speaking, it should be possible to reach a large measure of agreement about what that common reader knows.

Such agreement about literate culture should, in theory, enable a random group of literate Americans to compile a list of its core contents. Their compilation, despite its inevitable defects, might yield practical benefits to American education. In 1983 I persuaded two of my colleagues at the University of Virginia, Joseph Kett, chairman of the department of history, and James Trefil, professor of physics, to help me compile such a list. My field is the humanities, Kett is a historian with a special interest in the history of American education, and Trefil is a highly literate scientist who is well known both for his experimental work and for his ability to communicate technical information to the general public. Our expertise was useful in *generating* candidate items for the list, but it was not decisive in judging whether the items were the possession of the common reader. In fact, experts may be quite unreliable judges of items within their own domains, because their daily experiences within special fields may distort their estimates of what is and is not familiar.

Each of us took the primary responsibility for developing the vocabulary within his field, consulting numerous sources — indexes, reference books, textbooks, general books, magazines; one combed through a large dictionary page by page. Our growing lists were criticized by the other two, who brought to bear their own sense of the basic vocabulary of our culture. When we finished the first version of our list, we submitted it to more than a hundred consultants outside the academic world.

The three of us have also been at work on a large explanation of the listings, which we are calling a dictionary. Its definitions consist of the associations that each item tends to call forth in the minds of literate persons. We attempt to reproduce the shared cultural schemata that underlie literate communications of the present day. The list reproduced here as an appendix is a provisional index to the forthcoming larger work.

In consulting others about our initial list we did in fact discover a strong consensus about the significant elements in our core literate vocabulary. My colleagues and I were not surprised at this agreement, but we were gratified to find that the consensus did indeed exist far beyond our narrow circle and extended to educated Americans of different ages, sexes, races, and ethnic origins.

We do not claim that the initial list is definitive. Such an assertion, even for a longer version, would be rash, because of human variations. Nonetheless, the consensus we found has made us confident that our list provides a fairly reliable index to the middle-level information that is shared by most literate people but remains largely unfamiliar to most illiterate people. This unspecialized middle domain, the homeland of the common reader, must, in the nature of things, have fuzzy edges.

Another reason our list could not be definitive is that its design must be somewhat arbitrary for mechanical reasons alone. Further words that literate people associate with individual items could be represented by further entries. The difficulty of deciding between main and subordinate items is one faced by all encyclopedists. To appreciate that fact, one need only compare the huge number of items listed in the index to the *Encyclopaedia Britannica* with the modest number of main entries in that same work. In our selections we gave priority to words and phrases found in the front pages and editorial columns of serious newspapers and in the pages of serious books and magazines. Unfortunately, no systematic studies exist of the information that is assumed without explanation in magazines like *The Atlantic* and general-circulation books. We therefore had to rely on our own experience and judgment in deciding what is central and what is subordinate in compiling such a list.

Early in our project, my colleagues and I decided that our list should aim to represent but not to alter current literate American culture. The only exception to this principle that we have permitted is in the domain of scientific literacy. It is widely agreed that our shared knowledge of science and technology ought to be enhanced, because of their growing importance in our lives. But beyond this small attempt to improve scientific literacy, we have tried to avoid any of the prescriptiveness that is inherent in cultural politics, the aims of which are fundamentally different from those of teaching literacy. A chief goal of cultural politics is to change the content and values of culture. But the principal aim of schooling is to promote literacy as an enabling competence. Although our public schools have a duty to teach widely accepted cultural values, they have a duty *not* to take political stands on matters that are subjects of continuing debate. Only a descriptive list accords with these fundamental goals of universal education.

Of course, even a descriptive list cannot be entirely neutral with respect to cultural politics; it must necessarily emphasize traditional materials, because widely shared information is not likely to be new. The traditionalism inherent in our project may make the list seem to some an obstacle to desirable change. But wise change comes from competence, and that is what our list really addresses.

My colleagues and I decided also that the first version of the list should represent a high school level of literacy. Most Americans now complete high school, a level of schooling that ought to guarantee true literacy. We hoped our list might help educators and publishers develop methods and materials for primary and secondary education, as well as create a sound foundation for later education in college.

Having written for general-circulation newspapers and magazines, we had gained a sense of the assumptions that can be made in addressing literate American audiences. We are aware that the suspicion may be entertained that our list is merely academic or male or white, and so on, just because we are. But a similarity of shared knowledge is inherent to national literacy, and this fact controverts the ad hominem assumption that, because a list was made by so and so, it merely reflects so and so's view of American literate culture. The proof that this is not the case is the wide agreement we found.

Indeed, it would have been highly surprising if literate people from different parts of the country, different generations, different ethnic groups, different areas of employment, and different political allegiances had not confirmed almost all of our selections. But decisions about many items are not clear cut. The inclusion or exclusion of such borderline items must be matters of judgment; we must draw a northerly border, above which lies specialized knowledge, and a southerly one, below which lies knowledge so obvious and widely known that its inclusion would make the list unusably long. There are also easterly and westerly borderline areas. To the east lie materials that are still too new to have passed into general currency. For instance, only a few years ago that would have been the case with *AIDS* or *Ayatollah Khomeini*. To the west are items, like *Sherman Adams*, which have passed from view and are now known only by older generations.

To take a minor but characteristic instance of the problems we encounter in the full dictionary, consider Superman. One can argue that he is so widely known to people of different generations that he lies well below the southern border and needn't be included at all. But maybe that judgment is premature. As a mythical figure, Superman is likely to be used allusively in all sorts of writings. But just how far will those allusions reasonably go? What associations properly belong in an entry under *Superman*? Certainly we should include Clark Kent and the blue-and-red suit with the flowing cape, but what about Lois Lane, kryptonite, and the *Daily Planet*?

Such subtle problems are closely analogous to those confronted by makers of ordinary dictionaries when they must decide which rare or obsolete words to leave out of high school or college or even unabridged editions, or when they deal with words that have begun to take on meanings that are not yet universally accepted. At what point should new, questionable meanings be included, and when should they be accepted as correct? One method that lexicographers have devised for dealing with borderline cases is to audit their use in a representative group of sources. Needless to say, diverse sources produce somewhat different evidence, with the result that there is not, even in theory, a definitive right answer in borderline cases.

Such problems occur throughout our cultural lexicon, where even such unquestionable entries as *Abraham Lincoln* and *gravity* present difficulties. Should all the following associations be listed under *Lincoln*?

> Gaunt face with a beard; log cabin; Honest Abe; debates with Douglas; Gettysburg Address; stovepipe hat; Emancipation

Proclamation; "With malice toward none, with charity for all"; John Wilkes Booth; "Tell me what brand of whiskey Grant drinks, so I can get it for my other generals"; "One aye, seven noes, the ayes have it."

Where should such associations stop? How many are generally known by literate people? Or take *gravity*. What is the extent of the knowledge of literate people about it? Does it include Newton's apple, celestial orbits, the law of inverse squares, relativity, the weak force, the unified field theory? Are those associations too many or too few? As my colleagues and I proceed with our work on the lexicon and develop the clusters that surround each entry on our list, we reach points of uncertainty that cannot be definitively resolved. At that point we enlist the help of a panel of advisers.

PUTTING CULTURAL LITERACY TO WORK

What application could be made of this dictionary? An obvious possibility would be to develop a national core curriculum from the material, but this approach seems neither desirable nor feasible. We wish to preserve the choice and variety that a locally controlled educational system allows us.

Nonetheless, American schools should be able to devise an *extensive* curriculum based on the national vocabulary and arranged in a definite sequence. This aim could be accomplished with a great diversity of schoolbooks and teaching methods. But while the methods of conveying cultural literacy can and should vary from school to school, an agreed-upon, explicit national vocabulary should in time come to be regarded as the basis of a literate education.

Such a plan is not really radical or new. In earlier days, when the school curriculum was based upon the materials set forth in Blair's *Rhetoric* and the textbooks of his imitators, we had no need for self-conscious agreement about the extensive curriculum, because the common vocabulary of cultural literacy was explicitly provided in Blair's and similar books. Now, after many decades of skills-oriented textbooks, we must take a more deliberate approach to the problem of shared information.

Naturally, schools and school boards cannot be expected to introduce a change of this magnitude unless parents and citizens want it. But once people perceive the need for shared content, students as well as parents may demand it. The effect of student opinion on educational reform should not be underestimated. Not long after *Newsweek* published a cover article titled "Why Johnny Can't Write," students flocked into college writing courses in numbers that overwhelmed departments of English. This was an unpredictable, startling phenomenon, because, in the past, composition had been a subject most college students were eager to avoid. Clearly, the students had been persuaded that they needed to learn how to write, and largely on their own, they increased the demand for writing instruction.

One can't foresee all the ways in which reforms in the extensive part of the school curriculum might come about. The process may be more subtle and complex than any specific proposal or prediction I can outline here. But suppose that after a time people did come to agree on the specific items of information that literate people currently share and on the necessity of communicating them in education. What practical measures could be taken to create useful school materials?

The single most effective step would be to shift the reading materials used in kindergarten through eighth grade to a much stronger base in factual information and traditional lore. At present, heavy emphasis is placed on stories, on chapters from novels (with bridging introductions and conclusions), on essays about human feelings, and other selections of the kind. All these texts convey information, but rarely the kinds most necessary for future literacy. What is needed are reading texts that deliberately convey what children need to know and include a substantially higher proportion of factual narratives.

This will not be a simple change to make. What is called for is an alteration in the convictions of educational administrators. Most of the teachers I have talked with would welcome the change, and they have indeed urged me to try to bring it about. In making this recommendation, I focus on reading instruction, because reading is the principal subject in elementary schools and retains a high importance in middle school and junior high.

The requisite information should be conveyed in an orderly, coherent way. How is that coherence to be obtained? One method would be for each publisher of multigrade materials to develop its own sequence of presentation. But that would limit the flexibility of the school system in its selection of materials and put children who move from one system to another at a disadvantage. A better solution would be for publishers and educators to reach an accord about the contents of the national vocabulary and a good sequence for presenting it. The agreement needn't specify anything about the way the sequenced materials should be presented or the percentage of time to be spent on them. But such an agreement would ensure that any child who graduated from an elementary, junior high, or high school would share with others a minimal core of background information.

State systems of education are not only independent but independent-minded. It would be difficult to induce them to agree on a year-by-year sequence for imparting the national vocabulary from kindergarten to grade twelve, since any such sequence would be arbitrary (though, by the same token, any thoughtful sequence would be as satisfactory as another, and the choice of a common sequence would carry enormous benefits to our children). It might be valuable, therefore, to convene a distinguished group of educators and public leaders to develop a model grade-by-grade sequence of core information. Their recommendations could carry only the force of personal authority, which is sometimes effective, sometimes not.

Another, supplementary, way in which we might develop a consensus about teaching core information would be to develop general knowledge tests for three different stages of schooling, each based upon an agreed-on body of information. The three tests would be specified for particular grades — say, five, eight, and twelve. Ideally, they would also be devised by an independent group of scholars, educators, and concerned citizens and serve a variety of purposes. For instance, they would be helpful for diagnosing areas of a student's knowledge and ignorance. Their use would, of course, be left entirely to state and local discretion.

In some European countries, common information is taught just by virtue of the existence of national tests. The O- and A-level exams in Britain shape the elementary and secondary curricula, respectively, and I am told that they encourage the teaching of some degree of common information throughout the country. We are not likely to accept such tests, but general-knowledge examinations wouldn't need to be compulsory to exert a normalizing effect on the extensive curriculum. If school administrators knew that some of their students might want to take one or more of the tests, they might adjust their curricula accordingly for all students. Similarly, the mere existence of such tests might encourage publishers, as a matter of commercial prudence, to include in their textbooks the core information upon which the tests were based.

The information would be relatively stable and known by everyone in advance. Although individual versions of the tests would change from year to year, most of the information the tests sampled would remain the same over many years, because the central components of cultural literacy change rather slowly. General-knowledge tests made in this rational way and based on published lists and dictionaries would be inherently less arbitrary than the verbal SAT, because they would openly depend on the realities and requirements of national literacy.

Although the verbal SAT is fundamentally a vocabulary test, its makers have never defined the specific vocabulary on which it is based. That task is left to special companies, which have learned how to prepare students who can afford to pay their fees. Consequently, the verbal SAT remains a dark mystery to disadvantaged students: an obstacle to and a subverter of confidence and hope.

There are many things to be said against making a list, and in the past two years I have heard them. Ideological objections to codifying and imposing the culture of the power structure have been among them. These are objections to the whole concept of spreading cultural literacy and are consequently objections to spreading literacy itself, not to making lists. A sounder objection is that the very existence of a list will cause students merely to memorize the bare items it contains and learn nothing significant at all. Students will trivialize cultural information without really possessing it.

How can I deny that such misuse of the list is not only a danger but a near certainty? Whole sections of our bookstores are already devoted to paring down complex information into short, easily digested summaries — crib sheets for every school subject. (If such cribs and trots did not exist in many other countries, one might think they reflected a uniquely American optimism.) Could anyone learn or remember anything from a mere list? Won't the whole project end up just as a large-scale crib sheet for general-knowledge tests? And won't seventeen-year-olds, after they take the tests, promptly forget everything they momentarily crammed into their heads?

Maybe, but that wouldn't be the only result. A better, and more likely, consequence of publishing this material will be that children and parents will desire it to be used in a truly effective way in school. If the list is found to be defective, they will demand a better one. But the mere existence of the list and the full dictionary will help people perceive that our previous reluctance to identify core information has seriously hindered the effective teaching of literacy. It's not the list that is dangerous to serious education; its explicitness is dangerous to the inadequate, skills-oriented educational principles of the recent past. The list is an implicit challenge to supporters of those principles to be equally explicit.

Not least among the virtues of a list of cultural literacy is the fact of its finiteness. As soon as one thinks about it, it is obvious that shared information in a large nation like ours must be limited in extent. Each of us shares an immense amount of information with small circles of intimates and cospecialists, and the smaller the circle, the greater the amount shared. But what we share with the very large circle of literate persons throughout the nation cannot be huge. Just to illustrate the finiteness of literate culture is useful. It should energize people to learn that only a few hundred pages of information stand between the literate and the illiterate, between dependence and autonomy. Moreover, the cost of recognizing this fact, if it is a cost at all, will be rather low — simply the demystification of literate culture. The benefit could be very great indeed — the achievement of significantly greater social and economic equity.

I hope that anyone who has read this book will see that the educational reforms it advocates are based upon reason and strong evidence. The reforms are meant to raise the reading levels of all students and to break the cycle of illiteracy that persists from parent to child under our current school curriculum. By stressing the essential role of content in reading, this book should have punctured the myth that reading and writing are like bike riding or map reading, skills that require only a narrow range of specific information plus some practice. I hope it has also punctured the myth that our schools need only teach techniques of decoding, or techniques of thinking, or techniques of looking up information that might later be needed. The skills model of education is illusory, because it overlooks the fact that reading and thinking skills alike depend upon a wide range of specific, quickly available information. Every citizen needs to have immediately at hand a critical mass of specific information in order to possess that skill of skills which is literacy.

Since these fundamental facts about reading are no longer subjects of debate among reading researchers, the question of specific content can no longer be ignored in American education. The question "Who is to say what that content shall be?" must not be allowed to serve its traditional role as a debate stopper. To suggest that it is undemocratic or intolerant to make nationwide decisions about the extensive school curriculum must not any longer be allowed to end the discussion. The "pluralistic," laissez-faire view itself implies a nationwide extensive curriculum — the curriculum of cultural fragmentation and illiteracy. To repudiate the idea of a shared extensive curriculum is necessarily to accept the idea of an *unshared* extensive curriculum. And that is precisely the extensive curriculum our schools now offer. We must not allow the suggestion to go unchallenged that this fragmented curriculum isn't really a curriculum at all but only a method for developing skills. That position is, as we know, an evasion, an abdication of our responsibility to make decisions about curricular content. It invites somebody else to decide.

And in each classroom somebody always does decide what material our children will be storing in their minds in the name of skills acquisition. All too often it is content for which our children will have no use in the future. If the contents of our existing extensive curriculum were listed openly, as in the Appendix, we would see that much of the information now being conveyed to our children is wasteful of precious opportunities, particularly in the early grades. The choice that this book offers is not a narrow, either-or choice between the specific list of items given here or the current state of curricular fragmentation. Rather, it presents a broad challenge: to bring the currently hidden curriculum out in the open where it belongs and to make its contents the subject of democratic discussion. Those who might consider our specific recommendations to be defective are being challenged to improve upon them, but not to perpetuate the illusion that we can continue, in honesty, to avoid a discussion of the specific contents of the extensive curriculum.

I hope that in our future debates about the extensive curriculum, the participants will keep clearly in view the high stakes involved in their deliberations: breaking the cycle of illiteracy for deprived children; raising the living standard of families who have been illiterate; making our country more competitive in international markets; achieving greater social justice; enabling all citizens to participate in the political process; bringing us closer to the Ciceronian ideal of universal public discourse — in short, achieving fundamental goals of the Founders at the birth of the republic.

WHAT LITERATE AMERICANS KNOW: A Preliminary List

by E. D. Hirsch, Jr., Joseph Kett, and James Trefil

E. D. Hirsch, Jr., is William R. Kenan Professor of English, Joseph Kett is Chairman of the Department of History, and James Trefil is Professor of Physics, all at the University of Virginia, Charlottesville. This list is provisional; it is intended to illustrate the character and range of the knowledge literate Americans tend to share. More than one hundred consultants reported agreement on over 90 percent of the items listed. But no such compilation can be definitive. Some proposed items were omitted because they seemed to us known by both literate and illiterate persons, too rare, or too transitory. Moreover, different literate Americans have slightly different conceptions of our shared knowledge. The authors see the list as a changing entity, partly because core knowledge changes, partly because inappropriate omissions and inclusions are bound to occur in a first attempt. Comments and suggestions are welcome and should be sent to Dr. Hirsch at the Department of English, University of Virginia, Charlottesville, VA 22903. Correspondents should bear in mind that we do not seek to create a complete catalogue of American knowledge but to establish guideposts that can be of practical use to teachers, students, and all others who need to know our literate culture.

1. A NOTE ON LISTINGS IN LANGUAGE AND LITERATURE

E. D. Hirsch, Jr.

The geographical names, historical events, famous people, and patriotic lore need no special comment. They are words and phrases that appear in newspapers, magazines, and books without explanation. Famous persons are identified as they are normally alluded to, sometimes without first names, e.g., Cervantes rather than Miguel de Cervantes. We are not encyclopedists; we want to reflect the culture. We have provided a rather full listing of grammatical and rhetorical terms because students and teachers will find them useful for discussing English grammar and style.

Items from the field of literature require a special comment. In the minds of literary specialists, a literary work is a text, but that is not the cultural reality. The information about literature that exists in the minds of literate people may have been derived from conversation, criticism, cinema, television, or student crib sheets like *Cliffs Notes*. The American conception of Sherlock Holmes has been formed more by the acting of Basil Rathbone than by the writing of Conan Doyle. Judy Garland and Bert Lahr have fixed our conception of *The Wizard of Oz* more vividly than Frank Baum. Only a small proportion of literate people can name the Shakespeare plays in which Falstaff appears, yet they know who he is. They know what *Mein Kampf* is, but they haven't read it.

To reflect the cultural reality, we have listed literary terms in the same way as historical or geographical terms, that is, as words and phrases rather than as texts. For the few items that are widely read in their original texts, such as the Declaration of Independence and the Gettysburg Address, we indicate that fact by the word *text* in parentheses. But in the usual case, when people are likely to know the title of a work and just a few bits of associated information, we indicate that fact by using the word *title* in parentheses. And to avoid misleading our readers, we list all the entries in roman type. In some special cases, like those of Hamlet or Antigone, where the name of a character is also the title of a work, for the sake of efficiency we list the term only once.

2. A NOTE ON THE SCIENTIFIC TERMS

James Trefil

As poorly as we have served our students in the humanities and social sciences, we have served them even more poorly in the natural sciences.[1] The general level of scientific knowledge even among educated people is very low, a situation caused in part by the fact that science courses are perceived to be difficult and are therefore avoided by students. The maximum science load taken in high school seems to be set by the minimum requirements of entrance to state universities. Study beyond these is seldom demanded by our secondary schools.

This neglect has had a bad enough effect on general scientific knowledge, but still another policy in science education contributes just as much to scientific illiteracy. The policy is based on an assumption, seldom specifically stated, that bears close analogy to the doctrine of educational formalism described in Chapter 1 of this book. It is that science is a transferable skill, so that study of one branch provides the basic knowledge necessary to understand another one. Thus, a course in planetary astronomy is thought to impart a knowledge of "science" just as effectively as one in evolutionary biology, because in any science course one learns something called the scientific method.

I suspect that if this assumption were to be examined explicitly, it would be rejected by a majority of thoughtful people. But it is not examined, with the result that students are encouraged to pursue courses in only one or two sciences during their secondary education. Even students who receive exemplary instruction in particular scientific fields have major gaps in their knowledge of science as a whole. Someone may come out of high school or college with a good background in biology but no knowledge of physics, with an understanding of astronomy but none of geology, and so on.

Because there is little broad knowledge of science even among educated people, the kind of criteria used to compile our lists for the humanities and social sciences — for example, Would a literate person be familiar with this term? — simply can't be used for the natural sciences. The gap between the essential basic knowledge of science and what the general reader can be expected to know has become too large. Our criterion for choosing a science entry has been that the candidate must be truly essential to a broad grasp of a major science. This criterion may not assure true scientific literacy, but it should at least help overcome serious illiteracy.

A personal example will emphasize the necessity of making prescriptive decisions in the scientific part of the list. For over a decade I have been a regular contributor of science articles to *Smithsonian* magazine, which reaches a well-educated, highly literate readership. Yet even when writing for such an exceptional audience, I am reluctant to use a word like *proton* without glossing it ("one of the elementary particles that forms the nucleus of an atom"). I simply cannot assume that the term, standing alone, will be understood.

If a political scientist were to proceed on comparable assumptions, he or she would have to pause to explain every time a term like "United States Senate" appeared in the text.

In his famous essay on the "two cultures," C. P. Snow described the failure of his literary colleagues at Cambridge to recall, if they ever knew, the second law of thermodynamics. Chances are that the second law is no better known now than when he made his observation.[2] The science-related terms in our list represent the best judgments my colleagues, our advisers, and I can make about what literate Americans ought to know to achieve the levels of communication described in the text. People should know enough about the language of science to deal with the affairs of the polis on the pattern that Jefferson had in mind.

Although the true language of much science is mathematical, important elements of science can be expressed without the mathematical complexities that effectively move science beyond the understanding of all except specialists. Indeed, the goals of scientific literacy are no different from those of other kinds of cultural literacy: to provide each citizen with the basic framework of knowledge into which public debate can be placed. It is part of the basic responsibility of scientists to translate the essential elements of science into general, nontechnical terms. As we are unlikely to elect any presidents or members of Congress who have mastered advanced mathematics, let us hope this aim can be achieved.

I have not found it difficult to discover a consensus among scientists about what constitutes core knowledge in the different fields of science. Far more difficult is the choice of a limited set of terms for conveying that core knowledge to nonspecialists. Some basic terms will be familiar; others will seem technical. But yesterday's technical term is tomorrow's common parlance. Moreover, some essential scientific knowledge is tied to ordinary terms. We already know many of the words of science, but lack the appropriate concepts to go with them. For example, we know the words *sun* and *star*, but literate people do not universally know that the sun is a star or that the human body is composed of cells. All literate people know the word *energy*, but not all know that it is conserved and that its forms are interchangeable. It is necessary to know that an atom, like a cell, has a nucleus. A number of highly familiar words are listed, but they stand for scientific concepts that are less familiar than they should be.

Some of my scientist colleagues are inclined to talk vaguely about the desirability of citizens acquiring the competence to make technical judgments. In reality, the true benefits to be gained from a broad improvement in scientific literacy do not derive from that ability. Scientists who do not specialize in a precise field in which a technical question arises are scarcely better equipped than laypeople to reach technical judgments in that field. But all citizens must be equipped to make nontechnical judgments about technical questions.

For example, in the debate over the Strategic Defense Initiative ("Star Wars"), it is a serious error to expect literate citizens, including nonspecialist scientists, to make highly specialized technical decisions. Instead, their education should simply have provided them with the general facts and principles needed to understand the terms of the debate — how a satellite works, what a laser is and can do, and under what conditions such a system would be likely to succeed or fail. Similarly, in the great nuclear safety debates of the 1970s, all participants had to use the same basic scientific background for their arguments, and the real debate centered on whether the admittedly small risks of accident were acceptable in light of the benefits. Once basic technical issues are understood, policy questions become ethical and political, not technical.

Should we therefore conclude that science education is useless in producing informed citizens? Of course not. One might just as well argue that because the details of constitutional law can be understood only by legal experts, it's not necessary for citizens to know anything about the Constitution. We understand broad issues of national law because we have been taught the main principles of the Constitution and can make broad judgments on the basis of that elementary knowledge. Similarly, if we gain basic scientific literacy, we can make intelligent judgments about broad issues of technology.

Some scientists may feel that we are trying to combat scientific illiteracy in an inappropriate way. Lists of facts and concepts just don't reflect the true character of science. Granted, but a large part of any science can be learned without mathematics, and that part is precisely the content that is likely to be most important to the general public. A useful analogy here is the study of literature in translation. We cannot fully understand Tolstoy unless we read him in Russian, but obviously we gain a great deal from reading *War and Peace* in translation. We would think it absurd to withhold Homer or Goethe from students who haven't spent years learning Greek or German by declining to offer those authors in English. Why should we deny our students scientific knowledge just because it has been translated from mathematics into English? Something may be lost in translation, but not enough to make the translation worthless.

Some specialists can be expected to repeat the familiar objection that merely teaching scientific facts and concepts will fail to convey the nature of "scientific method." That seems to us a misguided objection. Some of our best philosophers of science rightly reject what Hilary Putnam calls "method fetishism" as necessary to an understanding of science.[3] To claim that the paramount goal of teaching basic science is to convey the scientific method is to make the same formalistic mistake as to claim that the main goal of reading instruction is to teach reading strategies. You cannot study "scientific method" in the abstract; you can only study scientific methods in specific instances, and in order to understand those instances you need to know the scientific facts and concepts represented in our list. Can anyone seriously argue that a student can understand how scientific method operates in nuclear physics if he or she doesn't know that the atom has a nucleus?

In the end, the purely instrumental utility of scientific knowledge may be less important than the wider value to be gained from being acquainted with science as one of the great expressions of the human spirit. Science has been and continues to be one of the noblest achievements of mankind. From a humanistic point of view, its attainments are on a par with great achievements in art, literature, and political institutions, and in this perspective, science should come to be known for the same reasons as these other subjects.[4]

THE LIST

1066
1492
1776
1861–1865
1914–1918
1939–1945
1984 (title)

Aaron, Hank
Abandon hope, all ye who enter here.
abbreviation
Aberdeen
abolitionism
abominable snowman
abortion
Absence makes the heart grow fonder.
absenteeism
absolute monarchy
absolute zero
abstract art
abstract expressionism
academic freedom
a capella
accelerator, particle
accounting
acculturation
AC/DC
Achilles
Achilles' heel
acid
acid rain
acquittal
acronym
acrophobia
Acropolis
Actions speak louder than words.
act of God
actuary
acupuncture
A.D.
ad absurdum
adagio
Adam and Eve
Adams, John
Adams, John Quincy
adaptation
Addams, Jane
Addis Ababa
Adeste Fideles (song)
ad hoc
ad hominem
adieu
ad infinitum
adiós
Adirondack Mountains
adjective
Adonis
adrenal gland
adrenaline (fight or flight)
adultery
adverb
AEC (Atomic Energy Commission)
Aegean, the
Aeneas
Aeneid, The (title)
aerobic
Aeschylus
Aesop's fables
aesthetics
affirmative action
affluent society
Afghanistan

aficionado
AFL-CIO
Africa
Agamemnon
Age cannot wither her, nor custom stale/Her infinite variety.
aggression
agnosticism
agreement
agribusiness
Ahab, Captain
AIDS
air pollution
Air Quality Index
Akron, OH
Alabama
à la carte
Aladdin's lamp
Alamo
Alaska
Alaskan pipeline
Alas, poor Yorick . . .
Albania
Albany, NY
albatross around one's neck
Albuquerque, NM
alchemy
Alcott, Louisa May
Aleutian Islands
Alexander the Great
Alexandria, Egypt
al fresco
algae
Alger, Horatio
Algeria
Algiers
alias
Alice in Wonderland (title)
Alien and Sedition Acts
alienation
Ali, Muhammad
alkaline
Allah
All animals are equal, but some animals are more equal than others.
Allegheny Mountains
allegory
allegro
Allen, Woody
allergy
Alliance for Progress
alliteration
alloy
All roads lead to Rome.
All's fair in love and war.
All's well that ends well.
All that glitters is not gold.
all the news that's fit to print
All the world's a stage.
all things to all men
allusion
All work and no play makes Jack a dull boy.
alma mater
alpha and omega
alpha radiation
Alps, the
alter ego
alternating current (AC)
alternator
alto
altruism
Alzheimer's disease
a.m.
Amazing Grace (song)
Amazonian
Amazon (myth)
Amazon River
America
American Gothic (image)
American Legion

American Revolution
American Stock Exchange
America the Beautiful (song)
amicus curiae
amino acids
Amish
amnesia
amnesty
amniotic sac
amoeba
amok, run
amortization
amp (ampere)
ampersand (&)
amphibians
amplifier
Amsterdam
anaerobic
analogy
anal personality
An apple a day keeps the doctor away.
anarchy
An army travels on its stomach.
Anchorage, AK
ancien régime
andante
Anderson, Hans Christian
Andromeda
And thereby hangs a tale.
anecdote
anemia
Angelou, Maya
Anglican church (Church of England, Episcopal church)
Angola
angst
animal kingdom
animal/vegetable/mineral
animism
Ankara
Annapolis
Ann Arbor, MI
anno domini (A.D.)
annuity
annus mirabilis
anon.
anorexia
Antarctica
antebellum
Anthony, Susan B.
anthropology
anthropomorphism
antiballistic missile (ABM)
antibiotic
antibody
anticlericalism
antigen
Antigone (myth)
Antigone (title)
antimatter
antiparticle
antipodes
anti-Semitism
antitrust legislation
Antony and Cleopatra (title)
antonym
Antony's speech at Caesar's funeral
anxiety
any port in a storm
aorta
Apache Indians
apartheid
aphorism
aphrodisiac
Aphrodite (Venus)
apocalypse
apocryphal
Apollo
Apollo program
Apostles, the Twelve

apostrophe (')
Appalachian Mountains
appeals, court of
appeasement
appendix (anatomy)
Appleseed, Johnny
Appomattox Court House
apportionment
appraisal
appropriation
April showers bring May flowers.
apropos
Aquinas, Saint Thomas
Arabia
Arabian Nights
Arab-Israeli conflict
arbitration
arch
Archduke Francis Ferdinand
archetype
Archimedes
archipelago
Arctic, the
Arctic Circle
Arctic Ocean
Argentina
aria
aristocracy
Aristophanes
Aristotle
Arizona
Arkansas
Armageddon
Armenian massacres
armistice
Armstrong, Louis
Arnold, Benedict
arrivederci
Artemis (Diana)
arteriosclerosis
artery
art for art's sake
arthritis
article (grammar)
Articles of Confederation
artificial intelligence (AI)
Art is long, life is short.
asceticism
ascorbic acid
asexual reproduction
As flies to wanton boys are we to the gods.
Asia
Asia Minor
Ask, and it shall be given.
Ask not what your country can do for you . . .
assessment
assimilation
Astaire, Fred, and Ginger Rogers
asteroid belt
as the crow flies
astrology
asymmetry
As you make your bed so must you lie in it.
atheism
Athena (Minerva)
Athens
A thing of beauty is a joy forever.
Atlanta, GA
Atlantic Charter
Atlantic City, NJ
at large
Atlas
atlas
atmosphere
atmospheric pressure
atoll
atom
atomic bomb (A-bomb)
atomic number

atomic weight
atom smasher
atrium (of heart)
attaché
AT&T
Attila the Hun
attorney general of the United States
Auckland
audit
auditory nerve
Audubon
auf Wiedersehen
Augean stables
Augustine, Saint
Augustus Caesar
Auld Lang Syne (song)
au revoir
auricle
aurora borealis (northern lights)
Auschwitz
Austen, Jane
Austin, TX
Australia
autistic
autobiography
autocracy
automation
autonomic nervous system
auxiliary verb
A word to the wise is sufficient.
axiom
Axis powers
azimuth
Azores
Aztecs

Baa, Baa, Black Sheep (text)
Babbitt (title)
Babel, Tower of
Babylon
bacchanalian
Bacchus (Dionysus)
Bach, Johann Sebastian
bacillus
Back to the drawing board.
Baconian method
Bacon, Sir Francis
bacterium
Bad news travels fast.
bad penny always turns up., A
bad workman always blames his tools., The
Baez, Joan
Baghdad
Bahamas
baker's dozen
Bakke case
balanced diet
balance of nature
balance of payments
balance of power
balance of terror
balance sheet
Balboa
balkanization
Balkans
ballad
ballerina
ballet
ballistic missile
Baltimore, MD
Balzac, Honoré de
banana republic
Bangkok
banjo
bank run
bankruptcy
Banneker, Benjamin
baptism
Baptist
Barber of Seville, The (title)
Barcelona
Bard of Avon, the

baritone
bark is worse than his bite., His
bar mitzvah
Barnum, P. T.
barometer
baroque
barrier island
Barrymores, the
Bartlett's Familiar Quotations (title)
Barton, Clara
basal metabolism
basalt
base
basilica
Basque
bas-relief
bass
bass drum
bass fiddle
basso
bassoon
basta
Bastille, fall of the
baton
battery
Battle of Britain
Baudelaire, Charles
Bauhaus movement
Bavaria
Bay of Biscay
Bay of Pigs
bayou
Beale Street
bear market
beat around the bush
Beatitudes (text)
Beatles, the
beaucoup
Beauty and the Beast (title)
Beauty is but skin deep.
Becket, Thomas à
bed; You've made your ——, now you must lie in it.
bee in your bonnet
Beethoven, Ludwig von
Beggars can't be choosers.
beginning, In the
beg the question
behaviorism
Beijing (Peking)
Beirut
Belfast
Belgium
Belgrade
Bell, Alexander Graham
bell curve
benign
Bergen
Bering Sea
Berkeley, CA
Berkshire Hills
Berlin
Berlin, Irving
Berlin airlift
Berlin Wall
Bermuda
Bernhardt, Sarah
Bernstein, Leonard
Berry, Chuck
best-laid plans of mice and men oft' go awry., The
best of friends must part
best things in life are free., The
beta radiation
bête noire
Bethlehem
Bethune, Mary
Better late than never.
Better safe than sorry.
between a rock and a hard place
Beverly Hills, CA
Beware of Greeks bearing gifts.
Beware the Ides of March.

Bible Belt
bibliography
bicameral legislature
big bad wolf
big bang theory
Big Ben
big board
Big Brother is watching you.
big business
Big Dipper, the
bigger they come, the harder they fall., The
big-stick diplomacy
bilateralism
bile
Bill of Rights
Billy the Kid
biochemistry
biofeedback
biography
biology
biomass
biosphere
Birch Society, John
bird in the hand is worth two in the bush., A
Birds of a feather flock together.
Birmingham, AL
birth control
birthday suit
Birth of a Nation, The (title)
Birth of Venus, The (image)
bishop
Bismarck, Otto
bit between your teeth
bit (computer term)
bite the bullet
bite the dust
biting the hand that feeds you
Bizet, Georges
Black, Hugo
blackball
blackbody radiation
Black Boy (title)
black cat
Black Death
Black Hills, the
black hole
Black Hole of Calcutta
blacklist
black market
Black Muslims
black power
Black Sea
black sheep
Blake, William
blank verse
Blarney Stone
blasé
blind leading the blind
blitzkrieg
Blood is thicker than water.
blood, sweat, and tears
blood type
blow hot and cold
Blue and the Gray, the
Bluebeard
blue-chip stock
blue-collar
blue laws
Blue Ridge Mountains
Blue-tailed Fly (song)
boat people
Boers
Bogart, Humphrey
bohemian
Bohr, Niels
Bohr atom
boiling point
Boleyn, Anne
Bolivia
Bolsheviks

bolt from the blue
Bombay
bona fide
bond (business)
bond (chemical)
bone to pick
bonjour
Bonn
bonus
Book of Common Prayer
boom (business)
boom (sonic)
Boone, Daniel
Booth, John Wilkes
Bordeaux
Borgia, Cesare
Borgia, Lucretia
born-again Christian
Borneo
born with a silver spoon in one's mouth
Bosporus, the
Boston, MA
Boston Massacre
Boston Tea Party
botany
Botticelli
bottleneck
bottom line
botulism
bounty
Bourbon
bourgeois
bowdlerize
Bowery, the
boycott
Boy Scouts of America
Boys will be boys.
Boy Who Cried "Wolf," The (title)
brackets ([ ])
Bradley, Omar
Brahmin
Brahms, Johannes
Braille
brain trust
brainwashing
Brasilia
brass band
brave new world
Brazil
breach of contract
bread and circuses
break the ice
Brer Rabbit
Brevity is the soul of wit.
brinkmanship
Brisbane
Britain
Britain, Battle of
British Columbia
Broadway
broker
bronchial tubes
Brontë, Charlotte and Emily
Bronx, The
Bronze Age
Brooklyn
Brooklyn Bridge
Brooks, Gwendolyn
brother's keeper?, Am I my
Brown, John
Brownian movement
Browning, Elizabeth Barrett
Browning, Robert
Brown v. Board of Education (Brown decision)
Brueghel, Pieter (the Elder)
Brussels
Brutus
Bryan, William Jennings
bubble (business)

bubble chamber
Bucharest
buck stops here., The
Budapest
Buddha
Buddhism
Buenos Aires
Buffalo, NY
Buffalo Bill
buffer
building castles in the air
Bulgaria
Bulge, Battle of the
bull in a china shop
bull market
Bull Run, Battle of
Bumpo, Natty
Bunche, Ralph
Bundestag
Bunker, Archie
Bunker Hill, Battle of
Bunyan, Paul
buoyancy
bureaucracy
Burke, Edmund
Burma
burning the candle at both ends
burning the midnight oil
Burns, Robert
burnt child fears the fire., The
burn with a hard, gemlike flame
Burr, Aaron
Burr-Hamilton duel
bury the hatchet
business before pleasure
business cycle
bust (business)
Butter wouldn't melt in her mouth.
buyer's market
buying a pig in a poke
Byron, Lord
Byronic
byte
Byzantine complexity
Byzantine Empire

cabinet
cadre
Caesar, Julius
caesarean section
Cain and Abel
Cairo
cajun
calculus
Calcutta
Calder, Alexander
Calhoun, John C.
California
Caligula
calling a spade a spade
calls the tune
calorie
Calvary
Calvin, John
cambium
Cambodia
Cambridge, MA
Cambridge University
Camelot
Camptown Races (song)
Canada
Canal Zone
Canberra
Candide (title)
canine
Canterbury Tales, The (title)
can't fit a round peg in a square hole
can't have your cake and eat it too
can't hold a candle to
can't make a silk purse from a sow's ear
can't see the forest for the trees
Canton

capacitor
Cape Cod
Cape Hatteras
Cape Town
capillary
capital expenditure
capital gains
capitalism
capital letter
capital punishment
Capitol Building
Capitol Hill
Capone, Al
Capri
captain of industry
Caracas
carbohydrates
carbon cycle
carbon dioxide (CO_2)
carbon-14 dating
carbon monoxide
carcinogen
cardinal number
Caribbean Sea
caricature
Carmen (title)
Carnegie, Andrew
Carnegie, Dale
carnivorous
carpetbaggers
Carroll, Lewis
carry a torch for
carrying coals to Newcastle
carte blanche
cartel
Carter, James Earl (Jimmy)
cartilage
Caruso, Enrico
Carver, George Washington
Casablanca
Casanova
Casey at the Bat (title)
Casey Jones (song)
Cassandra
caste
cast pearls before swine
Castro, Fidel
cast thy bread upon the waters
catalyst
Catch-22 (title)
catch-as-catch-can
Catcher in the Rye, The (title)
catharsis
Catherine the Great
Cather, Willa
cathode ray tube (CRT)
Catholicism, Roman Catholicism
Cato
CAT scan
Caucasus, the
caucus
cause célèbre
causistry
caveat emptor
CD (certificate of deposit)
CD (compact disc)
cell differentiation
cello
cellulose
cell wall
Celsius
center of gravity, center of mass
centigrade
centimeter
Central America
Central Intelligence Agency (CIA)
Central Park
centrifugal force
Cerberus
cerebellum
cerebral cortex
Ceres (Demeter)
Cervantes
C'est la vie.

Ceylon
Cézanne, Paul
cf.
chain reaction
chain store
Chamberlain, Neville
change of phase
Chapel Hill, NC
Chaplin, Charlie
Charge of the Light Brigade, The (title)
charisma
Charlemagne
Charles I
Charleston (dance)
Charleston, SC
Charleston, WV
Charlotte, NC
Charon
Chartres, cathedral of
Chattanooga, TN
Chaucer, Geoffrey
chauvinism
checks and balances
chef d'oeuvre
Chekhov, Anton
chemical bond
chemical element
chemical equilibrium
chemotherapy
Chernobyl
Cherokee Indians
cherubim
Chesapeake Bay
Cheshire cat
Chiang Kai-shek
Chicago, IL
Chicanos
chickens come home to roost
chief business of the American people is business., The
child labor laws
Chile
chimera
China
chip on one's shoulder
Chippendale
chip (silicon chip)
chivalry
chloroform
chlorophyll
cholesterol
Chopin, Frédéric
chordates
choreography
chosen people
Chou En-lai (Zhou En-lai)
Christianity
Christian Science
Christie, Agatha
Christmas Carol, A (title)
chromosomes
Chungking
Churchill, Winston
chutzpah
Cicero
Cid, The (title)
Cincinnati, OH
Circe
circuit, electric
circuit court of appeals
circumcision
circumference
circumlocution
cirrus clouds
civil disobedience
civil rights movement
civil service
Civil War
clarinet
class consciousness
classical music
classical mythology
classicism

class struggle
clause
claustrophobia
Clay, Henry
clean bill of health
Cleanliness is next to godliness.
clean slate
clear and present danger
Clemenceau, Georges
Clemens, Samuel (Mark Twain)
Clementine (song)
Cleopatra
Cleveland, Grover
Cleveland, OH
cliché
climate
clockwork universe
clone
closed shop
cloture
cloud chamber
cloud seeding
coalition
coals to Newcastle
Coast Guard
coat of many colors
Cobb, Ty
cobbler should stick to his last., The
cock and bull
cockles of the heart, warm the
COD
coda
coexistence (peaceful)
cognitive development
Cohan, George M.
coherence
cold-blooded
cold hands, warm heart
cold shoulder, the
cold war
Coleridge, Samuel Taylor
collateral
collective bargaining
collective farm
collective unconscious
College of Cardinals
Cologne
Colombia
colon (anatomy)
colon (:)
colonialism
Colorado
Colorado River
coloratura
Colosseum, the
Columbia River
Columbia, the Gem of the Ocean (song)
Columbus, Christopher
Columbus, OH
combustion
come full circle
Come live with me and be my love.
comet
comma
comme il faut
commissar
commission (business)
commissioned officer
commodity
common carrier
common denominator
common law
common-law marriage
Common Market
Common Sense (title)
communicative diseases
communism
Communist Manifesto, The (title)
Comparisons are odious.
compass
complex sentence

composite materials
compound-complex sentence
compound interest
compound sentence
compulsion
computer
Conan Doyle, Sir Arthur
concentration camp
concerto
concierge
conciseness, concision
Concord, Battle of
condensation point
conditioned reflex
conduction
Coney Island, NY
Confederacy, the
confederation
Confessions (title) (Rousseau)
Confessions (title) (St. Augustine)
confirmation hearings
conflict of interest
conformity
Confucius
congenital disease
conglomerate
Congo River
Congress
Congressional Medal of Honor
Congressional Record
Congress of Vienna
conjunction
Connecticut
connotation
conquistadores
Conrad, Joseph
conscientious objector (CO)
consent of the governed
conservation of energy, law of
conservatism
consonant
conspicuous consumption
Constable, John
constant dollars
Constantine the Great
Constantinople
constellation
Constitutional Convention
constitutional monarchy
Constitution of the United States
consumerism
consumer price index
containment
contempt of Congress
contempt of court
Continental Congress
continental divide
continental drift
continental shelf
contraband
contraception
contraction (grammar)
contralto
Cook, Captain
Coolidge, Calvin
coolie
cool your heels
Cooper, James Fenimore
coordination
Copenhagen
Copernicus
copulation
copyright
coral reef
core
Corinthian
cornea
Cornwallis, Lord
coronary artery
corporal punishment
corporation
Cortés, Hernán

cosmic rays
cosmology
Cossacks
Costa Rica
cost-of-living allowance
cotton to
counterfeit
counterinsurgency
counterpoint
Counter Reformation
coup
coup de grace
couplet
course of true love never did run smooth., The
court of appeals
Court of St. James's
court packing
covalent bond
covenant
covered wagon
Crash of 1929
crater
Crazy Horse
Creation, the
creationism
creature comforts
creditor
credit rating
credit union
crème de la crème
Creole
crescendo
Crete
Crick, Francis, and James Watson
Crimea
Crime and Punishment (title)
Crimean War
critical mass
Crockett, Davy
crocodile tears
Croesus, rich as
Cro-Magnon man
Cromwell, Oliver
Crosby, Bing
crossing the Rubicon
cross of gold
Cross that bridge when you come to it.
cross to bear
crown of thorns
Crucifixion, the
cruel and unusual punishment
Crusades
Crusoe, Robinson
Crystal Palace
Cuba
Cuban missile crisis
cubism
Cullen, Countee
cult
cultivate one's garden
cultural imperialism
culture
Cumberland Gap
Cumberland Mountains
cum laude
cummings, e. e.
cumulus clouds
Cupid (Eros)
cupola
Curie, Marie
current, electric
curriculum vitae
curry favor
Custer's last stand
cut off your nose to spite your face
cut the Gordian knot
cyclone
Cyclops

cyclotron
cymbal
Cyprus
Cyrillic alphabet
cytoplasm
czar
Czechoslovakia

dacha
Dachau
Daedalus
Daley, Mayor Richard
Dali, Salvador
Dallas, TX
Damascus
Damn the torpedoes. Full speed ahead.
damn with faint praise
Damocles, sword of
Daniel in the lions' den
danke schön
Dante Alighieri
Danton
Danube River
Dark Ages
dark horse
Darrow, Clarence
Darwin, Charles
dash (—)
data
date which will live in infamy
David (Bible)
David Copperfield (title)
David of Michelangelo, the (image)
Davis, Jefferson
Davy Jones's locker
DC
D-Day
dead bury their dead., Let the
dead heat
dead languages
Dead Sea
Dead Sea Scrolls
Death of a Salesman (title)
Death Valley
Debs, Eugene
debtor nation
decadence
decibel
deciduous
Declaration of Independence
declarative sentence
deduction
de facto segregation
default
defense mechanism
deficit financing
definite article
deflation
Degas, Edgar
de Gaulle, Charles
De gustibus non est disputandem.
deism
déjà vu
de jure
Delaware
Delhi
Delphic oracle
delusion
demagogue
Demeter (Ceres)
De Mille, Cecil B.
democracy
Democratic party
demography
demonstrative pronouns
Demosthenes
Denmark
denotation
denoument
Denver, CO
Department of Agriculture
Department of Commerce

Department of Defense (DOD)
Department of Education
Department of Housing and Urban Development (HUD)
Department of the Interior
Department of Justice
Department of Labor
Department of State
Department of the Treasury
Department of Transportation
dependent clause (grammar)
depletion allowance
deposit (geology)
depreciation
Depression, the Great
de rigueur
desalinization
Descartes, René
Des Moines, IA
despotism
de-Stalinization
détente
determinism
deterrence
Detroit, MI
deus ex machina
devaluation
developing nation
developmental psychology
devil can cite Scripture., The
Dewey, John
diabetes
dialectic
dialectical materialism
dialysis
diameter
diamond in the rough
Diana (Artemis)
Diary of a Young Girl (title)
Dickens, Charles
Dickinson, Emily
dictatorship
diction
Dido
diehards
dielectric
Dien Bien Phu
diffraction
diffusion
Dillinger, John
dinosaur
Diogenes
Dionysus (Bacchus)
diplomatic immunity
direct object
direct primary
disciples
discount
Discretion is the better part of valor.
disenfranchise
Disney, Walt
Disraeli, Benjamin
dissidents
distillation
district attorney
District of Columbia
divestiture
dividend
Divine Comedy, The (title)
divine rights of kings
divinity that shapes our ends., There's a
division of labor
DNA (deoxyribonucleic acid)
Dr. Jekyll and Mr. Hyde (title)
Doctor Livingstone, I presume?
dog days
dog in the manger
dog is a man's best friend., A
dogma
dollar diplomacy
Doll's House, A (title)
dominant trait

Dominican Republic
domino theory
Donald Duck
Don Giovanni (title)
Don Juan
donkey
Donne, John
donnybrook
Do not go gentle into that good night.
Don Quixote (title)
Don River
Don't count your chickens before they hatch.
Don't cry over spilled milk.
Don't fire until you see the whites of their eyes.
Don't give up the ship.
Don't hide your light under a bushel.
Don't judge a book by its cover.
Don't look a gift horse in the mouth.
Don't put all your eggs in one basket.
Don't put the cart before the horse.
Doppler effect
Doric
Dos Passos, John
Dostoyevsky, Fyodor
Double, double, toil and trouble.
double entendré
double helix
double indemnity
double jeopardy
doubting Thomas
doughboy
Douglas, Stephen A.
Douglas, William O.
Douglass, Frederick
Do unto others as you would have them do unto you.
doves and hawks
Dow-Jones average
Down in the Valley (song)
down payment
Down's syndrome (mongolism)
draconian
Dracula
draft (military)
draft dodger
Drake, Sir Francis
dramatis personae
Dred Scott decision
Dreyfus affair
Drink to me only with thine eyes . . .
drive a nail into one's coffin
dualism
Dublin
Du Bois, W.E.B.
due process of law
dumping
Dunbar, Paul Laurence
Dunkirk
duodenum
Dürer, Albrecht
dust bowl
Dust thou art and unto dust shalt thou return.
Dutch treat
Dylan, Bob
dyslexia

eardrum
Earhart, Amelia
early bird catches the worm., The
Early to bed and early to rise, / Makes a man healthy, wealthy, and wise
Earp, Wyatt
earthquake
easier said than done
Easter

Easter Bunny
Eastern bloc
Eastern Establishment
East is East, and West is West, and never the twain shall meet.
Easy come, easy go.
eat crow
Eat, drink, and be merry, for tomorrow we die.
eaten out of house and home
eat humble pie
Ecclesiastes, The Book of
eclecticism
eclipse
ecological niche
ecosystem
Ecuador
ecumenism
Eddy, Mary Baker
Eden, Garden of
Edinburgh
Edison, Thomas A.
editorial
Edwardian
Edwards, Jonathan
e.g.
ego
egocentric
egomania
Egypt
Eichmann, Adolf
Eiffel Tower
Einstein, Albert
Eisenhower, Dwight D.
elasticity
Elbe River
El Dorado
electoral college
electric charge
electric field
electrocardiograph
electrolysis
electromagnet
electromagnetic radiation
electron microscope
electroplating
elegy
Elegy Written in a Country Churchyard (title)
Elementary, my dear Watson.
elementary particles
elephant never forgets., An
eleventh hour
Eliot, George
Eliot, T. S.
elite
Elizabethan period
Elizabeth I
Elizabeth II
ellipse
ellipsis (. . .)
Ellis Island
El Paso, TX
Elysian Fields
Emancipation Proclamation
embargo
embezzlement
embryo
embryology
Emerson, Ralph Waldo
eminence grise
eminent domain
empathy
Emperor's New Clothes, The (title)
Empire State Building
Empyrean
enclosures
encyclical
endocrine
enfant terrible
Engels, Friedrich
England
English Channel

Enlightenment, the
en masse
entangling alliances with none
entourage
entrepreneur
entropy
Environmental Protection Agency (EPA)
environment/heredity controversy
enzyme
epic
Epicurean
epidemic
epidermis
epigram
epistemology
e pluribus unum
epoxy
Equal Employment Opportunity Commission (EEOC)
equal protection of the laws
equal time
equation
equator
equilibrium
equity
Erasmus
ergo
Erie Canal
Eros (Cupid)
erosion
esprit de corps
Essay on Liberty (title)
established church
Establishment, the
estrogen
estuary
etching
ethanol
ethical relativism
ethics
Ethiopia
ethnocentrism
ethos
ethyl alcohol
Et tu, Brute.
Euclid
eugenics
euphemism
Euphrates River
Eurasia
eureka
Euripides
Eurocommunism
European Common Market
Eustachian tube
euthanasia
evangelist
evaporation
Everybody talks about the weather, but nobody does anything about it.
Every cloud has a silver lining.
Every dog has his day.
every inch a ____
eviction
evolution
ex cathedra
exchange rate
excise tax
exclamation point
executive branch
exeunt
existentialism
Exodus, The Book of
ex officio
expanding universe
expatriation
expense account
Experience is the best teacher.
expletive
exponential growth

export quota
ex post facto
expressionism
expropriation
extended family
extortion
extradition
extrasensory perception (ESP)
extraterrestrial
extrovert/introvert
eye for an eye, an
eye of a hurricane

Fabian tactics
face that launched a thousand ships?, Was this the
faction
Fagin
Fahrenheit
fair exchange is no robbery., A
fair-weather friends
fait accompli
faith, hope, and charity
Falkland Islands
fallacy
Fall of France
Fall of Man
Fall of Rome
Fall of the House of Usher, The (title)
fallopian tubes
Falstaff
Familiarity breeds contempt.
Faraday, Michael
Far East
Farewell Address of Washington
far from the madding crowd
farm bloc
Farragut, Admiral David G.
Far West
fascism
fatalism
Fates, the
father of his country
fathom
Faulkner, William
fault (geology)
fauna
Faust (title)
FDA recommended intake
featherbedding
feather in your cap
feather your own nest
Federal Bureau of Investigation (FBI)
Federal Deposit Insurance Corporation (FDIC)
federalism
Federalist Papers, The (title)
Federal Republic of Germany
Federal Reserve (the "Fed")
Feed a cold and starve a fever.
feedback loop
feet of clay
fellow traveler
felony
female of the species is more deadly than the male., The
feminism
Ferdinand and Isabella
fermentation
Fermi, Enrico
fertilization
fetish
fetus
feudalism
fiber optics
fibrous root
fiction
fiddle while Rome burns
fief

Fielding, Henry
Fields, W. C.
fiesta
fife
Fifteen men on the Dead Man's Chest — yo-ho-ho, and a bottle of rum!
Fifth Amendment (taking the Fifth)
fifth column
fifth wheel
Figaro
filibuster
Final Solution
Finders keepers, losers weepers.
fin de siècle
fine arts
Finland
fireside chat
First Amendment
first come, first served
First in war, first in peace, and first in the hearts of his countrymen.
first-strike capability
fiscal policy
Fish or cut bait.
fission, nuclear
fits and starts
Fitzgerald, Ella
Fitzgerald, F. Scott
fjord
flapper
flash in the pan
Flaubert, Gustave
Florence
Florida
Florida Keys
flute
fly-by-night
flying buttress
flying saucers
folklore
follow your nose
food chain
fool and his money are soon parted., A
foolish consistency is the hobgoblin of little minds., A
Fools rush in where angels fear to tread.
footprints on the sands of time
forbidden fruit
For Brutus is an honorable man.
Ford, Gerald
Ford, Henry
foreclosure
Foreign Relations Committee
Foreign Service
forgive and forget
Forgive them, for they know not what they do.
fornication
forte
fortissimo
Fort Sumter
Fortuna (goddess of fortune)
Fortune 500
Fort Worth, TX
forty-niners
forty winks
For want of a nail the kingdom was lost.
for whom the bell tolls
fossil fuel
fossil record
Foster, Stephen
Founding Fathers
Four Freedoms
four-letter words
Fourteen Points
Fourteenth Amendment
Fourth of July

Fox and the Grapes, The
Frailty, thy name is woman.
France
franchise (economics)
franchise (politics)
Francis of Assisi, Saint
Franco, Francisco
Frank, Anne
Frankenstein's monster
Franklin, Benjamin
Freedman's Bureau
freedom of religion
freedom of speech
freedom of the press
Freedom Riders
free enterprise
free fall
free market
Freemasons (or Masons)
free trade
free verse
free will
freezing point
French and Indian War
French horn
French Impressionism
French Revolution
frequency modulation (FM)
fresco
Fresno, CA
Freud, Sigmund
Freudian slip
friar
friction
friend in need is a friend indeed., A
friend of the court
Friends, Romans, countrymen, lend me your ears.
Friends, Society of
frieze
fringe benefit
From little acorns grow mighty oaks.
From the sublime to the ridiculous is but a step.
front (frontal zone)
frontier
Frost, Robert
fruits shall ye know them., By their
Fulbright scholarship
fulcrum
full employment
Fulton, Robert
functionalism (architecture)
fundamentalism
Furies, the
fusion, nuclear

Gable, Clark
Galahad, Sir
galaxy
Galileo
gall bladder
gallstone
Gallup Poll
galvanize
game is not worth the candle., The
gamma rays
gamut, running the
Gandhi, Indira
Gandhi, Mohandas (Mahatma)
Ganges River
Gang of Four
gangrene
Garbo, Greta
gargoyle
Garibaldi, Menotti
Garland, Judy
Garrison, William Lloyd
Garvey, Marcus

gas (physics)
gasohol
Gather ye rosebuds while ye may.
Gauguin, Paul
gay rights
Gehrig, Lou
Geiger counter
geisha
gene
gene pool
general anesthetic
general strike
general theory of relativity
generating plant
generation gap
generator
Genesis, The Book of
genetic code
genetic engineering
genetics
Geneva
Geneva Convention
Genghis Khan
Genius is one percent inspiration and ninety-nine percent perspiration.
genocide
genotype
genre
Gentile
genus
geology
geometric progression
George III
Georgia
geothermal energy
German Democratic Republic
Germany
Geronimo
gerontocracy
gerrymander
Gershwin, George
gerund
gestalt psychology
Gestapo
gesundheit
get down to brass tacks
get out of bed on the wrong side, to
Get thee behind me, Satan.
Get thee to a nunnery.
getting a dose of one's own medicine
Gettysburg Address
Ghana
Gibbon, Edward
GI Bill
Gibraltar
GI Joe
Gilbert and Sullivan
gilded cage, a
Giotto
Girl Scouts of America
Give him enough rope and he'll hang himself.
Give me liberty or give me death.
Give me your tired, your poor . . .
Give my regards to Broadway.
give than to receive., It is better to
giving the Devil his due
glacier
glad hand
Gladstone
Glasgow
global village
Glorious Revolution
glossary
glucose
glut
God Bless America (song)
God helps those who help themselves.
God's in his heaven — All's right with the world.

Goebbels, Joseph
Goethe, Johann Wolfgang
Golan Heights
Goldberg, Rube
golden calf
golden fleece
Golden Gate Bridge
golden mean
Golden Rule
Goldilocks and the Three Bears
gold rush, the
gold standard
Golgotha
Gompers, Samuel
gonads
Gone With the Wind (title)
Gonna lay my burden down.
Good fences make good neighbors.
Good Friday
good man is hard to find., A
Good Neighbor Policy
good Samaritan
goosestep
goose who laid the golden eggs
GOP
Gordian knot, cutting the
Göring, Hermann
Gospel
gothic
go to pot
Go west, young man.
Goya, Francisco
graçias
gradualism
graft (politics)
Graham, Billy
grain of salt, with a
Granada
Grand Canyon
grand jury
Grandma Moses
granite
Grant, Ulysses S.
Grapes of Wrath, The (title)
grass is always greener on the other side., The
gravity
grazie
Great Depression
greatest good for the greatest number
Great Expectations (title)
Great Gatsby, The (title)
Great Lakes
Great oaks from little acorns grow.
Great Plains
Great Proletarian Cultural Revolution
Great Salt Lake
Great Smoky Mountains
Great Society
Great Wall of China
Great War, The
Greco, El
Greece
Greek Orthodox Church
Greeley, Horace
greenbacks
green-eyed monster, the
greenhouse effect
Greenland
green revolution
Greenwich mean time
Greenwich Village
gremlins
Grenada
Gresham's law
Griffith, D. W.
Grimm brothers
Grim Reaper, the (image)
Grinch Who Stole Christmas, The (title)

gringo
Gross National Product (GNP)
groundwater
guerrilla war
Guiana
guild
guilt by association
gulag
Gulf of Mexico
Gulf Stream
Gulliver's Travels (title)
gunboat diplomacy
Gunga Din (title)
gung-ho
guru
Gutenberg, Johannes
Guthrie, Woody

H_2O
habeas corpus
habitat
H-bomb
Hades
Had we but world enough, and time . . .
Hague, The
Hail-fellow-well-met
hairsplitting
Haiti
Hale, Nathan
Half a loaf is better than none.
half-life
hallucination
Hamburg
Hamilton, Alexander
Hamlet (title)
hammer and sickle
Hancock, John
Handel
handwriting on the wall, the
Hannibal
Hanoi
Hansel and Gretel (title)
Hanukkah
hara-kiri
Harding, Warren G.
hard water
hardwired
Hare and the Tortoise, The (title)
Harlem, NY
Harpers Ferry
harpsichord
harpy
Hartford, CN
Haste makes waste.
Hastings, Battle of
Havana
Hawaii
hawks and doves
Haydn, Joseph
hearsay
Hearst, William Randolph
heat capacity
heat of fusion
heat of vaporization
heavy water
Hector
hedonism
Heep, Uriah
Hegel, Georg
Heisenberg uncertainty principle
Helen of Troy
helium
Hell hath no fury like a woman scorned.
Helsinki
Hemingway, Ernest
hemisphere
hemoglobin
hemophilia
Henry, Patrick
Henry VIII

Hepburn, Katharine
Hera (Juno)
herbaceous
herbivore
Hercules
heredity
heretic
Here today, gone tomorrow.
Here We Go Round the Mulberry Bush (song)
Hermes (Mercury)
Herodotus
herpes
hertz (Hz)
heterogeneity
heterosexuality
He that is not with me is against me.
He who hesitates is lost.
He who laughs last laughs best.
Hey, Diddle Diddle (text)
Hiawatha (title)
hibernation
Hickory, Dickory, Dock (text)
hieroglyphics
highbrow/lowbrow
Highlands, the
high tech
Himalayas
Himmler, Heinrich
Hinduism
hippies
Hippocratic oath
Hiroshima
Hiss, Alger
hit below the belt
Hitchcock, Alfred
Hitch your wagon to a star.
Hitler, Adolf
hitting the nail on the head
Hobbes, John
Ho Chi Minh
hoi polloi
hoist with his own petard
holding company
holistic
Holland
Hollywood, CA
Holmes, Oliver Wendell, Jr.
Holmes, Oliver Wendell, Sr.
Holmes, Sherlock
Holocaust, the
Holy Grail
Holy Roman Empire
Holy See
holy writ
homage
Home is the sailor, home from sea . . .
Home on the Range (song)
homeostasis
Homer
Homer, Winslow
Homestead Act
Home, Sweet Home (song)
homicide
homogeneity
homonym
homophone
Homo sapiens
homosexuality
Honduras
Honesty is the best policy.
Hong Kong
Honolulu, HI
Hoosier
Hoover Dam
Hoover, Herbert
Hoover, J. Edgar
Hope, Bob
Hope springs eternal in the human breast.

Horace
hormones
hornet's nest, stir up a
horns of a dilemma, on the
horror! The horror!, The
horse! A horse! my kingdom for a horse!, A
horticulture
Houdini, Harry
house arrest
"house divided" speech
House of Commons
House of Lords
House of Representatives, the U.S.
Houston, Sam
Houston, TX
How sharper than a serpent's tooth it is/ To have a thankless child.
How you gonna keep 'em down on the farm after they've seen Paree?
hubris
Huckleberry Finn (title)
Hudson Bay
Hudson River
hue and cry
Hughes, Langston
Hugo, Victor
Huguenots
humanist
humanitarianism
humanities, the
Hume, David
humidity (relative and absolute)
Humpty Dumpty (text)
Hunchback of Notre Dame, The (title)
Hundred Years' War
Hungary
hung jury
Huns
hurricane
Huxley, Aldous
Huxley, Julian
hybridization
hydraulic
hydrocarbon
hydroelectric
hydrogen
hydrogen bomb (H-bomb)
hydrological cycle
hydroponics
hydropower
Hymen (mythology)
hymen (physiology)
hyperbola
hyperbole
hypertension
hyphen
hypnosis
hypochondriac
hypotenuse
hypothalamus
hypothesis
hysteria

Iago
iambic pentameter
I am the state. (L'état, c'est moi.)
I am the very model of a modern Major-General.
I-beam
ibid.
Ibsen, Henrik
I came, I saw, I conquered.
I cannot tell a lie.
Icarus
ice age
iceberg
Iceland
Idaho
ideal gas
ideology

Ides of March
idiom
id, the
i.e.
If at first you don't succeed, try, try again.
If music be the food of love, play on.
If the mountain will not come to Mohammed . . .
If you can't stand the heat, get out of the kitchen.
igloo
Ignatius of Loyola, Saint
igneous rock
Ignorance is bliss.
I Have a Dream (speech)
I have not yet begun to fight.
Iliad, The (title)
illegitimacy
Illinois
imagery
Imitation is the sincerest form of flattery.
Immaculate Conception
immigration
immune system
immunity (law)
impeachment
impedance
imperative (grammar)
imperialism
import quota
impresario
impressionism
Incarnation, the
Incas
incest
incumbent
indefinite article
indentation
indentured servant
Independence Day
Independence, MO
independent clause
Index, the
India
Indiana
Indianapolis, IN
Indian file
Indian summer
indirect object
individualism
Indochina
inductance
induction (philosophy)
indulgences
industrial relations
Industrial Revolution
I never met a man I didn't like.
inference
infinitive
inflammation
inflation
influenza
infrared
inhibition
injunction
in loco parentis
in medias res
in memoriam
inoculation/vaccination
Inquisition, the
in situ
insomnia
installment buying
instinct
insulator
insulin
insurance
integrated circuit
integration
intelligence quotient (IQ)
intelligentsia

intercontinental ballistic missile (ICBM)
interest rate
interference
interjection
intermediate range ballistic missile (IRBM)
internal combustion engine
Internal Revenue Service (IRS)
international law
International Monetary Fund
interrogative sentence
Interstate Commerce Commission
In the spring a young man's fancy/ Lightly turns to thoughts of love.
in toto
intransitive verb
intrauterine device (IUD)
introspection
introvert/extrovert
inventory
inversion (meteorology)
invertebrate
Invictus
In vino veritas.
invisible hand
Invisible Man, The (title)
in vitro
in vivo
Ionic (architecture)
ionic bond
ionization
I only regret that I have but one life to lose for my country.
ionosphere
IOU
Iowa
Iran
Iraq
Ireland, Republic of
Irish potato famine
Irish Republican Army (IRA)
Iron Age
Iron Curtain
irony
Iroquois Indians
irrational number
irregular verb
irrigation
Irving, Washington
Isaiah
I shall return.
Islam
isolationism
isomer
isotope
Israel
Istanbul
isthmus
It ain't a fit night out for man or beast.
italics
I think that I shall never see / A poem lovely as a tree.
I think, therefore I am.
It is a far, far better thing that I do, than I have ever done.
It was the best of times, it was the worst of times.
Ivan the Terrible
I've Been Working on the Railroad (song)
ivory tower
Ivy League
I wandered lonely as a cloud.
Iwo Jima

Jack and Jill (text)
Jack and the Beanstalk (title)
Jack Be Nimble (text)
Jack Frost

jack-of-all-trades, master of none
Jackson, Andrew
Jackson, Jesse
Jackson, Stonewall
Jacksonian democracy
Jacksonville, FL
Jack Sprat (text)
Jacob and Esau
Jacobin
Jacob's Ladder (song)
Jakarta
Jamaica
James, Henry
James, Jesse
James, William
Jamestown settlement
Janus
jargon
Jason and the Golden Fleece
Java
jazz
Jefferson, Thomas
Jehovah
Jehovah's Witnesses
Jekyll, Dr., and Mr. Hyde (title)
je ne sais quoi
Jeremiah
Jericho, Battle of
Jersey City, NJ
Jerusalem
Jesuits
Jesus Christ
jet stream
Jew
Jezebel
jihad
Jim Crow
jingoism
Joan of Arc
Job, The Book of
Johannesburg
John, Saint, Gospel according to
John Birch Society
John Brown's Body (song)
John Bull
John Doe
John Henry (song)
John Paul II, Pope
Johnson, Andrew
Johnson, Lyndon B. (LBJ)
Johnson, Samuel
John the Baptist
John XXIII, Pope
joie de vivre
Joint Chiefs of Staff
joint resolution
Jolly Roger
Jonah and the whale
Jones, John Paul
Joplin, Scott
Jordan
Jordan River
Joseph and his brothers
Joseph, Chief
Joseph, Saint
Joshua
Joshua Fit the Battle of Jericho (song)
journeyman
Joyce, James
Judaism
Judas Iscariot
Judge not, that ye be not judged.
Judgment Day
Judgment of Paris
judicial branch
judicial review
Julius Caesar (title)
Jung, Carl
Juno (Hera)
junta
Jupiter (planet)

Jupiter (Zeus)
justification by faith
justify the ways of God to men
juvenilia

Kabul
Kafka, Franz
Kafkaesque
Kamikaze
kangaroo court
Kansas
Kansas City, MO
Kant, Immanuel
Kapital, Das (title)
Karachi
Keats, John
keeping up with the Joneses
keep the wolf from your door
Keller, Helen
Kennedy, John F. (JFK)
Kennedy, Robert
Kent State
Kentucky
Kentucky Derby
Kenya
Kepler, Johannes
kettle drum
Key, Francis Scott
Keynes, John Maynard
KGB
Khomeini
Khrushchev, Nikita
kibbutz
Kidd, Captain William
kidneys
Kiev
Kilimanjaro
kill two birds with one stone
kill with kindness
kilogram
kilometer
kilowatt hour (kwhr)
kinetic energy
King Arthur stories
kingdom
kingdom come
King, Martin Luther, Jr.
King James Version (Bible)
King Kong
King Lear (title)
king's English, the
Kinsey, Alfred
kinship
Kipling, Rudyard
kitsch
Kitty Hawk
kleptomania
Klondike gold rush
knee-jerk reflex
Knesset
Knights of the Round Table
Knock on wood.
Knowledge is power.
Know-Nothing
Koran
Korea
Korean War
kosher
Kremlin
Ku Klux Klan (KKK)
Kuwait

Labor Day
labor-intensive
labor movement
labor union
Labrador
Labyrinth, the (mythology)
La Cucaracha (song)
lady doth protest too much., The
Lady Godiva
Lafayette, Marquis de

Lafayette, we are here.
La Fontaine, Jean de
La Guardia, Fiorello
laissez-faire
Lake Erie
Lake Huron
Lake Michigan
Lake Ontario
Lake Superior
Lake Victoria
Lamb of God
lame duck
Lancelot, Sir
land breeze
land flowing with milk and honey
land grant
Land Is Your Land, This (song)
Land of Nod
Land Was Ours, The (title)
Laocoön
Lao-tse
larceny
large intestine
La Scala
laser
last laugh, the
Last of the Mohicans, The (title)
last shall be first., The
last straw, the
Last Supper, the
Las Vegas, NV
latent heat
Latin
Latin America
latitude/longitude
Latter-Day Saints
lattice structure
Laugh, and the world laughs with you; weep, and you weep alone.
Laurel and Hardy
lava
Lavoisier, Antoine
law of contradiction
law of universal gravitation
Lawrence, D. H.
Lawrence of Arabia (T. E.)
layoff
Lay on, Macduff.
leading question
League of Nations
lean and hungry look
Leaning Tower of Pisa
leap year
lease
Leave no stone unturned
Leaves of Grass (title)
Leave well enough alone.
Lebanon
Leda and the swan
Lee, Robert E.
Left Bank
left-handed compliment
leftist
left-wing
legal tender
Legend of Sleepy Hollow, The (title)
legislative branch
legitimate government
Legree, Simon
Leibnitz
lemmings to the sea
Lenin, Vladimir
Leningrad
Lennon, John
Lent
Leonardo da Vinci
leopard doesn't change his spots., The
leprechaun
leprosy
lesbian

L'état c'est moi.
Let bygones be bygones.
Let me not to the marriage of true minds/Admit impediment.
Let sleeping dogs lie.
Letter from the Birmingham Jail (title)
letter killeth, but the spirit giveth life., The
let the cat out of the bag
Let them eat cake.
Let there be light.
Levant, the
Leviathan
Lewis, John L.
Lewis, Sinclair
Lewis and Clark expedition
Lexington and Concord, Battle of
liaison
libel
liberal
liberal arts
liberalism
Liberty, Statue of
Liberty Bell
libido
Library of Congress
Libya
lien
Lightning never strikes twice in the same place.
light-year
like a fish out of water
lilies of the field., Consider the
Lilliputian
Lima
Limbo
limerick
limestone
Lincoln, Abraham
Lincoln-Douglas debates
Lincoln Memorial
Lincoln's Second Inaugural Address
Lindberg, Charles A.
linear momentum
Linnaeus
lipid
Lippmann, Walter
lip service
liquid asset
liquidity
Lisbon
list price
Liszt, Franz
litany
literati
litmus test
Little Big Horn
Little Bo-Peep (text)
Little Boy Blue (text)
Little Eva
Little Jack Horner (text)
little learning is a dangerous thing., A
Little Miss Muffet (text)
Little pitchers have big ears.
Little Red Hen, The (title)
Little Red Riding Hood (title)
Little Rock, AR
Little strokes fell great oaks.
Little Women (title)
Live and learn.
Live and let live.
Liverpool
Lloyd George, David
loaves and fishes
lobby (politics)
lobotomy
local anesthetic
Loch Lomond
Locke, John

lock, stock, and barrel
locking the stable door after the horse is stolen
lockout
locus
lodestone
logarithm
logrolling (politics)
London
London Bridge Is Falling Down (song)
Long, Huey
Longfellow, Henry Wadsworth
Long Island, NY
longitude/latitude
Long March, the
Look before you leap.
looking out for number one
Lord's Prayer, The (text)
Lord, what fools these mortals be!
Los Angeles, CA
Lothario
Lot's wife
Louis, Joe
Louis XIV
Louisiana
Louisiana Purchase
Louisville, KY
Louvre, the
Love conquers all.
Love makes the world go round.
Love of money is the root of all evil.
Love thy neighbor as thyself.
lowbrow
lowercase
Lower East Side
lowest common denominator (LCD)
Loyola, Saint Ignatius of
Lucifer
Luddite
Luftwaffe
Luke, Saint, Gospel according to
lunatic fringe
Lusitania, sinking of the
Luther, Martin
Lutheranism
Luxembourg
lymph
lynch, lynch mob
lyric

MacArthur, Douglas
Macbeth (title)
Machiavelli
Mach number
macho
macrocosm
macroeconomics
Madagascar
mad as a hatter
Mad dogs and Englishmen (go out in the midday sun)
Madison, Dolley
Madison, James
Madison Avenue
Madonna, the
Madrid
maestro
Mafia
Magellan
Magellan, Strait of
Maginot Line
magma
Magna Carta
magna cum laude
magnetic field
magnetic north
magnetic pole
magnetic tape
magnum opus
Maine

mainframe
mainspring
mainstream
majority floor leader
make a clean breast of it
make a mountain out of a molehill
make a virtue of necessity
make ends meet
Make haste slowly.
Make hay while the sun shines.
make-work
malapropism
malaria
Malaysia
Malcolm X
mal de mer
malignancy
malnutrition
malpractice
Malthus, Thomas
mammal
Mammon
management
mañana
Manchester
mandate
Mandela, Nelson
Mandela, Winnie
Man doth not live by bread alone.
Manet, Edouard
man Friday (girl Friday)
Manhattan
Manhattan Project
mania
manic-depressive
Manifest Destiny
Manila
man is known by the company he keeps., A
Man is the measure of all things.
Mann, Horace
Mann, Thomas
manna from heaven
Man proposes, God disposes.
man's home is his castle., A
manslaughter
man's reach should exceed his grasp., A
mantle (geology)
manumission
Many are called, but few are chosen.
Many hands make light work.
Maoism
Mao Tse-tung (Mao Zedong)
Marat, Jean Paul
Marathon, Battle of
Marbury v. Madison
Marconi, Guglielmo
Mardi Gras
mare's nest
Marie Antoinette
Mark, Saint, Gospel according to
Marry in haste, repent at leisure.
Mars (Ares)
Mars (planet)
Marseilles
Marshall, Chief Justice John
Marshall, General George C.
Marshall Plan
Martha's Vineyard, MA
Marx, Karl
Marx Brothers
Marxism
Mary, Mary, Quite Contrary
Mary, mother of Jesus
Mary Had a Little Lamb (text)
Maryland
Mary Magdalene
M*A*S*H (title)
masochism
Mason-Dixon line

Masons, Freemasons
Mass
Massachusetts
massive resistance
massive retaliation
mass media
mass production
Mata Hari
materialism
Mather, Cotton
Matisse, Henri
matriarchy
matrilineal
Matterhorn
Matthew, Saint, Gospel according to
Maxwell, James Clerk
Mayan civilization
Mayflower, the
McCarthy, Senator Joe
McCarthyism
McCoy, the real
mea culpa
mean (statistics)
mean free path
measles
Mecca
mechanics
Medea
media, the
median
mediation
Medicare
Medici, the
medieval
medium is the message., The
Medusa
meek shall inherit the earth., The
meet one's Waterloo
megabyte
megalomania
megawatt
Mein Kampf (title)
Meir, Golda
melancholy
melanoma
Melbourne
meliorism
Mellon, Andrew
melodrama
melody
meltdown
melting point
melting pot, the
Melville, Herman
memento mori
Memphis, TN
Mencken, H. L.
Mendel, Gregor
Mendeleev, Dmitri
Mendelssohn, Felix
meningitis
Mennonites
menopause
menstrual cycle
Mephistopheles
mercantilism
mercator projection
Merchant of Venice, The (title)
merci
mercury (element)
Mercury (god — Hermes)
Mercury (planet)
merger
meridian
merit system
Merlin
Messiah
Messiah of Handel
metabolism
metamorphic rock
Metamorphoses (Ovid) (title)

metamorphosis
Metamorphosis, The (Kafka) (title)
metaphor
metaphysics
meteorites
meteorology
meteors
meter
method in his madness., There's
Methodism
Methuselah
métier
metric system
Metternich
Mexican War
Mexico
Mexico City
Miami, FL
Michelangelo
Michigan
Mickey Mouse
microchip
microclimate
microcosm
microeconomics
microfiche
microfilm
microorganisms
microscope
microwave communication
Midas
Middle Ages
Middle America
middle class
middle ear
Middle East
Middle West
Midsummer Night's Dream, A (title)
Midway, Battle of
midwife
Milan
milieu
militant
military-industrial complex
milk of human kindness
Milky Way
Mill, John Stuart
Miller, Arthur
Milton, John
Milwaukee, WI
mind/body problem
Mind your p's and q's.
Mine eyes have seen the glory . . .
mineral
Minerva (Athena)
minimum wage
Minneapolis, MN
Minnesota
minority floor leader
Minotaur
Minuteman
Miranda decision
misanthrope
miscarriage
misdemeanor
Misery loves company.
missing link, the
miss is as good as a mile., A
Mississippi
Mississippi River
Missouri
Missouri Compromise
Missouri River
Mitty, Walter
Moby Dick (title)
Model T
Modest Proposal, A (title)
modifier (grammar)
modus operandi (m.o.)
modus vivendi

Mohammed
Mojave Desert
molar
molecular biology
molecular weight
molecule
Molière
Molotov cocktail
Momaday, Scott
momentum
Mona Lisa (image)
monarchy
Monet, Claude
monetarism
monetary policy
money burning a hole in your pocket
Money is the root of all evil.
money market
Mongolia
mongolism
monism
Monitor versus Merrimack
monogamy
mononucleosis
monopoly
monotheism
Monroe, James
Monroe, Marilyn
Monroe Doctrine
monsieur
monsoon
montage
Montaigne, Michel Eyquem de
Montana
Mont Blanc
Montesquieu
Montessori, Maria
Montezuma
month of Sundays
Monticello
Montreal
moon made of green cheese
Moral Majority
moratorium
more sinned against than sinning
More, Sir Thomas
more the merrier., The
more things in heaven and earth, Horatio
Morgan, J. P.
Mormon
Morocco
Morpheus
morraine
Morse, Samuel F. B.
Morse Code
mortal sin, venial sin
mortgage
Mosaic Law
Moscow
Moses
Moslem
mosque
most unkindest cut of all
Mother Goose rhymes
motif
motor development
mountain labored and brought forth a mouse., The
Mount Everest
Mount Kilimanjaro
Mount McKinley
Mount Olympus
Mount Parnassus
Mount Rainier
Mount Rushmore
Mount Saint Helen
Mount Vernon
Mount Vesuvius
Mount Whitney
movement, symphonic

Mozambique
Mozart, Wolfgang Amadeus
Ms.
muckraking
mulatto
multilateral
multiple independently targeted reentry vehicle (MIRV)
Munich
mural
Murder will out.
Murphy's Law
muscular dystrophy
Muses, the
Music hath charms to soothe the savage breast.
music of the spheres
Mussolini, Benito
mutation
mutual fund
mutual insurance company
MX missile
my brother's keeper?, Am I
My Country 'Tis of Thee (song)
My Fair Lady (title)
My God, My God, why hast thou forsaken me?
My Lai massacre
myopia
mysticism
mythology

Nader, Ralph
Nagasaki
Nantucket, MA
Naomi
Naples
Napoleon Bonaparte
narcissism
Narcissus
Narrative of the Life of Frederick Douglass (title)
narrator
Nashville, TN
Nasser
Nation, Carrie
National Aeronautics and Space Administration (NASA)
national anthem, the
National Association for the Advancement of Colored People (NAACP)
National Guard
nationalism
Nationalist China
nationalization
National Labor Relations Board (NLRB)
national liberation movements
National Organization for Women (NOW)
National Weather Service
Native Son (title)
Nativity, the
naturalism
natural law
natural rights
natural selection
Nature abhors a vacuum.
nature-nurture controversy
Navaho Indians
Nazism
Nazi-Soviet nonagression pact
n.b.
Neanderthal man
Nebraska
nebula
Necessity is the mother of invention.
née
negative charge
negative income tax
Nehru, Jawaharal

Neither a borrower nor a lender be.
Nelson, Admiral Horatio
Nemesis
neoclassicism
neocolonialism
Nepal
nepotism
Neptune (Poseidon)
Nero fiddled while Rome burned.
Nestor
neuron
neurosis
neutron
Nevada
Never give a sucker an even break.
Never in the field of human conflict was so much owed by so many to so few.
Never leave put off until tomorrow . . .
Never-Never Land
never over 'til it's over., It's
never rains but it pours., It
Never say die.
never too late to mend., It's
New Amsterdam
Newark, NJ
new broom sweeps clean., A
New Deal
New Delhi
New England
Newfoundland
New Frontier
New Guinea
New Hampshire
New Haven, CT
New Jersey
New Left
New Mexico
New Orleans, LA
Newport, RI
New Right
New Testament
Newton, Sir Isaac
new wine in old bottles
New York, NY
New Yorker, The (title)
New York State
New York Stock Exchange
New Zealand
Niagara Falls, NY
Nicaragua
Nice
Nicholas, Saint
nicotine
Nietzsche, Friedrich
Nigeria
Night Before Christmas, The (text)
Nightingale, Florence
nihilism
Nile
nimbus clouds
nine days' wonder
Nirvana
Nisei
nitrogen fixing
nitrogenous wastes
Nixon, Richard
Noah and the Flood
Nobel laureate (Nobel Prize)
noble gas
noblesse oblige
noblest Roman of them all., This was the
Nobody knows the trouble I've seen.
Noël
no-fault insurance
nolo contendere
No man can serve two masters.
No man is an island.

nom de plume
nonaligned nations
non compos mentis
No news is good news.
nonperson
non sequitur
nonviolent resistance
No one ever went broke underestimating the intelligence of the American people.
Norfolk, VA
normal distribution
Norman Conquest
Norse mythology
North Atlantic Treaty Organization (NATO)
North Carolina
North Dakota
Northern Hemisphere
Northern Ireland
northern lights
North Korea
North Pole
North Sea
North Star (Polaris)
Northwest Passage, the
Norway
nose out of joint
nose to the grindstone
nothing good or bad, but thinking makes it so., There is
Nothing is certain but death and taxes.
Nothing succeeds like success.
Nothing ventured, nothing gained.
Nothing will come of nothing.
Notre-Dame cathedral
not with a bang but a whimper
noun
nouveau riche
nova
novel
Now I lay me down to sleep . . .
Now is the winter of our discontent.
NRA
nuance
nuclear energy
nuclear family
nuclear fission
nuclear-free zone
nuclear fusion
nuclear power
nuclear reactor
nuclear testing
nucleic acids
nucleotides
nucleus (atomic)
nucleus (cellular)
Nuremberg trials
nymphomania

Oakland, CA
Oakley, Annie
Oak Ridge
object
objet d'art
oboe
O brave new world!
obscenity laws
obsolescence
obtuse angle
O Captain! my Captain! (text)
Occident
O Come All Ye Faithful (Adeste Fideles) (song)
October Revolution
ode
Ode on a Grecian Urn (text)
Odyssey, The (title)
Oedipus complex
Oedipus Rex (title)

oeuvre
off-Broadway
Office of Economic Opportunity (OEO)
offshore drilling
Off with her head!
O'Hara, Scarlett
Oh beautiful for spacious skies.
Ohio
Ohio River
ohm
Oil and water don't mix.
oil sands (tar shales)
Okinawa
Oklahoma
Oklahoma! (title)
Oklahoma City, OK
old boy network
Old Glory
Old King Cole
Old Mother Hubbard
Old soldiers never die; they just fade away.
Old Testament
Old World
oligarchy
oligopoly
Oliver Twist (title)
Olympian heights
Omaha, NE
Omar Khayyám
ombudsman
omnivore
Once bitten twice shy.
once in a blue moon
Once more into the breach, dear friends.
one for all and all for one
One good turn deserves another.
One if by land, two if by sea.
O'Neill, Eugene
One man's meat is another man's poison.
One picture is worth a thousand words.
One rotten apple spoils the barrel.
One swallow does not make a summer.
one that loved not wisely but too well
on its last legs
only thing we have to fear is fear itself., The
Ontario
on tenterhooks
on the Hill
Ontogeny recapitulates phylogeny.
On Top of Old Smokey (song)
op art
OPEC
Open Door policy
open primary
open sesame
open shop
opera
operetta
Oppenheimer, J. Robert
opposable thumbs
optic nerve
optics
oral personality
orbit
order of magnitude
ore (ore deposit)
Oregon
Oregon Trail
Orestes
organic chemistry
organic molecule
organization man
Organization of American States (OAS)

Orient
original sin
Origin of Species, The (title)
Orion
O Romeo, Romeo! wherefore art thou Romeo?
Orpheus
Orwell, George
Oslo
osmosis
ostracism
Oh! Susannah (song)
Othello (title)
Ottawa
Ottoman Empire
ounce of prevention is worth a pound of cure., An
our country, right or wrong
Out, damned spot!
Out of sight, out of mind.
out of the frying pan into the fire
Oval Office
ovarian cycle
ovary
overdraft
overhead
overkill
Over There (song)
overture
Ovid
ovum (ova)
Owens, Jesse
Oxford and Cambridge universities (Oxbridge)
oxidation
oxygen
oxymoron
ozone layer

Pacific Islands
pacifism
Pacific Ocean
pagoda
Paine, Thomas
Painted Desert
Pakistan
paleontology
Palestine
Palestine Liberation Organization (PLO)
Palm Sunday
Pan
panacea
Panama
Panama Canal
pancreas
pandemonium
Pandora's box
pantheism
Panza, Sancho
papacy
papal infallibility
parables
parabola
paradigm
Paradise Lost (title)
paradox
paragraph
Paraguay
parallelogram
parameter
paranoia
paraphrase
parapsychology
parentheses
pariah
Paris
Paris (Greek myth)
parity price
Parkinson's Law
parliament
Parnassus

parody
parole
Parthenon
participle
particle accelerator
Parting is such sweet sorrow.
partition
partnership
parts of speech
parvenu
Pascal, Blaise
passé
passim
passing the buck
passive resistance
passive voice
Passover
Pasteur, Louis
pasteurization
pastoral
patience of Job
patience of Penelope
patriarchy
patronage
Patton, General George
Paul, Saint
Paul Revere's ride
pauper
Pavlov's dog
pax romana
pay the piper
pay through the nose
Peace Corps, the
peaceful coexistence
Pearl Harbor
pearl of great price
pearls before swine
peasant
pediatrics
peeping Tom
Pegasus
Peirce, Charles Sanders
Peking (Beijing)
pell-mell
Peloponnesian War
penance
Penelope
penicillin
peninsula
penis envy
pen is mightier than the sword., The
Penn, William
Pennsylvania
Pennsylvania Dutch
penny saved is a penny earned., A
pension
Pentagon
Pentagon Papers
peonage
People's Republic of China
People who live in glass houses shouldn't throw stones.
per capita
percentage
percussion
per diem
perfectibility of man
Pericles
perimeter
periodic table of the elements
period
Perish the thought.
Perón, Eva
Perón, Juan
perpetual motion machine
Pershing, General John "Black Jack"
Persian Empire
person (grammar)
personal computer (PC)
personal pronoun

persona non grata
perspective
Peru
Peter, Saint
Peter Pan
Peter Piper
Peter Principle
Peter Rabbit
Peter the Great
Petrified Forest
petrochemical
phallic symbol
Pharaoh
Pharisees
phase change
Phi Beta Kappa
Philadelphia, PA
philanthropy
Philippines, the
Philistine
philistinism
philosopher king
philosopher's stone
phobia
Phoenicia
Phoenix, AZ
phoenix (myth)
photoelectric effect
photon
photosynthesis
pH
phrase
phylum
Physician, heal thyself.
physics
pianissimo
piazza
Picasso, Pablo
piccolo
Pickwickian
pièce de résistance
Pied Piper of Hamelin, The (title)
pie in the sky
Pietà (Michelangelo)
pig in a poke, buy a
Pike's Peak
Pilate, Pontius
pilgrims
Pilgrim's Progress, The (title)
pill, the
Pinocchio (title)
pistil
Pitt, William (the Elder)
Pittsburgh, PA
pituitary gland
place for everything and everything in its place., A
placenta
plagiarism
plagues of Egypt
Planck's constant
plane geometry
planet
planetarium
planned economy
planned obsolescence
plant kingdom
plasma
platelets
plate tectonics
platform
Plato
platonism
play second fiddle
playwright
pleasure principle
plebiscite
Pledge of Allegiance (text)
Plessy vs. Ferguson
plot
plural
pluralism

Plutarch
Pluto (myth)
Pluto (planet)
plutocracy
Plymouth Rock
p.m.
pneumonia
Pocahontas
Poe, Edgar Allan
poetic justice
poet laureate
poetry
Poets are born, not made.
pogrom
polarization
police state
polio
Politburo
political machine
political science
Politics makes strange bedfellows.
Polk, James K.
polka
pollination
Pollock, Jackson
poll tax
pollution
Pollyanna
Polo, Marco
polygamy
polymer
Polynesia
polytheism
polyunsaturated
Pompeii
Ponce de León, Juan
pontiff
pony express
Pooh-Bah
Poor Richard's Almanack (title)
pop art
Pope, Alexander
Pope, the
pop the question
populism
Populist party
pork-barrel legislation
pornography
Porter, Cole
Portland, OR
Portugal
Poseidon (Neptune)
positive charge
possessive (grammar)
Post, Emily
postmaster general
post mortem
postulate
potato famine, Irish
pot calling the kettle black
potluck
Potomac River
pound of flesh
pour oil on troubled waters
power of the purse
Power tends to corrupt and absolute power corrupts absolutely.
Practice makes perfect.
Practice what you preach.
pragmatism
Prague
prayer rug
Preamble to the Constitution
precedent
precipitate (chemistry)
precipitation
predestination
predicate
preemptive strike
prefix
prejudice
premier (prime minister)

première
preposition
pre-Raphaelite
Presbyterian
Presley, Elvis
pressure group
Pretoria
prevailing westerlies
Priam
Pride and Prejudice (title)
Pride goeth before a fall.
priest (minister)
prima ballerina
prima donna
primate
prime minister
prime number
prime rate
primitivism
primogeniture
primrose path
Prince, The (title)
Prince Albert
Prince of Wales
Princess and the Pea, The (title)
principal (monetary term)
prism
private enterprise
private sector
probate court
probation
Procrastination is the thief of time.
Procrustes' bed
prodigal son, the
profit sharing
pro forma
prognosis
programming language
progressive education
Progressive movement
progressive tax
Prohibition
Prokofiev, Sergei
proletariat
Prometheus
Promised Land
pronoun
proof of the pudding is in the eating., The
propaganda
prophet is not without honor save in his own country., A
proportional representation
pro rata
prose
prosecution
prostate gland
protagonist
protective tariff
protectorate
protein
pro tempore (pro tem)
Protestant
Protestant ethic (work ethic)
proton
protoplasm
protozoa
Proust, Marcel
proverb
Providence, divine
Providence, RI
proxy
pseudoscience
psychedelic
psychiatry
psychic research
psychoanalysis
psychology
psychopath
psychosis
psychosomatic
Ptolemy

public be damned., The
public defender
public utility
public works
Puccini, Giacomo
Puerto Rico
Pulitzer Prize
pulmonary artery
pulpwood
pulsar
pumice
pump priming
pun
purgatory
purge
Puritans
purple passage
Pushkin, Aleksandr
Puss-in-Boots (title)
Pygmalion (title)
Pyramids, the
Pyrenees
pyromania
Pyrrhic victory

quadratic equation
Quaker
quality of mercy is not
  strain'd . . . , The
quantum leap
quantum mechanics
quarantine
quark
quasars
quasi
Quebec
Queen Elizabeth I
Queen Elizabeth II
Queen Victoria
question mark (?)
quid pro quo
quintet
Quisling
quixotic
quod erat demonstrandum
  (Q.E.D.)
quorum
quota
quotation marks (" ")
quotient

rabbi
Rabelaisian
rabies
racism
raconteur
radar
radiation damage
radical (chemistry)
radical (politics)
radioactive dating
radioactive waste
radio frequency
radio waves
RAF (Royal Air Force)
ragtime
rainbow
raining cats and dogs
raison d'être
Raleigh, Sir Walter
Ramadan
RAM (random access memory)
rank and file
ranking member
Raphael
rapprochement
Rapunzel
rare bird
Rasputin
rate of exchange
ratification
Raven, The (title)

reactionary
reactor
read between the lines
read the riot act
Reagan, Ronald
realism
realpolitik
real property
rebate
rebuttal
recession
recessive trait
recognition
recombinant DNA
recorder
Red Badge of Courage, The (title)
red blood cells
Red China
Red Cross
Red Guards
red herring
Red River Valley
Red Sea
Red Sea, parting of
red shift
Red Square
red tape
reductio ad absurdum
reduction (chemistry)
redundancy
reference works
referendum
reflex (psychology)
Reformation, the
refraction
refugee
regressive tax
regret that I have but one life to lose for my country., I only
regular verb
Reign of Terror
relative humidity
relativism
relativity, special theory of
relief (art)
Rembrandt van Rijn
Remember Pearl Harbor!
Remember the Alamo!
Remember the Maine!
Renaissance, the
Renaissance man
Render therefore unto Caesar the things which are Caesar's.
renewable resource
Renoir, Pierre Auguste
Reno, NV
reparation
reports of my death are greatly exaggerated., The
reprisal
reptiles
republican government
Republican party
requiem
Resistance, French
resistance (electric)
respiration
Restoration (of the British monarchy)
Resurrection, the
retail
Revelation
Revelation, The Book of
revenue sharing
Revere, Paul
revivals
Revolutionary War
Revolutions of 1848
rhetoric
rhetorical question
rheumatic fever
rheumatoid arthritis

Rhine River
Rhode Island
Rhodesia
Rhodes scholarships
Rhone River
rhyme
ribonucleic acid
Richard the Lion-Hearted
Richelieu, Cardinal
Richmond, VA
Richter scale
Ride a Cock Horse (song)
rider (politics)
right angle
right to bear arms
right-to-work law
right triangle
right wing
rigor mortis
Rime of the Ancient Mariner (text)
Ring around the Rosies (text)
Rio de Janeiro
Rio Grande
R.I.P.
Rip Van Winkle (title)
risk capital (venture capital)
Risorgimento
risqué
Rivera, Diego
Riviera, the
RNA
Road Not Taken, The (title)
road to hell is paved with good intentions., The
Roaring Twenties
robber barons
Robert's Rules of Order
Robeson, Paul
Robespierre, Maximilien
Robin Hood (title)
Robinson, Jackie
Robinson Crusoe (title)
rob Peter to pay Paul
Rochester, NY
Rock-a-Bye-Baby (song)
Rockefeller, John D.
Rock of Gibraltar
Rockwell, Norman
Rocky Mountains
rococo
Rodgers and Hammerstein
Rodin, Auguste
Rogers, Will
role conflict
role model
rolling stone gathers no moss., A
ROM (read only memory)
roman à clef
Roman Catholic Church
romance
Roman Empire
Romanesque
Romania
Roman numerals
romanticism
Romeo and Juliet (title)
Rome wasn't built in a day.
Romulus and Remus
Roosevelt, Eleanor
Roosevelt, Franklin Delano (FDR)
Roosevelt, Theodore (Teddy)
Roots (title)
Rorschach test
Rose is a rose is a rose is a rose.
Rosenberg case
Roses, Wars of the
Rosetta stone
Rosh Hashanah
Ross, Betsy
Rossini, Gioacchino
Rotterdam

Rough Riders
Rousseau, Jean Jacques
Row, Row, Row Your Boat (song)
royalty (business)
R.S.V.P.
Rubáiyát of Omar Khayyám, The (title)
Rubens, Peter Paul
Rubicon, cross the
rugged individualism
rule of thumb
rule the roost
Rumpelstiltskin (title)
run of the mill
run-on sentence
Russell, Bertrand
Russia
Russian Revolution
Russo-Japanese War
Ruth
Ruth, Babe

Sabbath, the
Sacco-Vanzetti case
sacrament
Sacramento, CA
Sacramento Valley
sacred cow
Sade, Marquis de
sadism
Sahara Desert
Saigon
Saint George and the dragon
Saint Lawrence River
Saint Louis, MO
Saint Paul, MN
Saint Paul's Cathedral
Saint Petersburg, FL
Saint Peter's Church
Saint Sophia (basilica)
salad days
Salem witch trials
Salk vaccine
Salome
salon
Salt Lake City, UT
salt of the earth
salt on a bird's tail
salvation
Salvation Army
Samson and Delilah
San Andreas Fault
San Antonio, TX
sanctions
sanctum sanctorum
Sand, George
Sandburg, Carl
San Diego, CA
San Francisco, CA
San Francisco Bay
sang froid
San Joaquin Valley
San Jose, CA
San Salvador
Sanskrit
Santa Fe, NM
Santa Fe Trail
Santiago
São Paulo
Sappho
Sarajevo
Saratoga, NY
sarcasm
Sardinia
Sartre, Jean-Paul
Satan
satellite (politics)
satellite (technology)
satire
saturated fatty acid
Saturn (myth)
Saturn (planet)

satyr
Saudi Arabia
savanna
savings and loan association
savings bond
savoir-faire
Savonarola, Girolamo
saxophone
scab (labor)
Scandinavia
scapegoat
Scarlet Letter, The (title)
Scheherazade
Schiller, Friedrich von
schism
schizophrenia
scholasticism
Schubert, Franz
Schweitzer, Albert
sciatica
science fiction
scientific method
Scopes trial (monkey trial)
Scotland
Scotland Yard
Scott, Sir Walter
Scrooge
Scylla and Charybdis
sea legs
seamy side
seasonal unemployment
Seattle, WA
secession
Second Coming, the
Second Inaugural Address
second sight
second wind
Secret Life of Walter Mitty, The (title)
Secret Service
sect
secular
Securities and Exchange Commission (SEC)
Security Council
sedimentary rock (sedimentation)
sedition
Seeing is believing.
segregation
Seine River, the
seismology (seismograph)
Seize the day. (Carpe diem.)
Selective Service
self-incrimination
Self-Reliance (title)
seller's market
Selma, AL
semantics
semicolon (;)
Seminole Indians
Semite, Semitic
semper fidelis
Senate, the U.S.
seniority
señor
señora
señorita
sentence
Seoul
separate but equal
separation of church and state
separation of powers
Sequoyah, Chief
serfdom
Sermon on the Mount
Serpent, the
Serra, Junipero
service industry
Sesame Street (title)
settlement houses
set your teeth on edge
Seuss, Dr.

seven deadly sins
Seventh-Day Adventists
Seven Wonders of the World
Seville
sexism
sex-linked trait
sexual reproduction
Shakespeare, William
shale
Shall I compare thee to a summer's day?
shalom
Shanghai
Shangri-la
sharecropping
Shaw, George Bernard (GBS)
Shawnee Indians
Shelley, Percy Bysshe
Sherman Anti-Trust Act
Sherman's march to the sea
Sherwood Forest
shibboleth
shipshape
ships that pass in the night
shock therapy
Shoot, if you must, this old gray head . . .
short circuit
short story
shout fire in a crowded theater
show must go on., The
Shreveport, LA
Siberia
sic
Sicily
sickle-cell anemia
Sic transit gloria mundi.
Sierra Madre
Sierra Nevada
siesta
sign of the cross
signor
signora
signorina
Silence is golden. (Speech is silver.)
silent majority
Silent Night (song)
silicates
silicon chip
Silicon Valley
simile
simple sentence
Simple Simon (text)
Sinai
Sinatra, Frank
sine die
sine qua non
Singapore
Sing a Song of Sixpence (song)
singular
sinking fund
Sink or swim.
Sioux Indians
Sirens, the
Sistine Chapel
Sisyphus
sitcom (situation comedy)
sit-ins
sit on the fence
Sitting Bull
skepticism
Skinner, B. F.
skin of your teeth
skull and crossbones
skyscrapers
slang
slavery
slave trade, the
Sleeping Beauty (title)
sliding scale
slow but sure
smallpox

smell a rat
Smith, Adam
Smith, Captain John
Smithsonian Institution
smog
Snow White (title)
social gospel
socialism
social science
Social Security
Society of Friends
sociobiology
sociology
sociopath
Socrates
Sodom and Gomorrah
soft answer turneth away wrath., A
software
solar cell
solar system, the
solid South
solipsism
Solomon
Something is rotten in the state of Denmark.
sonata
sonic boom
sonnet
sophist
Sophocles
soprano
Sorbonne
sound mind in a sound body, a
soup to nuts
sour grapes
Sousa, John Philip
Sousa marches
South Africa
South America
South Carolina
South Dakota
Southeast Asia
Southern Hemisphere
South Korea
South Sea Islands
South Seas
sovereignty
Soviet bloc
Soviet Union
space shuttle
space station
space telescope
Spain
Spanish-American War
Spanish Armada
Spanish Civil War
Spanish Inquisition
Spare the rod and spoil the child.
Sparta
Speaker of the House
Speak softly and carry a big stick.
Speech is silver; silence is golden.
speed of light
sperm whale
sphere
Sphinx, the
Spinoza, Baruch
Spirit of '76 (image)
Spirit of St. Louis
split hairs
split infinitive
Spock, Dr. Benjamin
spoils system
spontaneous combustion
spore
spreading yourself too thin
sputnik
Sri Lanka
staccato
staff of life
stagflation

stalactite
stalagmite
Stalin, Josef
Stalingrad, Battle of
Stalinism
stamen
Stamp Act
standard deviation
standard of living
standing orders
stanza
Star Chamber
star-crossed lovers
stare decisis
Stars and Stripes Forever (song)
Star-Spangled Banner, The (song)
Star Trek (title)
Star Wars (title)
State of the Union Address
states' rights
static electricity
statistics
Statue of Liberty
status quo
status symbol
statute of limitations
steal (someone's) thunder
Stein, Gertrude
Stendhal
Step on a crack, break your mother's back.
steppe
stereotype
Stevenson, Robert Louis
Stewart, Jimmy
Still waters run deep.
stitch in time saves nine., A
stock exchange/stock market
stoicism
stomach (anatomy)
Stone Age
Stonehenge
Stone walls do not a prison make.
Stopping by Woods on a Snowy Evening (title)
storage battery
Stowe, Harriet Beecher
Stradivarius
strain at a gnat and swallow a camel
strange bedfellows
Strategic Arms Limitation Treaty (SALT)
strategic defense initiative (SDI)
strategy/tactics
stratification
stratosphere
stratus clouds
Strauss, Johann
Strauss, Richard
Strauss waltzes
Stravinsky, Igor
straw in the wind
straw man
streamline
stream of consciousness
Streetcar Named Desire, A (title)
strike
strikebreaker
Strike while the iron is hot.
Strindberg, August
string quartet
strip mining
Stuart, Gilbert
Stuttgart
Sturm und Drang
Stuyvesant, Peter
Styx, River
subconsciousness
subject (grammar)
subjunctive

sublimation (chemistry)
sublimation (psychology)
subordination (grammar)
subpoena
subsidy
subsistence farming
suffer fools gladly
suffix
suffrage
suffragette
sui generis
sulfa drug
summa cum laude
summit meeting
Sumter, Fort
Sun Also Rises, The (title)
Sun King
superconductor
superego
superlative (grammar)
Superman
supernova
supersonic
supply and demand
supply-side economics
Supreme Court
surface tension
surrealism
surtax
swastika
sweatshop
Sweden
sweetness and light
Swift, Jonathan
swing
Swing Low, Sweet Chariot (song)
Switzerland
Sword of Damocles
Sydney
symphony
synagogue
syndrome
synfuel
synonym
syntax
syphilis
Syracuse, NY
Syria

taboo
tabula rasa
Taft, William Howard
Taft-Hartley Act
Taipei
Taiwan
Taj Mahal
take-home pay
Take Me Out to the Ball Game (song)
takes a heap o' livin' to make a house a home., It
takes a thief to catch a thief., It
takes two to tango., It
take the bitter with the sweet
take the bull by the horns
Tale of Two Cities, A (title)
tall tale
Talmud, the
Taming of the Shrew, The (title)
Tampa, FL
tangent
tango
Tantalus
Tanzania
Taoism
taproot
tar and feather
tariff
tarred with the same brush
Tarzan
taste bud

Taxation without representation is tyranny.
tax deduction
tax haven
tax loophole
taxonomic classification
tax shelter
Tchaikovsky, Pyotr
Teapot Dome scandal
technocracy
technological unemployment
tectonic plates
teeny-bopper
Teflon-coated
Teheran
telemetry
telepathy
telephoto
telescope
Tell, William
Teller, Edward
telling tales out of school
Tempest, The (title)
tempest in a teapot
temple
Temple, Shirley
tempo
tenant farming
Ten Commandments, the
tenderfoot
Tennessee
Tennessee River
Tennessee Valley Authority (TVA)
Tennyson, Alfred Lord
tenor
tense
tenure
terra firma
terrorism
tertiary recovery
testosterone
tetanus
tête-à-tête
Tet offensive
Texas
Thailand
thalidomide
Thames River
Thatcher, Margaret
That way madness lies.
theocracy
therapy
There are lots of fish in the sea.
There are more things in heaven and earth . . .
There is a tide in the affairs of men . . .
There is no joy in Mudville.
There is nothing good or bad, but thinking makes it so.
There is nothing new under the sun.
There's a divinity that shapes our ends.
There's a special providence in the fall of a sparrow.
There's many a slip twixt the cup and the lip.
There's method in his madness.
There's more than one way to skin a cat.
There's no disputing about taste.
There's no fool like an old fool.
There's no place like home.
There was a little girl (text)
There was an old woman who lived in a shoe (text)
thermal equilibrium
thermal pollution
thermodynamics
thermonuclear
thermostat

These are the times that try men's souls.
thesis
They shall not pass.
thiamine
thing of beauty is a joy forever., A
Thinker, The (image)
Third Reich
Third World
Thirteen Colonies
Thirty days hath September . . .
thirty pieces of silver
Thirty Years War
This land is your land, this land is my land.
This Little Piggy Went to Market (text)
This was the most unkindest cut of all.
This was the noblest Roman of them all.
Thomas, the doubting Apostle
Thomism
Thor
Thoreau, Henry David
Thorpe, Jim
Those who cannot remember the past are condemned to repeat it.
Three Bears, The (title)
Three Blind Mice (song)
three-D
Three Mile Island
Three Little Pigs, The (title)
three sheets to the wind
thrombosis
through a glass darkly
Through the Looking Glass (title)
through thick and thin
throwing out the baby with the bath water
thrown to the lions
throw weight
Thucydides
Thurber, James
thyroid
Tibet
ticker-tape parade
tied to his mother's apron strings
Tiffany glass
Tiger, Tiger, burning bright.
till the cows come home
tilting at windmills
Timbuktu
time and motion study
Time and tide wait for no man.
time dilation
time exposure
Time heals all wounds.
Time is money.
Time is of the essence.
time is out of joint., The
Times Square
time's winged chariot
time to be born and a time to die
Tin Pan Alley
Tintoretto
tip of the iceberg
tip of the tongue phenomenon
Tiresias
Titanic, the
Titans, the
tit for tat
tithe
Titian
Tito
titration
Tobacco Road (title)
To be, or not to be: that is the question.
Tocqueville, Alexis de
To err is human; to forgive divine.
tokomak

Tokyo
Toledo, OH
Tolstoy, Leo
Tom, Dick, and Harry
tommy gun
Tomorrow, and tomorrow, and tomorrow . . .
Tom Sawyer (title)
Tom Thumb
Too many cooks spoil the broth.
too many irons in the fire
tooth and nail
topic sentence
topsoil
Torah, the
tornado
Toronto
Torquemada, Tomós de
torque
Tortoise and the Hare, The (title)
totalitarianism
to the manner born
touch and go
touché
touchstone
tour de force
town and gown
trachea
Trafalgar, Battle of
tragedy
Trail of Tears
transformer
transistor
transitive verb
transubstantiation
transvestite
trapezoid
Trappist monks
trauma
Treasure Island (title)
Tree of Knowledge of Good and Evil
trench warfare
trial and error
trial balloon
Tripoli
Trojan Horse
Trojan War
trombone
troposphere
Trotsky, Leon
troubadours
Troy
Truman, Harry
trump card
trumpet
trust
trust busting
Truth, Sojourner
Truth is stranger than fiction.
Truth will out.
tuba
Tubman, Harriet
Tudor monarchy
Tulsa, OK
tumor
tundra
Turkey in the Straw (song)
Turn about is fair play.
Turner, J.M.W.
Turner, Nat
turn over a new leaf
turn the other cheek
Tucson, AZ
Tutankhamen
Twain, Mark
Tweed, Boss
Tweedledum and Tweedledee
Twenty-third Psalm
Twinkle, Twinkle, Little Star (song)
Two China policy
Two heads are better than one.
Two's company, three's a crowd.

two shakes of a lamb's tail
Two wrongs don't make a right.
tycoon
tympani (music)
tympanum
typhoid fever
Typhoid Mary
typhoon
typhus

U-boats
UFO
Uganda
Ugly Duckling, The (title)
UHF (ultrahigh frequency)
ukelele
ulcer
Ulster
ultimatum
Ulysses
umbilical cord
un-American
uncertainty principle
Uncle Remus stories
Uncle Sam (image)
Uncle Tom
Uncle Tom's Cabin (title)
underdog
Underground Railroad
understatement
Uneasy lies the head that wears the crown.
UNESCO (United Nations Educational, Scientific, and Cultural Organization)
unicorn
unilateral
Union, the
union shop
Unitarian church
United Kingdom
United Nations
United States Information Agency (USIA)
universal gravitation
unsaturated fatty acid
uppercase
uppercrust
upward mobility
uranium
Uranus
urbanization
urban renewal
Ursa Major
Ursa Minor
usury
Utah
uterus
utilitarianism
utility (business)
utopia
utopianism

vaccine
vacuum
valence
Valentino, Rudolph
Valhalla
Valkyrie
Valley Forge
valley of the shadow of death
Van Allen Belt
Vancouver
Vandals
Vanderbilts, the
Van Gogh, Vincent
vanishing point
Vanity Fair (title)
vaporization
vapor pressure
Variety is the spice of life.
vasectomy
vassal
Vatican, the

Vatican II
vector
V-E Day
velocity
venereal disease
Venezuela
venial sin
Veni, vidi, vici.
Venice
ventricle
Venus (Aphrodite)
Venus (planet)
Venus di Milo (image)
verb
Verdi, Giuseppe
Vermeer, Jan
Vermont
Verne, Jules
Versailles, Treaty of (16th and 20th centuries)
vertebrate
vestal virgins
vested interest
Veterans Administration (VA)
Veterans of Foreign Wars (VFW)
veto
VHF (very high frequency)
vice versa
Vichy
vicious circle
Victoria, Queen
Victorian
Vienna
Viet Cong
Vietnam
Vietnam War
vigilantes
Vikings, the
Viking spacecraft
Village Blacksmith, The (title)
viola
violin
VIP
Virgil
virgin birth
Virginia
Virgin Islands
virtual image
virus
vis-à-vis
visual aid
visual field
vital statistics
vitamin
vivisection
V-J Day
voilà
volcano
Volga River
Volstead Act
volt
voltage
Voltaire
Voting Rights Act of 1965
vowels
Vox populi vox dei.
voyeurism
Vulcan (Hephaestus)
vulcanization
Vulgate Bible

wage scale
Wagner, Richard
Wailing Wall
wake (Irish)
Walden (title)
Wales
walkie-talkie
walking papers
walking under a ladder
walkout (labor)
Wallace, George

Walls have ears.
Wall Street
wampum
wanderlust
War and Peace (title)
war crimes
war hawks (hawks)
Warhol, Andy
warhorse
War is hell.
warm-blooded
War of 1812
war on poverty
warp and woof
warpath, on the
warranty
Warren Court
Warsaw Pact
Wars of the Roses
washing dirty linen in public
Washington, Booker T.
Washington, George
Washington, D.C.
Washington and the cherry tree
Washington Crossing the Delaware (image)
Washington Mall
Washington Monument
Washington State
WASP (white Anglo-Saxon Protestant)
Waste Land, The (title)
Waste not, want not.
watched pot never boils., A
Watergate
Waterloo, Battle of
Water Music of Handel
water off a duck's back
water pollution
watershed
water softener
water table
Water, water everywhere, nor any drop to drink.
Watson, Doctor
Watson, James, and Francis Crick
watt
Watt, James (steam engine)
Watts riots
wavelength
wave-particle duality
Way down upon the Swanee River
Wayne, John
Ways and Means Committee
way to a man's heart is through his stomach., The
We are such stuff as dreams are made on.
weather map
weather satellite
weather service
Webster, Daniel
Webster, Noah
We have met the enemy, and they are ours.
Weimar Republic
welfare state
Well begun is half done.
Wellington, Duke of
Wells, H. G.
We Shall Overcome (song)
West, Mae
West Bank
Western Europe
West Germany
West Indies
Westminster Abbey
West Point
West Virginia
wetback
wet behind the ears
Wharton, Edith

What is good for General Motors is good for the country.
What's in a name?
What will be will be.
wheel is come full circle., The
wheel of fortune
When in Rome do as the Romans do.
When it rains it pours.
When the cat's away, the mice will play.
When the Saints Go Marching In (song)
Where are the snows of yesteryear?
Where there's a will there's a way.
Where there's smoke there's fire.
Whig party
While there's life, there's hope.
Whistler's Mother (image)
white blood cells
White Christmas (song)
white-collar worker
white dwarf
White House
white man's burden, the
Whitman, Walt
Whitney, Eli
Whoever loved that loved not at first sight?
Who laughs last laughs best.
wholesale
whooping cough
Who pays the piper calls the tune.
Wichita, KS
wide-angle lens
Wild Bill Hickok
wildcat strike
Wilde, Oscar
Wild West
William and Mary
Williams, Roger
Williams, Tennessee
William the Conqueror
Wilson, Woodrow
windfall
winter of our discontent
Win this one for the Gipper.
wiretapping
Wisconsin
wishbone
wishing well
wish is father to the thought., The
wish upon a star
witchcraft
witch hunt
withdrawal symptoms
withholding tax
Wittgenstein, Ludwig
Wizard of Oz, The (title)
wolf in sheep's clothing
Women's Christian Temperance Union (WCTU)
women's liberation movement
Woodstock
woodwinds
Woolf, Virginia
Wordsworth, William
word to the wise is sufficient., A
work ethic
workmen's compensation
Works Progress Administration (WPA)
World Court
world must be made safe for democracy., The
World Trade Center
World War I
World War II
worm turns., The
worship the golden calf
worth his salt

Wren, Sir Christopher
Wright, Frank Lloyd
Wright, Richard
Wright brothers
write-in candidate
Wuthering Heights (title)
Wyatt Earp
Wyeth, Andrew
Wynken, Blynken, and Nod (text)
Wyoming

X chromosome
xenophobia
X-ray
xylem

Yalta agreements
Yangtze River
Yankee
Yankee Doodle (song)
Y chromosome
Yellow Peril
yellow press
Yellowstone National Park
Yes, Virginia, there is a Santa Claus.
yin/yang
yoga
Yom Kippur
Yorktown, Battle of
Yosemite National Park
You Are My Sunshine (song)
You can catch more flies with honey than with vinegar.
You can lead a horse to water, but you can't make him drink.
You can't go home again.
You can't have your cake and eat it too.
You can't make an omelet without breaking eggs.
You can't make a silk purse out of a sow's ear.
You can't serve both God and Mammon.
You can't squeeze blood from a turnip.
You can't take it with you.
You can't teach an old dog new tricks.
You can't unscramble an egg.
You'll take the high road, and I'll take the low road . . .
You may fire when ready, Gridley.
Young, Brigham
Young Turk
You're never too old to learn.
Youth will have its fling.
Yucatán
Yugoslavia
Yukon
yuppies

Zambia
Zapata
Zeitgeist
Zen
zero-sum (game)
Zeus (Jupiter)
Zimbabwe
Zionism
zodiac
Zola, Emile
zoning
Zurich

NOTES

PREFACE

1. John Dewey and Evelyn Dewey, *Schools of To-morrow* (New York: Dutton, 1915 [14th printing, 1924]), 13.
2. Plato, *The Republic,* II, Stephanus 377, X, Stephanus 608.
3. Dewey, *Schools of To-morrow,* 13.

CHAPTER I

1. For rising standards of literacy, see R. L. Thorndike, *Reading Comprehension Education in Fifteen Countries: An Empirical Study* (New York: Wiley, 1973). On the connection between high literacy and Japan's economic performance, see Thomas P. Rohlen, "Japanese Education: If They Can Do It, Should We?" *American Scholar* 55, 1 (Winter 1985–86): 29–44. For American literacy rates see Jeanne Chall, "Afterword," in R. C. Anderson et al., *Becoming a Nation of Readers: The Report of the Commission on Reading* (Washington, D. C.: National Institute of Education, 1985), 123–24. On "world knowledge" in literacy, see Jeanne S. Chall, *Stages of Reading Development* (New York: McGraw-Hill, 1983), 8.
2. The two classical discussions of the stabilizing effects of mass literacy on oral speech are Henry Bradley, *The Making of English,* revised edition by Simeon Potter (London: Macmillan, 1968), and Otto Jespersen, *Mankind, Nation, and Individual from a Linguistic Point of View,* Midland edition (Bloomington: Indiana University Press, 1964). Wider bibliographical references to this subject may be found in the first two chapters of my *Philosophy*

of Composition (Chicago: University of Chicago Press, 1977).

3. The experiment is described in R. M. Krauss and S. Glucksberg, "Social and Nonsocial Speech," *Scientific American* 236 (February 1977): 100–105.
4. National Assessment of Educational Progress, *Three National Assessments of Reading: Changes in Performance, 1970–1980* (Report 11-R-01) (Denver: Education Commission of the States, 1981). The percentage of students scoring at the "advanced" level (4.9 percent) has climbed back to the very low levels of 1970. See *The Reading Report Card: Progress Toward Excellence in Our Schools, Trends in Reading Over Four National Assessments, 1971–1984* (Princeton, N.J.: Educational Testing Service No. 15-R-01, 1986).
5. John B. Carroll, "Psychometric Approaches to the Study of Language Abilities," in C. J. Fillmore, D. Kempler, and S.-Y. Wang, eds., *Individual Differences in Language Abilities and Language Behavior* (New York: Academic Press, 1979), 29.
6. The College Board, *College-Bound Seniors: Eleven Years of National Data from the College Board's Admission Testing Program, 1973–83* (New York, 1984). The College Board has sent me further details from an unpublished report that shows the breakdown of scores over 600 between 1972 and 1984. The percentage of students who scored over 600 was 7.3 percent in 1984 and 11.4 percent in 1972. The percentage scoring over 650 was 3.0 percent in 1984 and 5.29 percent in 1972.
7. Benjamin J. Stein, "The Cheerful Ignorance of the Young in L.A.," *Washington Post,* October 3, 1983. Reprinted with the kind permission of the author.
8. *Changes in Political Knowledge and Attitudes, 1969–76: Selected Results from the Second National Assessments of Citizenship and Social Studies* (Denver: National Assessment of Educational Progress, 1978).
9. The Foundations of Literacy Project under a grant from the National Endowment for the Humanities, has commissioned NAEP, now conducted by the Educational Testing Service of Princeton, to probe the literary and historical knowledge of American seventeen-year-olds.

10. I am breaking no confidences as a member of the NAEP panel in revealing these pretest figures. They were made public on October 8, 1985, in a press release by NEH Chairman John Agresto, which stated in part: "Preliminary findings indicate that two-thirds of the seventeen-year-old students tested could not place the Civil War in the correct half century; a third did not know that the Declaration of Independence was signed between 1750 and 1800; half could not locate the half century in which the First World War occurred; a third did not know that Columbus sailed for the New World 'before 1750'; three-fourths could not identify Walt Whitman or Thoreau or E. E. Cummings or Carl Sandburg. And one-half of our high school seniors did not recognize the names of Winston Churchill or Joseph Stalin."
11. See Chapter 2, pages 42–47.
12. Orlando Patterson, "Language, Ethnicity, and Change," in S. G. D'Eloia, ed., *Toward a Literate Democracy: Proceedings of the First Shaughnessy Memorial Conference, April 3, 1980,* special number of *The Journal of Basic Writing* III (1980): 72–73.
13. Letter to Colonel Edward Carrington, January 16, 1787, taken from *The Life and Selected Writings of Thomas Jefferson,* ed. A. Koch and W. Peden (New York: Random House, 1944), 411–12.
14. W. C. Sellar and R. J. Yeatman, *1066 and All That: A Memorable History of England, Comprising All the Parts You Can Remember, Including 103 Good Things, 5 Bad Kings, and 2 Genuine Dates* (London: Methuen, 1947).
15. Melvin Durslag, "To Ban the Beanball," *TV Guide,* June 8–14, 1985, 9.
16. H. Putnam, "The Meaning of Meaning," in *Philosophical Papers, Volume 2: Mind, Language and Reality* (Cambridge: Cambridge University Press, 1975), 227–48.
17. See M. S. Steffensen, C. Joag-Des, and R. C. Anderson, "A Cross-Cultural Perspective on Reading Comprehension," *Reading Research Quarterly* 15, 1 (1979): 10–29.
18. This is fully discussed in Chapter 3.
19. See H. J. Walberg and T. Shanahan, "High School Effects on

Individual Students," *Educational Researcher* 12 (August–September 1983): 4–9.

20. "Up to about ten hours a week, there is actually a slight positive relationship between the amount of time children spend watching TV and their school achievement, including reading achievement. Beyond this point, the relationship turns negative and, as the number of hours per week climbs, achievement declines sharply." R. C. Anderson et al., *Becoming a Nation of Readers,* 27.
21. Walberg and Shanahan, "High School Effects on Individual Students," 4–9.
22. Arthur G. Powell, Eleanor Farrar, and David K. Cohen, *The Shopping Mall High School: Winners and Losers in the Educational Marketplace* (Boston: Houghton Mifflin, 1985), 1–8.
23. The neutrality and avoidance of the schools are described in detail in *The Shopping Mall High School.*
24. Patterson, "Language, Ethnicity, and Change," 72–73.
25. Oscar Wilde, "The Decay of Lying" (1889).
26. Jeanne S. Chall, "Afterword," in R. C. Anderson et al., *Becoming a Nation of Readers,* 123–25.
27. J. S. Chall, C. Snow, et al., *Families and Literacy,* Final Report to the National Institute of Education, 1982.
28. R. L. Thorndike, *Reading Comprehension Education in Fifteen Countries: An Empirical Study* (New York: Wiley, 1973). There is also recent evidence that advanced reading skills have declined in the United States while elementary skills have risen. See J. S. Chall, "Literacy: Trends and Explanations," *Educational Researcher* 12 (1983): 3–8, and R. C. Anderson et al., *Becoming a Nation of Readers,* 2.
29. *Human Relations Area Files,* microfiches (New Haven: Human Relations Area Files, 1899–1956).
30. Ibid. My examples are from more than two hundred entries, stretching from 1899 to 1949, under the topics "Educational Theories and Methods" and "Transmission of Beliefs."
31. L. A. Cremin, *The Transformation of the American School: Progressivism in American Education, 1876–1957* (New York: Knopf, 1964).

CHAPTER II

1. R. Glaser, "Foreword," in R. C. Anderson, E. H. Hiebert, J. A. Scott, and I. A. G. Wilkinson, *Becoming a Nation of Readers* (Washington, D.C.: U.S. Department of Education, 1985), viii.
2. G. A. Miller, "The Magical Number Seven, Plus or Minus Two," *Psychological Review* 63 (1956): 81–97.
3. T. G. Bever, "Perception and Thought in Language," in J. Carroll and R. D. Freedle, eds., *Language Comprehension and the Growth of Knowledge* (Washington, D.C., 1972), 104.
4. J. S. Sachs, "Recognition Memory for Syntactic and Semantic Aspects of Connected Discourse," *Perception and Psychophysics* 2 (1967): 437–42.
5. S. Fillenbaum, "Memory for Gist: Some Relevant Variables," *Language and Speech* 9 (1966): 217–27.
6. M. A. Just and P. A. Carpenter, "The Relation Between Comprehending and Remembering Some Complex Sentences," *Memory and Cognition* 4 (1976): 318–22.
7. W. F. Brewer, "Memory for Ideas: Synonym Substitution," *Memory and Cognition* 3 (1975): 458–64.
8. E. Wanner, *On Remembering, Forgetting, and Understanding Sentences* (The Hague: Mouton, 1974).
9. W. J. M. Levelt and G. Kempen, "Semantic and Syntactic Aspects of Remembering Sentences: A Review of Some Recent Continental Research," in *Studies in Long Term Memory,* ed. A. Kennedy and A. Wilkes (London, 1975), 201–218.
10. J. R. Barclay, J. D. Bransford, and J. J. Franks, "Sentence Memory: A Constructive versus Interpretive Approach," *Cognitive Psychology* 3 (1972): 193–209.
11. R. J. Spiro, "Constructive Processes in Prose Comprehension and Recall," in *Theoretical Issues in Reading Comprehension,* ed. R. J. Spiro, B. C. Bruce, and W. F. Brewer (Hillsdale, N.J.: Erlbaum, 1980), 248.
12. J. D. Bransford and M. K. Johnson, "Contextual Prerequisites for Understanding: Some Investigations of Comprehension and

Recall," *Journal of Verbal Learning and Verbal Behavior* 11 (1972): 717–26.

13. J. D. Bransford and M. K. Johnson, "Consideration of Some Problems of Comprehension," in W. Chase, ed., *Visual Information Processing* (New York: Academic Press, 1973).
14. Adapted from Bruce Catton, *Centennial History of the Civil War,* vol. 3, *Never Say Die* (Garden City, N.Y.: Doubleday, 1965).
15. Adapted from a student essay.
16. This research is reported in two places: E. D. Hirsch, Jr., and David Harrington, "Measuring the Communicative Effectiveness of Prose," in J. Dominic, C. Fredricksen, and M. Whiteman, eds., *Writing* (Hillsdale, N.J.: Erlbaum, 1981), 189–207, and in E. D. Hirsch, Jr., "Culture and Literacy," *The Journal of Basic Writing* III, 1 (Fall and Winter 1980): 27–47.
17. Graphs taken from Hirsch, "Culture and Literacy," 27–47.
18. R. C. Omanson, W. H. Warren, and T. Trabasso, "Goals, Inferential Comprehension, and Recall of Stories by Children," *Discourse Processing* 1 (1978): 337–54.
19. P. D. Pearson, J. Hanson, C. Gordon, "The Effect of Background Knowledge on Young Children's Comprehension of Explicit and Implicit Information," *Journal of Reading Behavior* 11 (1979): 201–209. See also T. Nicholson and R. Imlach, "Where Do Their Answers Come From? A Study of the Inferences Which Children Make When Answering Questions about Narrative Stories," *Journal of Reading Behavior* 13 (1981): 111–29.
20. E. Rosch, C. B. Mervis, W. Gray, D. Johnson, and P. Boyes-Braem, "Basic Objects in Natural Categories," *Cognitive Psychology* 8 (1976): 382–439.
21. E. Rosch, "Human Categorization," in N. Warren, ed., *Advances in Cross-Cultural Psychology,* vol. I (London: Academic Press, 1977).
22. E. Rosch, "Cognitive Representation of Semantic Categories," *Journal of Experimental Psychology* 104 (1975): 192–233.
23. E. Rosch, "On the Internal Structure of Perceptual and Semantic Categories," in T. E. Moore, ed., *Cognitive Development and the Acquisition of Language* (New York: Academic Press, 1973), 111–44. See also L. J. Rips, E. J. Shoben, and E. E. Smith,

"Semantic Distance and the Verification of Semantic Relations," *Journal of Verbal Learning and Verbal Behavior* 14 (1975): 1–20.

24. Hilary Putnam, "The Meaning of Meaning," in *Philosophical Papers,* vol. II (Cambridge: Cambridge University Press, 1975), 215–71.
25. Jean Piaget's notion of assimilation, and its contrast with accommodation, are still highly useful concepts. We assimilate present experiences to past structures, but we also accommodate past structures to present experiences, and thereby add new structures. See Jean Piaget, *The Child's Construction of Reality,* trans. Margaret Cook (New York: Basic Books, 1954), and the report on the important debate between Piaget and Chomsky, set forth in M. Piattelli-Palmarini, ed., *Language and Learning: The Debate between Jean Piaget and Noam Chomsky* (Cambridge: Harvard University Press, 1980).
26. See the excellent book-length discussion of this subject by P. N. Johnson-Laird, *Mental Models: Towards a Cognitive Science of Language, Inference, and Consciousness* (Cambridge: Harvard University Press, 1983).
27. For the word *cup* see W. Labov, "The Boundaries of Words and Their Meanings," in C. J. Baily and R. Shuy, eds., *New Ways of Analyzing Variation in English* (Washington, D.C.: Georgetown University Press, 1973). For the word *eat,* see R. C. Anderson and A. Ortony, "On Putting Apples into Bottles — A Problem of Polysemy," *Cognitive Psychology* 1 (1975): 167–180. For the word *red,* see H. Halff, A. Ortony, and R. C. Anderson, "A Context-sensitive Representation of Word Meanings," *Memory and Cognition* 4 (1976): 378–83. For the word *held,* see R. C. Anderson, J. W. Pichert, E. T. Goetz, and D. L. Shallert, "Instantiation of General Terms," *Journal of Verbal Learning and Verbal Behavior* 15 (1976): 667–79.
28. R. C. Anderson, Z. Shifrin, "The Meaning of Words in Context," in Spiro, Bruce, and Brewer, *Theoretical Issues in Reading Comprehension* (Hillsdale, N.J.: Erlbaum, 1980), 331–47.
29. Much recent work in psycholinguistics has shown that typical or literal meanings are not always the ones that are first activated.

The initial posit strongly depends upon context. R. W. Gibbs, "Contextual Effects in Understanding Indirect Requests," *Discourse Processes* 2 (1979): 1–10; G. B. Simpson, "Meaning, Dominance, and Semantic Context in the Processing of Lexical Ambiguity," *Journal of Verbal Learning and Verbal Behavior* 20 (1981): 120–36; P. Gildea and S. Glucksberg, "On Understanding Metaphor: The Role of Context," *Journal of Verbal Learning and Verbal Behavior* 22 (1983): 577–90.

30. A good review article on this subject is M. J. Adams, "Failures to Comprehend and Levels of Processing in Reading," in Spiro, Bruce, and Brewer, *Theoretical Issues in Reading Comprehension,* 11–32.
31. By far the best general discussion of the nature of these mental representations is Johnson-Laird, *Mental Models.*
32. The most interesting treatment of this subject is still that of Ernst Cassirer, "The Problem of 'Representation' and the Structure of Consciousness," in his *Philosophy of Symbolic Forms,* vol. 1, trans. Ralph Mannheim (New Haven: Yale University Press, 1953), 93–104.
33. F. Wulf, "Über die Veränderung von Vorstellungen," in W. D. Ellis, trans., *A Sourcebook of Gestalt Psychology* (London: Routledge, 1938).
34. F. C. Bartlett, *Remembering* (Cambridge: Cambridge University Press, 1932).
35. Ibid., 206.
36. B. H. Ross and G. H. Bower, "Comparisons of Associative Recall," *Memory and Cognition* 9 (1981): 1–16.
37. Johnson-Laird, *Mental Models,* 146–243.
38. J. R. Anderson and G. H. Bower, *Human Associative Memory,* (New York: Wiley, 1973).
39. A. M. Collins and M. R. Quillian, "Retrieval Time from Semantic Memory," *Journal of Verbal Learning and Verbal Behavior* 8 (1969): 240–47.
40. R. C. Anderson and P. D. Pearson, "A Schema-theoretic View of Basic Processes in Reading Comprehension," in P. D. Pearson, ed., *Handbook of Reading Research* (New York: Longman, 1984), 255–91. I am indebted to this excellent review for the example.

41. A highly informed and very succinct account of this movement in educational theory is presented in R. Glaser, "Education and Thinking: The Role of Knowledge," *American Psychologist* 39 (January 1984): 93–104.
42. Herbert Simon and his colleagues make this remark in J. Larkin, J. McDermott, D. P. Simon, and H. A. Simon, "Expert and Novice Performance in Solving Physics Problems," *Science* 208 (1980): 1335–42. Molière's satire of medical pretension in *Le Malade Imaginaire* goes: "Pourquoi l'opium c'est-il dormir? Parcequ'il a une virtue dormative."
43. J. Larkin et al., "Expert and Novice Performance in Solving Physics Problems," 1335–42.
44. A. de Groot, *Het Denken van den Schaker*, 1946. English: *Thought and Choice in Chess* (The Hague: Mouton, 1965).
45. W. G. Chase and H. A. Simon, "Perception in Chess," *Cognitive Psychology* 4 (1973): 55–81.
46. A. Newell and H. A. Simon, *Human Problem Solving* (Englewood Cliffs, N.J.: Prentice-Hall, 1972). G. R. Norman, L. L. Jacoby, J. W. Feightner, and E. J. M. Campbell, "Clinical Experience and the Structure of Memory," *Proceedings of the Eighteenth Annual Conference on Research in Medical Education* (Washington, D.C., 1979).
47. A review of work on this question, with a focus on reading, may be found in D. E. Rummelhart, "Schemata: The Building Blocks of Cognition," in Spiro, Bruce, and Brewer, *Theoretical Issues in Reading Comprehension,* 33–58. Also E. Golding, "The Effect of Past Experience on Problem Solving," Annual Conference of the British Psychological Society, 1981, cited in Johnson-Laird, *Mental Models,* 33, and D. E. Rummelhart and D. A. Norman, "Analogical Processes in Learning," in J. R. Anderson, ed., *Cognitive Skills and Their Acquisition* (Hillsdale, N.J.: Erlbaum, 1981).
48. J. H. Larkin, *Skilled Problem Solving in Experts* (Technical Report, Group in Science and Mathematics Education, University of California, Berkeley, 1977). Norman et al. "Clinical Experience and the Structure of Memory."
49. R. C. Anderson, a cognitive psychologist, makes the following

relevant observation: "The full development of schema theory as a model for representing how knowledge is stored in human memory had to await the revolution in our conception of how humans process information spurred by the thinking of computer scientists doing simulations of human cognition." Anderson and Pearson, "A Schema-theoretic View of Basic Processes in Reading Comprehension," 259.

50. Larkin et al., "Expert and Novice Performance in Solving Physics Problems," 1335–42.
51. H. A. Simon and M. Barenfield, "Information-Processing Analysis of Perceptual Processes in Problem Solving," *Psychological Review* 76 (1969): 473–83.
52. The iceberg model: a small index that activates a bigger memory store is the one that best fits the current laboratory evidence. A detailed account of the structure of the process may be found in Newell and Simon, *Human Problem Solving;* J. R. Anderson and G. H. Bower, *Human Associative Memory* (New York: Wiley, 1973).
53. See the discussion of basic categories, pp. 49–52, above. Rosch et al., "Basic Objects in Natural Categories," 382–439; Rosch, "Human Categorization"; Rosch, "Cognitive Representation of Semantic Categories," 192–233.
54. The great Danish linguist Otto Jespersen notes that speech is cumbersome even in its grammatical forms when the unspoken conventions of a culture are just being developed. When the community shares more secure implicit conventions (more securely shared schemata) languages begin to drop their cumbersome redundancies, as the Middle Ages began to drop such explicit expressions of concord as *multorum virorum antiquorum*. But classical Latin was simple in this respect compared to nineteenth-century forms of Bantu. See O. Jespersen, *Language: Its Nature, Development and Origin*, 1922 (London: Allen and Unwin, 1969).
55. R. M. Krauss and S. Glucksberg, "Social and Nonsocial Speech," *Scientific American* 236 (February 1977): 100–105.
56. The contrast between the performances of adults and children parallels the contrasts Basil Bernstein has discovered between literate and nonliterate responses to verbal tasks. Bernstein has

associated these contrasts with social and economic class, but the operative principle is national socialization versus local socialization. See B. Bernstein, "Social Class, Language and Socialization," in *Language and Social Context,* ed. P. P. Giglioli (Harmondsworth: Penguin, 1972), 157–78.

57. Krauss and Glucksberg, "Social and Nonsocial Speech," 103.
58. This conjecture has been confirmed by Trabasso and his colleagues. See R. C. Omanson, W. H. Warren, and T. Trabasso, "Goals, Inferential Comprehension, and Recall of Stories by Children," *Discourse Processing* 1 (1978): 337–54.
59. Krauss and Glucksberg, "Social and Nonsocial Speech," 104.
60. Bernstein, "Social Class, Language and Socialization," 166. See also E. D. Hirsch, Jr., *The Philosophy of Composition* (Chicago: University of Chicago Press, 1977), 25–26. The state of current work on literacy in sociolinguistics is reviewed by D. Bloom and J. Green, "Directions in the Sociolinguistic Study of Reading," in Pearson, *Handbook of Reading Research*, 395–422.

CHAPTER III

1. This chapter brings together in brief compass some materials that are not usually correlated in histories of national languages and are rarely considered in histories of the English language. Scholars may therefore wish to consult the relevant background sources to the chapter.

   Specialists have disagreed about the importance of early language standardizers in England. But their decisive importance in Italy, France, Spain, Germany, and much later, in Czechoslovakia, and in the twentieth century in Norway, is well attested to and agreed upon. See Karl W. Deutsch, "The Trend of European Nationalism: The Language Aspect," *American Political Science Review* 36 (1942): 533–41; K. W. Deutsch, *Nationalism and Social Communication: An Inquiry into the Foundations of Nationality* (Cambridge: MIT Press, 1953); P. S. Ray, "Language Standardization," in F. A. Rice, ed., *Study of the Role of Second Languages in Asia, Africa, and Latin*

America (Washington, D.C.: Center for Applied Linguistics of the Modern Language Association, 1962); and E. Haugen, "Linguistics and Language Planning," in *Sociolinguistics,* ed. W. Bright (The Hague: Mouton, 1966). The lack of a consensus among historians of the English language regarding the importance of early schoolmasters, grammarians, and dictionary makers is an anomaly that calls for an explanation.

The first scholar to set forth the decisive importance of the early prescriptive writers for modern standard English, both spoken and written, was Henry Bradley, a brilliant philologist and sometime chief editor of the *Oxford English Dictionary.* He understood that universal education and the spread of literacy had caused the grammar of the English language, as codified by eighteenth-century prescriptivists, to be permanently fixed. He thought that universal education would cause any tendency to deviate from the eighteenth-century norm to be sternly repressed by schoolmasters and schoolmistresses. In 1904 he had the courage to make the following prophecy in *The Making of English,* rev. ed., ed. S. Potter (London: Macmillan, 1968): "On the whole, it is probable that the history of English grammar will for a very long time have few changes to record later than the nineteenth century" (52–53).

Bradley then made the same prophecy about the permanence of then current spelling and pronunciation of English, and for the same reason, the spread of literacy, in *On the Relations Between Spoken and Written Language, With Special Reference to English* (Oxford: Oxford University Press, 1919). The probability that Bradley's prophecies will continue to hold true becomes ever greater as time passes and literacy spreads. The only exceptions to them that opponents have been able to cite are rare and trivial — well within the compass of his predictions.

Why have the dominant historians of the English language failed to develop, or even discuss, Bradley's ideas? I believe the reasons are two. (1) Historians of English have been trained principally in the earlier periods of the language, before the rise of universal literacy, and have therefore underestimated the decisive linguistic importance of that epochal event. (2) Their predisposition was reinforced by the revolution in linguistics, led by Edward Sapir (*Language* [New York: Harcourt-Brace, 1921]) and Leonard Bloomfield (*Language* [New York: Holt, Rinehart and Winston, 1933]), away from an emphasis on written language in favor of the view that the true form of language is oral, that writing is unimportant and secondary, and that the universal law of language is constant change. This American Revolution in linguistics informed the thinking of American language historians, including the most influential historian of English, Albert C. Baugh, who mentions Bloomfield with enthusiasm in his *History of the English Language* (New York: Appleton-Century, 1935), 17. In discussing the seventeenth- and eighteenth-century movements to standardize English, Baugh observed somewhat scornfully:

> It is curious that a number of men notable in various intellectual spheres in the late seventeenth and early eighteenth centuries should have been blind to the testimony of history and believed that by taking thought it would be possible to suspend the processes of growth and decay that characterize a living language (322).

Later linguists have returned to Bradley's view. For instance, Dwight Bollinger speaks with a wryness equal to Baugh's of traditional philologists who view "linguistic change as if it were as inexorable as the drift of time, which no amount of tampering could prevent" in his *Aspects of Language* (New York: Harcourt, Brace and World, 1968), 284. Another important recent discussion of the subject, in opposition to the doctrines of Sapir and Bloomfield, may be found in Fred Householder's essay "The Primacy of Writing" in his *Linguistic Speculations* (Cambridge: Cambridge University Press, 1971).

For a fuller account of the relations between early language standardizing, literacy, and the stability of grammar, spelling, and pronunciation in modern national languages, I refer the reader to two chapters, "Distinctive Features of Written Speech" and "The Normative Character of Written Speech" in my book on theoretical aspects of writing, which contains further bibliographical references to the literature on language standardization. See E. D. Hirsch, Jr., *The Philosophy of Composition* (Chicago: University of Chicago Press, 1977). The later work of F. Furet and J. Ozouf, *Reading and Writing: Literacy in France from Calvin to Jules Ferry* (Cambridge: Cambridge University Press, 1982) may also be consulted with profit.

M. S. Zengel, "Literacy as a Factor in Language Change," *American Anthropologist* 64 (1962): 132–39, is another valuable source.

2. A good brief discussion of isoglosses and dialectal variation in medieval and modern times may be found in M. A. K. Halliday, A. McIntosh, and Peter Strevens, *The Linguistic Sciences and Language Teaching* (London: Longman, 1964), 81–90. See also A. McIntosh, "The Analysis of Written Middle English," *Transactions of the Philological Society* 34 (1956): 26–56.
3. Henry Sweet, "The Principles of Spelling Reform" (1877). Reprinted in Henry Sweet, *The Indispensable Foundation,* ed. E. J. A. Henderson (London, 1971), 220.
4. Alexander Pope, "Essay on Criticism" (1711), ll. 482–83.
5. Ernest Gellner, *Nations and Nationalism* (Ithaca, N.Y.: Cornell University Press, 1983).
6. See Deutsch, "The Trend of European Nationalism" and *Nationalism and Social Communication.*
7. Gellner, *Nations and Nationalism,* 27.
8. Ibid., 35.
9. Ibid., 36.
10. Even earlier than this, in the sixteenth and seventeenth centuries, the diffusion of printed books in the national languages had started the process of language standardization. The agitation in England for language standardization is well documented in W. F. Bolton, ed., *The English Language: Essays by English and American Men of Letters, 1490–1839* (Cambridge: Cambridge University Press, 1966).
11. See R. Emerson, "Nation Building in Africa," in K. W. Deutsch and W. J. Foltz, eds., *Nation Building* (Englewood Cliffs, N.J.: Prentice-Hall, 1963), 110–14.
12. On the importance of schoolteachers in preserving pronunciation and spelling across time and space, see E. Haugen, "Plan-

ning for a Standard Language in Modern Norway," *Anthropological Linguistics* 1 (1959): 18. On the role of schoolmasters see also E. J. Dobson, *English Pronunciation 1500–1700,* 2d ed., 2 vols. (Oxford: Oxford University Press, 1968), especially vol. 1, *Survey of the Sources.*

13. See Halliday, McIntosh, and Strevens, *The Linguistic Sciences,* 81–90.
14. On the history of European academies, see the excellent article "Academies" by Francis Storr in the eleventh edition of the *Encyclopaedia Britannica.* See also Bollinger, *Aspects of Language,* 285.
15. Since Johnson's dictionary a small number of spelling reforms have become established both in Britain and America, often thanks to Noah Webster. See his "An Essay on the Necessity, Advantages and Practicability of Reforming the Mode of Spelling, and of Rendering the Orthography of Words Consistent to the Pronunciation," 1789, reprinted in Bolton, *The English Language,* 157–73. A good account of Webster's career and influence can be found in Baugh, *A History of the English Language,* 246–50. By far the best discussion of spelling and spelling reform is to be found in Bradley, *On the Relations Between Spoken and Written Language.*
16. See Johnson's justifications in his Preface, and those of early orthoepists and orthographers in Bolton, *The English Language,* and Dobson, *English Pronunciation.*
17. See Haugen, "Planning for a Standard Language in Modern Norway."
18. Otto Jespersen, *Language: Its Nature, Development, and Origin* (London: Allen and Unwin, 1922), 319–67. See also his *Efficiency in Language Change* (Copenhagen: Munksgaard, 1941).
19. See Bradley, *The Making of English,* 53.
20. Present-tense *be* in all persons is an oral dialectal form that goes back to medieval times. See A. McIntosh, "The Analysis of Written Middle English," *Transactions of the Philological Society* 34 (1956): 26–56.
21. Other examples of "learned spellings" that never had a connection with pronunciation are *debt* and *rhyme.* See Bradley,

On the Relations Between Spoken and Written Language, 15, and Dobson, *English Pronunciation,* vol. 1, 90, vol. 2, 1007–1010.

22. See Bradley, *On the Relations Between Spoken and Written Language,* 30–35. Some modern spellings such as *thru* and *slo* are perhaps found more on road signs than in printed English. For reasons which Bradley gives, they will probably be exceedingly few in number. Further reasons are offered by Householder, *Linguistic Speculations,* 244–64.
23. Haugen, "Linguistics and Language Planning," and Otto Jespersen, *Mankind, Nation and Individual from a Linguistic Point of View* (Bloomington: Indiana University Press, 1964).
24. M. M. Guxman, "Some General Regularities in the Formation and Development of National Languages," in *Readings in the Sociology of Language,* ed. J. A. Fishman (The Hague: Mouton, 1968), 773–76.
25. Because of the fundamental differences between oral and written languages, Haugen has coined the useful word *grapholect,* which effectively indicates a functional distinction without implying an inherent superiority of the standard written language over oral dialects. See Haugen, "Linguistics and Language Planning."
26. Jespersen stresses this point with unmatched learning and objectivity in *Mankind, Nation and Individual.*
27. Gellner, *Nations and Nationalism,* 56.
28. Ibid., 57.
29. On the arbitrariness of the early prescriptive orthographers in English, see R. L. Venezky, *The Structure of English Orthography* (The Hague: Mouton, 1970), as well as Dobson, *English Pronunciation,* and Bradley, *On the Relations Between Spoken and Written Language.*
30. For *monk* see Dobson, *English Pronunciation,* 953.
31. See David Potter, Preface, in Hugh Blair, *Lectures on Rhetoric and Belles Lettres,* ed. Harold F. Harding, 2 vols. (Carbondale: Southern Illinois University Press, 1965), vol. 2, 435.
32. Ibid.
33. Ruth Miller Elson, *Guardians of Tradition: American School-*

books of the Nineteenth Century (Lincoln: University of Nebraska Press, 1964), 337–42.

34. Ibid., 186–220.
35. Mason L. Weems, *The Life of George Washington* (1809), ed. Marcus Cunliffe (Cambridge: Harvard University Press, 1962), 4–5.
36. Ibid., 12–13.
37. Abraham Lincoln, "Autobiography Written for John L. Scripps" [June 1860], in *The Collected Works of Abraham Lincoln,* ed. Roy B. Basler, 8 vols. (New Brunswick, N.J.: Rutgers University Press, 1953), vol. 4, 62. Volney's *Ruins,* now forgotten but an influential book of the Enlightenment, was subtitled *Meditations on the Revolutions of Empires.* A translation from the French was begun by Thomas Jefferson, a friend of Volney's, and finished by Joel Barlow. See Constantin C. Volney, *A New Translation of Volney's Ruins in Two Volumes,* ed. Robert D. Richardson, Jr. (New York: Garland, 1979).
38. Lawrence A. Cremin, *American Education: The National Experience 1783–1876* (New York: Harper and Row, 1980), 499.
39. The tendency for frequently used words to become shortened is one of the few universals of language, and has been well studied since the pathbreaking work of G. K. Zipf, "Relative Frequency as a Determinant of Phonetic Change," *Harvard Studies in Classical Philology* 40 (1929): 1–95. See also A. Martinet, *A Functional View of Language* (Oxford: Oxford University Press, 1962). Martinet gives numerous examples and observes: "The unmistakable existence of an inverse relationship between frequency and linguistic complexity is a most precious discovery" (144).
40. See the article "Webster, Noah" in James D. Hart, ed., *The Oxford Companion to American Literature* (New York: Oxford University Press, 1956).
41. The term *bilingualism* is sometimes used with deliberate vagueness, and in a quite misleading way, to capitalize on our positive valuation of people who know more than one language. For those who really mean the word in this positive

sense, I suggest the term *biliteracy*. In current discussions, *bilingualism* is often used to describe people who are literate in no language.

42. See Jespersen, *Mankind, Nation and Individual.*

CHAPTER IV

1. See *College-Bound Seniors: 1972–1983* (New York: College Board, 1984), table 1, 6.
2. *Becoming a Nation of Readers: The Report of the Commission on Reading* (Washington, D.C.: National Institute of Education, 1984), 3. See also D. P. Resnick and L. B. Resnick, "The Nature of Literacy: An Historical Exploration," *Harvard Educational Review* 47 (1977), 370–85.
3. Eugen Weber, *Peasants into Frenchmen: The Modernization of Rural France 1870–1914* (Stanford: Stanford University Press, 1976), especially 377–497.
4. Erving Goffman, *The Presentation of Self in Everyday Life* (New York: Doubleday, 1959).
5. William Pitt (the Elder), Debate on the Excise Bill, 1763, quoted in C. A. Goodrich, *Select British Eloquence* (New York: Bobbs-Merrill, 1963), 65.
6. For an analysis of the dispersal of ethnic groups, beginning around 1910, see Olivier Zunz, *The Changing Face of Inequality: Urbanization, Industrial Development, and Immigrants in Detroit, 1880–1920* (Chicago: University of Chicago Press, 1982).
7. The classic, brief treatment of the subject of American civil religion is an essay by Robert Bellah, "Civil Religion in America," in *Religion in America*, ed. W. G. McLoughlin and R. Bellah (Boston: Houghton Mifflin, 1968), 3–23.
8. Charles Krauthammer, "Bennett and His Sectarian Allies," *Washington Post*, August 23, 1985.
9. H. S. Commager, ed., *Documents of American History* (New York: Appleton-Century, 1948), 169.
10. H. M. Kallen, *Cultural Pluralism and the American Idea: An Essay in Social Philosophy* (Philadelphia: University of Pennsylvania Press, 1956), 87–88.

11. David Hume, "Of the Standard of Taste," first published in *Four Dissertations* (Edinburgh, 1757).
12. O. Patterson, "Language, Ethnicity, and Change," *Journal of Basic Writing* 3 (1980): 62–73.
13. Otto Jespersen, *Mankind, Nation, and Individual from a Linguistic Point of View* (Bloomington: Indiana University Press, 1964), 33–73.
14. Ibid.
15. For the importance of Cicero to Jefferson and the other founders, see Michael Grant, ed., *Cicero on the Good Life* (Harmondsworth: Penguin, 1971), 42.

CHAPTER V

1. *The Washington Post,* September 16, 1985, A-19.
2. J. S. Chall, C. Snow, et al., *Families and Literacy,* Final Report to the National Institute of Education, 1982. Also, J. S. Chall, "Afterword," in R. C. Anderson, et al., *Becoming a Nation of Readers: The Report of the Commission on Reading* (Washington, D.C.: National Institute of Education, 1985), 123–24.
3. P. S. Anderson, *Language Skills in Elementary Education,* 2d ed., (New York: Macmillan, 1972), 209–10.
4. Ibid., 220.
5. James S. Coleman et al., *Equality of Educational Opportunity* (Washington, D.C.: Government Printing Office, 1966). For commentary, see Diane Ravitch, *The Troubled Crusade: American Education 1945–1980* (New York: Basic Books, 1983), 168–70.
6. C. Jencks et al., *Inequality: A Reassessment of the Effect of Family and Schooling in America* (New York: Basic Books, 1972). See also F. Mosteller and D. P. Moynihan, eds., *On Equality of Educational Opportunity* (New York: Random House, 1972), and D. M. Levine and M. J. Bane, eds., *The "Inequality" Controversy: Schooling and Distributive Justice* (New York: Basic Books, 1975).
7. Diane Ravitch, *The Schools We Deserve: Reflections on the*

Educational Crises of Our Times (New York: Basic Books, 1985), 106.

8. H. J. Walberg and T. Shanahan, "High School Effects on Individual Students," *Educational Researcher* 12 (1983): 4–9.
9. See Ravitch, "The Meaning of the New Coleman Report," in *The Schools We Deserve,* 100–111.
10. Walberg and Shanahan, "High School Effects," 4–9.
11. My understanding of this historical process is based chiefly on the following historical works to which the reader is referred for detailed accounts and interpretations: L. A. Cremin, *The Transformation of the School: Progressivism in American Education, 1876–1957* (New York: Knopf, 1964); Patricia A. Graham, *Progressive Education: From Arcady to Academe* (New York: Teachers College Press, Columbia University, 1967); E. A. Krug, *The Shaping of the American High School, Volume I: 1880–1920; Volume II, 1920–1941* (Madison: University of Wisconsin Press, 1969, 1972); Ravitch, *The Troubled Crusade;* David K. Cohen, "Origins," in A. G. Powell, E. Farrar, and David K. Cohen, *The Shopping Mall High School* (Boston: Houghton Mifflin, 1985), 233–308.
12. Powell, Farrar, and Cohen, *The Shopping Mall High School,* 3–7.
13. National Education Association, *Report of the Committee of Ten on Secondary School Studies* (Washington, D.C.: Government Printing Office, 1893), hereafter cited as Eliot, *Report of the Committee of Ten*; C. D. Kingsley, ed., *Cardinal Principles of Secondary Education: A Report of the Commission on the Reorganization of Secondary Education, Appointed by the National Education Association,* Bulletin, 1918, No. 35 (Washington, D.C.: Department of the Interior, Bureau of Education, Government Printing Office, 1918).
14. "The *Cardinal Principles* quickly became the bible of school reformers. It continues to attract enthusiasts today. It helped to popularize and rationalize the new studies and standards because it identified them with a great democratic advance." Cohen, "Origins," 256.
15. See Cremin, *The Transformation of the School.* The process

after 1957 is traced in Ravitch, *The Troubled Crusade,* especially chapter 2. A concise overview of the process (just 16 pages long) can be found in "The Continuing Crisis: Fashions in Education," the third chapter in Diane Ravitch, *The Schools We Deserve.*

16. Eliot, *Report of the Committee of Ten,* 94. Italics in the original.
17. Ibid., 56–57.
18. Kingsley, *Cardinal Principles,* 7.
19. See Cremin, *The Transformation of the School.*
20. William Wordsworth, "Ode. Intimations of Immortality from Recollections of Early Childhood," ll. 109–10.
21. J. J. Rousseau, *Emile ou De l'Education* (Paris, 1762). John Dewey and Evelyn Dewey, *Schools of To-morrow* (New York: Dutton, 1915), 5–14. A practicing psychologist has written an excellent, sensible critique of the modern educational doctrine of self-esteem. See Barbara Lerner, "Self-Esteem and Excellence: The Choice and the Paradox," *American Educator* 9 (Winter 1985): 10–17.
22. Wordsworth, "Intimations of Immortality," ll. 128–29. Dewey, *Schools of To-morrow,* 5–14.
23. Kingsley, *Cardinal Principles,* 7.
24. Cremin, *The Transformation of the School,* 110–15.
25. Kingsley, *Cardinal Principles,* 7–12.
26. Ibid.
27. "While Thorndike himself was not willing to move from a completely general to a completely particular position on transfer, some of his readers were; as early as 1913 he criticized certain 'careless thinkers' for rushing 'from the belief in totally general training to the belief that training is totally specialized.' . . . The attack on transfer provided too much ammunition to practicalists for qualifications to prevail, however, and even Thorndike's strictures were ignored." Cremin, *The Transformation of the School,* 113–14.
28. Kingsley, *Cardinal Principles,* 7–12.
29. "The general philosophy of the new education may be sound, and yet the difference in abstract principles will not decide the way in which the moral and intellectual preference involved shall be worked out in practice. There is always the danger in a new movement that in rejecting the aims and methods of that

which it would supplant, it may develop its principles negatively rather than positively and constructively. Then it takes its clew in practice from that which is rejected instead of from the constructive development of its own philosophy." John Dewey, *Experience and Education* (New York: Macmillan, 1938 [1951]), 6–7.

30. Powell, Farrar, and Cohen, *The Shopping Mall High School,* 1–7.
31. Kingsley, *Cardinal Principles,* 7–12.
32. U.S. Office of Education, *Life Adjustment Education for Every Youth* (Washington, D.C.: Government Printing Office, n.d.), 15. Quoted in Ravitch, *The Troubled Crusade,* 64–65.
33. Ravitch, *The Troubled Crusade,* 65.
34. Powell, Farrar, and Cohen, *The Shopping Mall High School,* 8–52.
35. Ravitch, *The Troubled Crusade,* 65, 67.
36. Charles Rathbone, "The Implicit Rationale of the Open Education Classroom," in *Open Education: The Informal Classroom,* ed. C. H. Rathbone (New York: Citation Press, 1971), 100, 104, quoted in Ravitch, *The Troubled Crusade,* 249.
37. Roland Barth, "Teaching: The Way It Is / The Way It Could Be," *Grade Teacher* (January 1970): 101, quoted in Ravitch, *The Troubled Crusade,* 249.
38. Patricia A. Graham, "Schools: Cacophony About Practice, Silence About Purpose," *Daedalus* 113 (Fall 1984): 29–57.
39. W. S. Gilbert, *Plays and Poems of W. S. Gilbert* (New York: Random House, 1932), 155–57.
40. B. Bloom, A. Davis, and R. Hess, *Compensatory Education for Cultural Deprivation* (New York: Holt, Rinehart and Winston, 1965), 4–23.
41. A. H. Thorndike and F. T. Baker, *Everyday Classics,* 9 vols. (New York: Macmillan, 1917–1922), preface to vol. 3.

APPENDIX

1. "A Nation at Risk: The Imperative for Educational Reform," a report to the secretary of education by the National Com-

mission on Excellence in Education (Washington, D.C.: Superintendent of Documents, Government Printing Office, 1983).

2. C. P. Snow, *The Two Cultures and the Scientific Revolution* (Cambridge: Cambridge University Press, 1959).
3. Hilary Putnam, *Reason, Truth, and History* (Cambridge: Cambridge University Press, 1981), 188–200.
4. For those interested in the humanistic aspects of science, I recommend Victor Weiskopf's "Is Physics Human?" *Physics Today* (June 1976): 23.

INDEX

AUTHOR'S NOTE

The index to twelfth-grade-level literate culture is undergoing constant scrutiny and revision. The present list is owned by the Cultural Literacy Foundation, a nonprofit educational foundation instituted to advance literacy in the United States. The foundation will soon publish the list arranged under twenty-three categories of knowledge. This systematic index will form the basis for twelfth-grade general-knowledge tests, to be issued twice-yearly. In all, the Foundation will create four levels of general-knowledge tests, for grades three, six, nine, and twelve. Prior notice of what the four levels of tests will probe over the years will be provided by four separate lists that indicate in advance the knowledge to be sampled. These indexes will be distributed at cost to any schools and publishers wishing to use them. The Foundation encourages publishers to create dictionaries that explain the items indexed by the lists, and to create textbooks and other school materials that effectively impart literate culture. The address of the Cultural Literacy Foundation is 2012-B Morton Drive, Charlottesville, VA, 22901. Gifts to the Foundation are tax-deductible.

ABOUT THE AUTHOR

E. D. Hirsch, Jr., is William R. Kenan Professor of English at the University of Virginia. His articles on cultural literacy have appeared in *The New York Times Education Supplement, The American Scholar,* and *American Educator,* and he speaks frequently on the subject. Dr. Hirsch is a member of the American Academy of Arts and Sciences, has been a Senior Fellow of the National Endowment for the Humanities, and is a member of the federally sponsored Foundations of Literacy project.